Measurement in
Physical Education
and Athletics

Measurement in Physical Education and Athletics

Clayne R. Jensen

Cyntha C. Hirst
Brigham Young University

Macmillan Publishing Co., Inc.
New York
Collier Macmillan Publishers
London

Copyright © 1980, Macmillan Publishing Co., Inc.

Printed in the United States of America

Macmillan Publishing Co., Inc.
866 Third Avenue, New York, New York 10022

Collier Macmillan Canada, Ltd.

Library of Congress Cataloging in Publication Data

Jensen, Clayne R
    Measurement in physical education and athletics.

    Includes bibliographies and index.
    1. Physical education and training—Statistical
methods.   2. Physical fitness—Testing.   I. Hirst,
Cyntha C., joint author.   II. Title.
GV342.5.S7J46   1980   613.7   79-4492
ISBN 0-02-360500-6

Printing: 1 2 3 4 5 6 7 8   Year: 0 1 2 3 4 5 6

Preface

Among the significant changes in physical education and athletics that have taken place in recent years is greater emphasis on sound testing procedures and useful statistical techniques. To be well prepared, today's physical education teachers and coaches must complete an adequate course in measurement techniques. Such a course requires an understanding of elementary statistics. Because measurement and statistics are closely related and interdependent, they are often included in a single course in the professional preparation program. When this is done, it is logical to devote the first part of the course to selected statistical techniques and the second part to learning how to conduct a program of measurement and how to use the results.

An important advantage of giving a combined course in statistics and measurement is that the statistical techniques are immediately used in connection with the instruction in measurement, rather than forgotten by the time a later course on measurement is given. Also, students in physical education find it especially meaningful to work problems in statistics using such scores as endurance and strength rather than scores that do not relate to motor performance.

This book is designed for a combined course in statistics and measurement, taught at the upper-division college level. The book includes carefully selected statistical techniques which have frequent application in the educational setting. The techniques are presented in logical sequence for learning and explained in a clear fashion. The numerous problem-solving assignments help students learn how to apply the techniques effectively. Further, the book includes valuable information about selecting, constructing, and administering tests and using test results. Many useful tests are described and some scoring tables are included.

Measurement Techniques in Physical Education and Athletics should be interesting and meaningful to students majoring in physical education and related fields, and to professional teachers, coaches, and school administrators.

C. R. J.
C. C. H.

v

Contents

vii

V Nonphysical Performance Measures

VI Construction and Application of Measurements

Measurement in
Physical Education
and Athletics

Orientation
and
Overview

1

Introduction to Measurement

Measurement is not new. From the beginning of recorded history man has devised and used tests of one sort or another to determine human ability in those factors considered important in the particular society. Crude measurements of strength, speed, endurance, and skill, for example, date back to antiquity.

Conversely, educational measurement, as we know it today, is relatively new. It has developed as a part of the elaborate and complex mass education system, and like other aspects of that system, is of relatively recent origin. The qualities that we measure today are numerous and precisely defined, and our techniques for making and recording these measurements are more exact than ever before.

Physical education requires a greater variety of measurements than do most fields of education. Measurements in physical education include: (1) timed measurements in which the least amount of time is the desired result, as in running, swimming, and skiing races; (2) timed measurements in which the greatest amount of time is the desired result, as in steady pace endurance tests and laboratory treadmill testing; (3) measurements of horizontal distance (usually in measured units of yards or meters) as in throwing for distance; (4) measurements of vertical distance, as in the pole vault or high jump; (5) measurements in scores as in archery or bowling where the highest number of points is desired, or in golf or cross country where the lowest score is the best; (6) measurements of accuracy as in the basketball free throw or passing in football; (7) measurements in judged events where errors in performance are deducted and a raw score is multiplied by a preassessed difficulty factor as in diving or gymnastics; (8) measurements of knowledge in which the scores are in

3

percentages or whole numeral points; and (9) measurements in laboratory tests that are recorded in liters and kilograms.

All of these types of measurements as well as others are important in the evaluation of performance, and the physical educator must be able to use the measurements and apply the tools of statistics to aid in evaluation of the results. Many of the measurement techniques and instruments used today have been developed during recent years. Likewise, the statistical techniques we use to analyze measurement results are relatively new.

Tests, measurements, and *evaluation* are commonly used terms with certain similarities and certain differences.

A **test** is an instrument requiring a performance by an individual being evaluated. The performer receives a score representing how well he or she has performed. The quality or quantity of an individual's strength, speed, jumping ability, knowledge, intelligence, and so on are determined by the use of specifically designed tests.

The term **measurement** deals with an immediate objective aimed toward a specific and tangible goal and includes all tests, but is not necessarily confined to the concept of testing. Some measurements do not require a performance by the person. For instance, measurements of body height, weight, and percent body fat are not tests.

Evaluation is an ongoing process aimed at appraising the progress of the individual or group and is broader and more inclusive in use than either of the above terms. It is a process of determining the status of something and of relating that status to some standard in order to make a value judgment. For example, evaluations are made of teaching methods, program content, and teaching effectiveness. Evaluation is often based on information secured from observations, interviews, questionnaires, and other measures.

Reasons for Measuring

Physical educators are concerned with student development and adjustment resulting from participation in activity. They are specifically concerned with the development of knowledge, concepts, and judgments; interests, attitudes, and ideals; strength and skill; and the development of the organic systems.

If a teacher is to design a high-quality instructional program and teach the students effectively, he or she must obtain considerable information about the students. The more information a teacher has about the students' performances, abilities, and needs, the better an effective program can be designed and conducted. Much of the needed information can be gathered with the use of tests and measurements. The need for precise measures calls for a well-designed program, including carefully selected and well-constructed tests.

Two general purposes for measurement in physical education are (1) to increase knowledge about the students, and (2) to improve instruction. Little is achieved unless the information gained through measurement is applied in useful ways.

There are six specific purposes of measurement:

1. *Diagnostic.* Measurement is necessary to diagnose the differences in abilities, interests, and needs of students in order to plan and conduct adequate programs. Objective knowledge about specific student deficiencies is essential to provide remedial programs, regular programs, and accelerated programs.
2. *Classification.* Sometimes it is an advantage to classify students into homogeneous or heterogeneous groups, whichever is desired for a particular type of instruction, competition, or experience. Such classification is often based on the results of appropriate measurements.
3. *Achievement.* It is important to obtain objective measures and to keep accurate records of student achievement and progress, because these records form the basis for the selection of program content, for the assignment of grades or marks and for the advancement of students.
4. *Administration.* Objective information obtained from measurements serve as a basis for determining the best methods of instruction and for guiding students into appropriate experiences. Accurate measurements help to determine the success of students and to learn whether students are ready to progress to the next higher level. Properly administered tests can help provide information needed and desired by students, teachers, parents, and school administrators.
5. *Supervisory.* Objective test results may be valuable in the evaluation of teachers and their teaching efficiency. The test results may be used to indicate if the objectives established by the teacher are being reached.
6. *Research.* The field of physical education is rich with opportunities for valuable research. For example, additional research is necessary on the effectiveness of various methods of instruction, on the rate of progress of students, on the physiological, psychological, and sociological values of the different activities, and on the evaluation of the entire school program in physical education. However, most scientific research can be performed effectively only with the use of appropriate tests.

Historical Overview

Familiarity with the historical development of a subject frequently results in a better appreciation of the subject and an understanding of its significance. In this light let us consider the major developments of measurement that have led to its present status in the field of physical education.

Physical education measurement is only one phase of educational measurement, since each subject in a field calls for evaluation techniques unique to that subject. Physical education tests frequently measure motor performances.

Measuring the structure and function of the human body is not new. Early civilized man used measures of strength, running, speed, endurance, specific skills, and body size and proportions. At first the measures were crude, but gradually they became more refined and more numerous until today a large number of useful measures of structure and function are available.

The history of measurement in physical education has occurred with the development in six distinct areas: anthropometric, strength, cardiac function, athletic ability, fitness, and motor skills.

Anthropometric Measurements

Measures dealing with structure and proportions of the body can be traced to ancient India where a treatise entitled "Silpi Sastri," describing the division of the body into 480 parts and explaining the structure and proportions of each part, was written. In an attempt to find one body part which would serve as a standard for measurement of all other parts, the ancient Egyptians divided the body into 19 equal segments, each of which was the length of the High Priest's middle finger.

Two ancient Greek sculptors, Phidias and Polyclitus, fashioned models in an attempt to demonstrate perfection in human proportions. Later, Roman sculptors developed human forms somewhat different from those created by the earlier Greeks. The Greek and Roman ideals of the perfect body form prevailed for centuries, during which time little was done in developing new ideas about human structure.

In 1770 Joshua Reynolds, an English painter, placed new emphasis on anthropometric measures. He called attention to the idea that body size and proportions are largely hereditary, that the individual has limited control over them, and that they change considerably from childhood to adulthood.

Around 1850 anthropometric measures began to be important in organized physical education programs. In 1860 Cromwell, an Englishman, studied the growth patterns of Manchester school children from ages eight to eighteen. He found that from ages eleven to fourteen girls were taller and heavier than boys at the same age. In 1861 Edward Hitchcock, at Amherst College, took careful measurements to establish standards of age; height; weight; girths of the chest, arm, and forearm; and strength of the upper arm. Later, on the basis of his findings he developed more than 50 standard measures of body proportions.

Soon after Hitchcock's studies Dudley A. Sargent at Harvard University began a systematic anthropometric measurement program. The data he gathered, published in 1893, created a wider interest in growth and structure. As a result of his report several other universities initiated measurement programs.

At about the turn of the century, Street developed the idea of a weight–height index. Later other researchers built on his idea and developed extensive weight–height indexes. These indexes became useful to educators and also to the public in general. They presumably indicated how much a person ought to weigh in relation to his or her height and body type. In 1902 D. W. Hastings at Springfield College made a study of the rate of growth of the human body from the fifth to the twenty-first birthday.

Following the turn of the century the use of anthropometric measures lagged, but in the late 1920s a new interest developed. In 1928 Clifford Brownell of Columbia University presented a series of posture silhouettes with which to detect postural deviations in boys, soon after which Charlotte G. MacEwan and Eugene C. Howe provided a more extensive set of posture silhouettes. Two years later R. C. Quimby developed his weight analysis scale for man, and subsequently Helen B. Pryor of Stanford University constructed the Pryor Width–Weight Tables. Then, William H. Sheldon published his rather elaborate system of somatotyping of the human body.

In 1947 Thomas Cureton at the University of Illinois devised a simplified somatotyping system, and Howard V. Meredith published his height–weight charts. In 1948, Norman Wetzel published the widely used Wetzel Grid. More recently, R. W. Parnell used height and weight, bone diameters, skinfold measures, and muscle girth to assess Sheldon's physique components. Heath and Carter modified the Parnell chart. Other significant events occurred along the way, but the aforementioned seem to be the milestones in the development of anthropometric measurements.

Interest in anthropometric measures has lessened during the last two decades. However, some measures still serve worthwhile purposes, especially those used as screening devices to identify the more extreme structural types.

Strength Tests

The idea that strength is fundamental to vigorous athletic performances has long been recognized, and for this reason strength testing has interested physical education teachers, and athletic coaches. The actual origin of strength testing is not known.

The first wave of enthusiasm for strength development and testing in the United States reached its peak in the period from 1860 to 1875 during which time George Winship toured the eastern part of the country lecturing on exercise and giving exhibitions of weight lifting. In about 1880 Sargent began his strength studies of Harvard University students in an attempt to determine standards for American college men. The studies resulted in Sargent's Intercollegiate Strength Test, which received extensive use.

In 1890 Francis Galton devised a test to measure physical efficiency, especially for business and civil service use. Among other items Galton's test included strength measures. Late in the 1880s and early in the 1890s J. H. Kellogg did work emphasizing the importance of exercise as a therapeutic measure. His work led to the invention of the universal dynamometer in 1896. With this instrument he could test the strength of different muscle groups.

During the early part of the twentieth century a brief lapse occurred in strength testing. It was generally thought that strength tests did not lend enough emphasis to measures of endurance and especially to heart and lung development. Also the idea that muscle boundness hindered an athlete's performance led to the temporary abandonment of strength testing.

While studying the effects of the Vermont polio epidemic in 1915, E. G. Martin recognized the need for a strength test that could be used for comparing normal and affected muscle groups. He developed the Martin Resistance Test based on the principle of resistance to a pull in contrast to the idea of voluntary strength exertion. The original test measured 11 muscle groups, but a shorter test was devised involving four muscle groups.

In 1925 Frederick R. Rogers revived interest in strength testing by developing the Strength Index and the Fitness Index. Rogers' work brought forth new evidence that strength correlates significantly with athletic ability.

After Rogers' work several new tests appeared. J. H. McCurdy developed his so-called Physical Capacity Test in which strength was an important item. In 1931 Charles H. McCloy revised the Rogers' Strength Index by devising his own formula for estimating arm strength. Rump's studies on strength testing indicated that pull-up and dip strength were good indicators of total strength.

During the 1940s Thomas DeLorme did considerable strength testing and strength building among wounded war veterans under rehabilitation treatment. He is often referred to as the father of modern isotonic weight training, for largely under his leadership the value of strength in athletic performance was established. More recently H. Harrison Clarke developed tests to measure the strength of muscle groups responsible for 38 different joint movements. In the late 1940s Leonard A. Larson developed his Dynamic Strength Test, consisting of pull-ups, dips, and vertical jumps. The test was designed to measure ability to do work against the resistance of one's own body weight.

Currently strength is recognized as a major contributor to athletic performance, and some leaders claim it is the most important single characteristic. The present popularity of strength testing stems from the extensive concentration on strength development in athletic conditioning. Many strength tests require a tensiometer and strap-and-cable arrangement to test strength of specific muscle groups. Also, tests that measure a combination of strength and endurance are often used. These tests consist of performances such as pull-ups, dips, and push-ups, in which the performer works against the resistance of his body weight.

There are now isokinetic strength training machines which have attachments for measuring strength throughout the range of motion. This kind of test provides two important results: the amount of strength, and the variations of strength at different positions (strength curve). Devices for measuring isokinetic strength are of recent origin and they are rapidly becoming popular.

Circulorespiratory (Cardiovascular) Tests

Angelo Mosso, the inventor of the ergograph, pointed out in 1884 that the ability of muscles to carry on sustained performance is related to the efficiency of the circulatory system. Thus attention turned toward more satisfactory methods of measuring cardiovascular condition. Subsequently significant strides were made in the development of procedures to measure blood pressure. In 1905 C. Ward Crampton used this knowledge to establish a rating scheme in order to obtain information about the general condition of a person by noting changes in cardiac rate and arterial pressure upon assuming the erect position.

In 1910 McCurdy devised a simple test of what he termed physical condition. He concluded that if the change in heart rate from the reclining to the erect position exceeded 15 to 18 beats per minute, the individual should be advised to consult a physician.

The next significant steps in cardiac function testing began in 1914 when G. L. Meylan, W. H. Foster, and J. H. Barach each reported a physical efficiency test. Meylan's test measured blood pressure, the reaction of the heart to exercise, the character of the pulse rate, and some other elements of general condition. Foster's test was similar to Meylan's test. Barach's test indicated the efficiency of the individual by means of the pulse rate and measures of diastolic and systolic blood pressure.

In 1916 T. B. Barringer attempted to show that physically deficient individuals displayed a delayed rise in blood pressure after completion of vigorous exercise. During and after World War I Campbell, an Englishman, developed a cardiovascular adjustment test involving breath holding and recovery of normal breathing rate after exercise. This test was later shortened to a pulse rate recovery test known as Campbell's Pulse Ratio Test.

In 1920 E. C. Schneider developed a test of physical efficiency to measure the effect of exercise on the cardiovascular system. The test was used extensively in aviation during World War II to determine the physical condition of flight personnel.

In 1931 W. W. Tuttle developed his pulse Ratio Test. The pulse ratio was interpreted as the ratio between the pulse rate at rest and the pulse rate after a given amount of exercise, with a low ratio indicating efficiency of the circulatory system. Soon after the publication of Tuttle's test, McCloy presented his Test of Present Condition. In 1935 the McCurdy–Larson Test of Organic Efficiency became available. Attention increased toward almost all types of organic function tests with the advent of World War II.

In 1943 Lucien Brouha at Harvard University developed the Harvard Step Test designed to indicate the ability of the body to adapt to strenuous work and to recover quickly after work. In this test the efficiency of the circulatory system is indicated by the increase in heart rate during exercise and the speed with which the heart rate returns to normal after exercise. The test is based on the principle that the rate at which the heart slows down after it has been accelerated by a standard amount of exercise gives a correct measure of a person's condition. Brouha also worked with J. R. Gallagher on two other tests which measure essentially the same qualities as the Harvard Step Test. These tests are the Gallagher and Brouha Test for High School Boys and the Gallagher and Brouha Test for High School Girls.

During World War II the Pack Test was developed by Craig Taylor for testing large groups of men on their ability to sustain heavy work. This test, also similar to the Harvard Step Test, was used extensively during the war. In 1945 H. C. Carlson reported the Carlson Fatigue Curve Test, ten-second bouts of in-place running followed by pulse counts taken at specific times after the exercise. The underlying principle of this test is essentially the same as the Harvard Step Test.

Recently, Astrand and Ryhming developed a nomogram for the calculation of aerobic capacity from the pulse rate during submaximal work. Balke developed a cardiac function test measured on a motor driven treadmill. The Ohio State University Step Test to measure submaximal cardiovascular work was developed by Kurucz, Fox, and Mathews. Cooper presented his work on aerobic measures, and this has become widely used.

Athletic Ability Tests

Strength tests were criticized as indicators of athletic ability because they measured strength primarily. Cardiac function tests were also considered inadequate as measures of athletic ability. Therefore, some physical educators felt the need for a different type of test, one which would measure several qualities important in athletic performance. General athletic (or motor) ability tests were designed to measure a combination of speed, power, agility, strength, endurance, and other important aspects of performance ability.

The beginning of athletic ability tests can be traced to the Normal School of Gymnastics at Milwaukee, where in 1894 the abilities of the students were measured in nine different test items and compared with their performances in athletic sports. In 1901 Sargent devised a test of six simple exercises which were continued for a period of 30 minutes. Those who completed the test were considered athletically fit. Three years later Meylan at Columbia University developed tests which incorporated items such as running, jumping, vaulting, and climbing. These tests were used widely in universities.

Use of athletic ability tests in the public school curriculum began in 1908 in the New York City and Cleveland schools. In 1910 the Cincinnati schools used the Button Test to measure all-round efficiency in athletic events. The Playground and Recreation Association of America (now the National Recreation and Park Association) published the Athletic Badge Test in 1913 to stimulate interest in achieving minimum athletic performance standards. These early tests aroused the interest of people in the public schools throughout the country.

The Decathlon Test, which originated with Hetherington and H. R. Stolz in California, soon spread throughout the nation. This test for high school boys gave a choice of 20 activities including such events as the sit-up, push-up, rope climb, pull-up, high jump, broad jump, 100-yard dash, shot put, and throws for accuracy and distance. Tests were also available for high school girls and for elementary school children. In 1927 the Brace Test of Motor Ability was published and became widely used in the public schools. This test consisted of 20 stunts, which were easy to administer to groups of students.

Between 1900 and 1930 the development of athletic ability tests in college paralleled the development of those for public schools. Sigma Delta Psi, a national athletic fraternity, was established in 1912. To gain membership a candidate had to pass a general performance test. In 1915 the University of California Classification Test gained acceptance. It measured agility, defense ability, and swimming ability. In 1921 the University of Oregon began using athletic ability tests as a basis for prescribing the physical education courses for students. Other colleges used similar tests.

In 1924 McCurdy, chairman of a national committee on motor ability tests, pointed out the desirability of extending testing to the various games and sports, particularly to the so-called major sports. He developed general ability tests for football, soccer, field hockey, basketball, and tennis. These developments, along with others, led to the Cozens—Neilson books containing achievement scales for individual athletic events and to a study by Frederick W. Cozens which resulted in the Cozens Test of General Athletic Ability. Cozens' test, developed in 1929, consisted of a battery of seven tests especially selected to measure the seven components which he and other experts thought most important in athletic performance. The test has been used extensively and is still considered one of the better tests of its type.

The Humiston Motor Ability Test for college women, published in 1937, consisted of seven items which correlated highly with athletic performances. Larson's Motor Ability Test originated in 1941 and included five items in the indoor version and four items in the outdoor version. Leonard A. Larson's test has also been widely used.

In 1954 McCloy at the State University of Iowa used a rather complex approach in what is known as McCloy's General Motor Ability Test. This prescribed battery is different for various ages. It consists of a combination of strength tests and performances in track and field events. In 1957 Barrow developed a general motor ability test for college men which consists of an indoor version of three test items and an outdoor version of six items.

Several other general athletic ability tests have been developed and used in the schools. Some of these are Newton's Motor Ability Test, Scott's Motor Ability Test, Carpenter's Motor Ability Test, Olympic Motor Ability Test, Oberlin College Test, and the Emory University Test. Some other tests are closely related to general athletic ability but have been given other names. Among these are Johnson's Test of Motor Educability, Metheny's Revision of the Johnson Test, Carpenter's Test of Motor Educability, and McCloy's Test of General Motor Capacity. The validity of measuring educability and capacity has been seriously questioned.

Almost all general athletic ability tests are similar in nature. They consist of several short test items selcted to measure specific qualities considered important in a variety of athletic performances.

Motor (Physical) Fitness Tests

The term *physical fitness* became popular during and following World War II and is used to refer to the individual's ability to perform multiple tasks requiring vigorous muscular activity. The emphasis is on the efficiency of the organic systems.

During World War II much emphasis was placed on the fitness of military men. This emphasis resulted in the development of fitness tests designed specifically for military personnel. Most prominent among these tests were the Army Physical Efficiency Test, the Navy Standard Physical Fitness Test, and the Army Air Force Physical Fitness Test. These tests were designed to measure strength, endurance, agility, speed and neuromuscular coordination. All three tests have been used extensively by the military and also in areas outside the military.

In 1943 Karl W. Bookwalter constructed the Indiana Physical Fitness Tests for high school boys and girls and for college men. These tests were designed to measure fitness with particular emphasis on administrative feasibility for large groups. They have been included in the Indiana Department of Public Instruction Bulletin on Physical Education and have also been used outside the state of Indiana. Two years later the Division of Girls' and Women's Sports of the American Association of Health, Physical Education and Recreation developed a test consisting of activities selected to measure power, agility, speed, strength, endurance, and coordination of high school girls. The test was used extensively until more recent tests became available. In 1947 Bernath E. Phillips reported the JCR (jump, chin, run) test which proved to be a popular test. In 1948, C. C. Franklin and N. G. Lehsten adapted the Indiana Physical Fitness Test for use in grades four through eight and developed norms for this age group.

In 1954 Hans Kraus and Ruth P. Hirschland used the Kraus–Weber Test of Minimum Strength to compare the fitness of American children with the fitness of children in other countries. The results indicated that the American children were relatively unfit. These findings caused a great upsurge in the development of fitness programs and in fitness testing in the United States.

Because of this emphasis on fitness, the American Association for Health, Physical Education and Recreation appointed a special committee in 1958 to develop a comprehensive fitness test. The test consists of six items especially selected to measure strength, endurance, agility, speed, power, and coordination. Two sets of norms, one based on the Neilson–Cozens Classification Index, were established. Probably this test has been more widely used in the schools than any other physical education test. The test was revised in 1977 under the leadership of Hunsiker.

In 1961 the President's Council on Youth Fitness constructed the Youth Physical Fitness Test, consisting of pull-ups for boys and flexed arm hang for girls, sit-ups, and squat thrusts. This easy-to-administer test has been used in schools and in recreation and scouting programs. The test was revised in 1973 and certificates and emblems are available.

Extensive research has been done by Cooper on circulorespiratory fitness of men and women. Doolittle and Bigbee used the 12 minute run–walk to measure oxygen intake of adolescent boys. Balke used a motor-driven treadmill for a test of oxygen intake. Astrand and Ryhming developed a nomogram to calculate an individual's maximal attainable oxygen intake during work.

In addition to the fitness tests already mentioned, other tests that have had less national appeal but have been used in certain localities include the Oregon Motor Fitness Test, University of Illinois Motor Fitness Test, Elder Motor Fitness Test, New York State Physical Fitness Test, California Physical Performance Test, and the AAU (Amateur Athletic Union) Junior Olympics. Currently, fitness testing is the most popular type of testing in physical education.

Motor Skill Tests

The Playground and Recreation Association of America developed the Athletic Badge Tests for volleyball, tennis, baseball, and basketball in 1913. In 1918 Hetherington developed the California decathlon. Since then many standardized sport skill tests have been developed and used extensively in physical education. Among those that have survived the test of time are the Hyde archery test, the French short serve and clear badminton tests, the Vanderhoof golf tests, the Fox swimming test, the Cornish handball test and the Dyer backboard tennis test.

As the skills of the sport changed so have the skill tests changed. Power volleyball of today demands different techniques for proficient play than did the two hit version of volleyball played in the 1950s. The skill tests must change and must include the actual skill level demanded by the game to be valid and reliable measures of skill evaluation. This kind of transition relative to improved skill tests is constantly in effect.

Other Kinds of Tests

Even though **power** events have been used in athletic competition for centuries, little attention was given to formally testing this characteristic until 1921 when Dudley Sargent attempted to standardize the vertical jump as a test of leg power. A decade later Charles McCloy gave additional attention to the vertical jump and other tests of power. Around 1950 Edward Capen did some useful research on the topic of power testing, and concurrently Edward Chui did research on how to develop and test power. The most useful developments on power testing during recent years have been done by Rodolfo Margaria in the development of the Margaria Anaerobic Power Test and by James Kalamen who did subsequent research that resulted in the Margaria-Kalamen Power Test.

Royal Burpee in 1935 devised the ten-second squat thrust test as a measure of **agility.** In the late 1930s and early 1950s Charles McCloy and his associates did considerable work in the testing of agility, and he and Norma Young devised several running agility tests. More recently, agility tests were developed by Barry Johnson and Jack Nelson in the late 1960s in the form of the Quadrangle Jump Test and the LSU Agility Test.

Very little formal testing of **flexibility** was done prior to 1941 when Thomas Cureton published several practical flexibility tests which became widely used. In 1942 Jack Leighton reported new measures of flexibility and he also developed the Leighton flexometer which made possible new approaches in flexibility measurement. Katherine Wells and Evelyn Gillan devised the Sit-and-Reach Flexibility Test in 1952. In 1966, Barry Johnson modified the Wells and Dillon Test. Also Johnson developed a testing instrument known as the Flexomeasurer along with several tests with which it can be used.

In 1951, Franklin Henry did significant research on the topic of measuring **reaction time** and **speed of movement,** and in 1961, he published research on the relationship between reaction time and movement time. In 1965, Fred Nelson constructed the Nelson Reaction Timer and tests with which it can be used. In 1969, Clayne Jensen developed the Four-way Alternate Response Test and he also developed the Hand and Arm Response Test.

One of the most useful early tests of **posture** was the Wesley test developed by Charlotte MacEwan and Eugene Howe in 1932. Wayne Massey developed the Massey Posture Test in 1943, and the Kraus-Weber Refined Posture Test was completed in 1945. In 1958, the New York State Fitness Test was developed and it includes a posture test which has turned out to be one of the most widely used posture screening tests yet developed.

One of the earliest **sports knowledge** tests was developed by J. G. Bliss in 1929. Since then, a rather large number of sports knowledge tests have been constructed in a variety of activities with some of the leading contributors being Katherine Fox, Esther French, Katherine Ley, Catherine Snell, Gail Hennis, Jack Hewitt, and Gladys Scott.

B. E. Blanchard was one of the pioneers in developing measures of **personality traits,** and in 1951 the Weir Attitude Inventory was developed. Cowell's Social Adjustment Index was completed in 1958. In 1961, the Mercer Attitude Inventory was published. Others who have contributed significantly to this field are Harold Barrow, Martha Carr, Marianne Kneer, Rosemary McGee, and Genevie Dexter.

Classification of Measurements

2

When a field of study is in its first stages of formulation, confusion frequently results from a lack of clearly defined relationships among the areas of knowledge. Well-established sciences are bodies of analyzed, systematized, classified knowledge. In botany, for instance, plants are classified, and in zoology animals are classified. Physical education consists of a number of areas which are in various stages of classification, so one might contend that physical education is in the process of becoming a science. One of the first steps to avoid confusion in the study of physical education measurement is to view and study the various ways in which measurements may be classified.

Measurements are designed to examine, test, measure, and evaluate human traits. All human traits may be classified under two general categories: structural traits and functional traits. Structure and function are dynamic, that is, subject to change. They are closely related and affect each other to some degree throughout the whole period of a person's growth and development. Both structural and functional traits may be analyzed, synthesized, and hence classified from the general to the specific and from the specific to the general.

People exhibit differences in many structural and functional traits. In general these differences may be classified according to race, sex, age, and individual traits. When they fall outside the range called normality, these differences are classified as divergencies, or anomalies. Six fingers on one hand, and one arm rather than two, are divergencies in structure. A broken leg, mitral insufficiency, and typhoid fever are examples of divergencies in function. Difficulties in testing may often be avoided by using tests constructed specifically for one sex, or for one age, when such groupings are important. Likewise, tests may be designed for children in elementary school, for boys or girls in junior or

15

senior high school, for college men or women, or for the middle-aged or even older adults.

A Method of Classifying Measurements

All measurements in physical education are of either **structural** or **functional** traits. Anthropometric measurements deal with structural traits. Tests of functional traits fall into four categories: interpretive traits (knowledge, concepts, beliefs, and so on), impulsive traits (feelings, interests, attitudes, and so forth), neuromuscular traits (nerve–muscle coordinations), and organic traits (functions of the organic systems).

Anthropometric Measurements

Anthropometric measurements are objective measurements of body structure. Height, weight, hip width, chest depth, and girth of the upper arm are examples of anthropometric measurements. Long before the Christian era the people of India, China, and Greece measured the size, form, and symmetry of the body and related these traits to beauty and function. Sculptors in Greece searched for a unit of measurement that could be used to find the correct proportions of the perfect man and woman.

Measurement in objective units is possible with such tools as scales, tape measure, calipers, stadiometer, and silhouetteograph. Helen B. Pryor's Width–Weight Tables and the Wetzel Grid have proved to be useful standards for finding the lower and upper limits of normal weight in terms of growth rate. Sheldon classified physique, or body type, as endomorphic, mesomorphic, or ectomorphic. Body build assumes importance as a facet of measurement because of its effect on motor performance. Certain body builds are advantageous to certain activities; a heavy build may help a football tackle, but is a hindrance to a distance runner.

Tests of Interpretive Traits

Interpretive traits include perceptions, ideas, concepts, understandings, knowledge, and judgments. Information or knowledge tests about the history of physical education; about the rules, techniques, and strategies which govern performance; about the environment which influences performance; and about oneself as a performer may be classified as tests of interpretive traits. These tests may be given orally, or they may require writing an essay or answering true–false, matching, multiple-choice, or completion questions. Tests of interpretive traits have been and may be constructed in a great variety of physical education activities.

Tests of Impulsive Traits

Tests, or ratings, of the degree of interest in physical education activities, of attitudes toward activities, of maturity of emotions, and of the quality of ideals held may be classified as tests of impulsive traits. These kinds of measurements are usually in the form of rating scales or check lists. They become subjective estimates of the traits under consideration. The rating scales relating to interest may use such headings as *excellent, above average, average, below average,* and *poor.* Relating to attitudes, the headings may be *always, usually, sometimes, rarely,* and *never;* or, *strongly agree, agree, undecided, disagree,* and *strongly disagree.* While little has been done to date, possibilities exist for the development of tests to measure the ideals and the emotional maturity as these factors relate to physical education.

Tests of Neuromuscular Traits

Neuromuscular tests include measurements of strength, specific skills, agility, power, reaction time, speed, balance, flexibility, and other qualities of performance which depend primarily upon the effective functioning of the nervous and muscular systems.

Individual strength tests have been devised for specific muscle groups, such as strength of arm and shoulder girdle, hand, back, abdomen, and legs. A general strength index may be determined with a battery of strength tests. Tests of other neuromuscular traits have also been developed, including tests of muscular (explosive) power, flexibility, speed, agility, reaction time, and balance.

Many tests of specific skills are available in the areas of individual events (100-yard run, long jump), elements in games (football kick for distance, softball throw for accuracy, base running against time, putting accuracy), individual sports (archery, bowling, golf, swimming), dual activities (badminton, handball, tennis), and team sports (baseball, basketball, field hockey, American football, rugby, softball, soccer, speedball, and volleyball).

Tests of Organic Traits

Organic traits include the physiological functions of internal organs and systems of organs (circulatory, respiratory, digestive, eliminative, and heat-regulating mechanisms). Physical educators are primarily interested in the efficiency of the circulatory and respiratory processes of organic systems.

There are two kinds of tests of endurance: tests of muscular endurance (static and dynamic) and tests of circulatory–respiratory endurance. Some activities emphasize muscular endurance (the ability to repeat muscular contractions many times), while other activities emphasize circulatory–respiratory endurance.

Batteries of Tests

Two or more different tests administered to a person within a short time is called a *battery of tests.* The tests might measure several traits, and the intercorrelations of the traits may be relatively low. A battery of tests may be given in one activity, such as soccer, it may include two or more activities, or it may test a series of traits within one aspect of development. The results of batteries of tests may be interpreted in relation to achievement, ability, and progress. Skill tests in individual athletic events may be combined into a pentathlon (five events) or decathlon (ten events).

Batteries of tests have been developed to measure such traits as general athletic ability, total body strength, and flexibility. In recent years several test batteries, labeled Tests of Physical Fitness, have been introduced.

Other Methods of Classification

Physical education measurements may also be classified according to (1) kind of activity (such as basketball tests or swimming tests), (2) type of test structure (such as true–false or essay), (3) purpose of test (such as diagnosis or motivation), and (4) traits to be measured (such as ability, achievement, or progress). A given test may fall under all four categories, for example, a **true–false** test of **ability** to remember certain rules of **basketball** given for **diagnostic** purposes to discover which rules need to be reviewed.

Kind of Activity

Tests named after specific physical education activities have been constructed and used in football, gymnastic activities, archery, badminton, baseball, basketball, bowling, dance, diving, fencing, golf, swimming, tennis, individual events in track and field, volleyball, wrestling, and a great variety of other activities appropriate for students in the elementary schools, secondary schools, and colleges.

Type of Test Structure

Written tests may consist of essay questions which are to be answered in paragraph form, statements which are to be answered true or false (true–false test), statements which are to be matched (matching test), several statements from which the most appropriate one is to be selected (multiple-choice test), and statements which are to be completed by inserting the missing words (completion test). A given test may be composed of one or more of these types of questions.

Purpose of Test

Tests may be given for different reasons, that is, for diagnostic, classification, administrative, motivational, supervisory, or research purposes. Tests given by physical education instructors to determine the needs of students for specific kinds of development serve a diagnostic purpose, and the results may be used to guide individuals into appropriate and meaningful experiences. Tests may also be used to classify students into homogeneous groups for purposes of instruction or competition. Tests have an administrative use when grading students and when evaluating methods of instruction. They have a supervisory use when evaluating the efficiency of teachers, and they may serve the purposes of research when the data obtained are needed for the solution of specific problems.

Traits Measured

Tests may be designed to measure performance, progress, achievement, ability, and capacity. The basic tool in determining values in any aspect of function (behavior) is the performance record. Performance scores are used as indicators of progress, achievement, ability, and capacity. But a given performance score is not necessarily an accurate measure of achievement, ability, or capacity.

Measurement of Performance. A sample performance record of a student is not necessarily his or her present ability or capacity to perform. Performance may depend on a number of factors, including motivation, emotional status, effort, organic condition, time of day, and even weather. Performance may also be influenced by sex, age, height, weight, body build, innate capacity, and degree of maturation. An individual's performance is what he or she does on a particular occasion, for example, five feet in the high jump.

Measurement of Progress. Two or more measures, separated by a period of time, are necessary to measure progress. For example, performance tests may be given at the beginning and again at the end of a course for the purpose of measuring the amount of progress made during the intervening time. Measuring progress is important because the results indicate whether certain kinds of development have occurred and at what rate.

Measurement of Achievement. When a student does a standing long jump of seven feet and then asks the instructor whether this performance is poor or good, the instructor may give a subjective evaluation (judgment based on past experience) or an objective evaluation if there is an achievement scale at hand. Measures of achievement are simply evaluations of performance in terms of what other students in a classified group can do. Measuring achievement is of primary value in motivating students to perform better.

Achievement scales may be constructed in individual games or sports (archery), in individual events (high jump), and in elements of games or sports (volleyball serve for accuracy). The necessary requirement is that the individual perform alone; that is, his or her performance should not depend upon the performance of others.

Measurement of Ability. In physical education the terms *ability* and *capacity* have sometimes been used interchangeably without regard to the differences in meaning. Capacity means potential, or the limits within which ability may be developed. Ability indicates the actual amount (expressed overtly in performance) to which capacity has been developed. Hence, an individual will probably always have a greater capacity to perform in a given activity than he or she has ability to perform. At any given time a person's ability is represented by his or her best performance record taken from numerous trials. Ability in activities may be modified considerably as a result of learning, practice, and conditioning.

Measurement of Capacity. The capacity to perform an activity is limited in part by heredity and in part by the development that occurs during the period of maturation. To some extent capacity is dynamic, a result of a number of factors. To illustrate, one's capacity to high jump at age 2 years, 20 years, and 80 years is not the same. Capacity is different from ability in that capacity represents the limits within which ability may be developed. At present it is doubtful whether there are any valid tests of capacity to perform in motor activities. Perhaps the best approach to estimating capacity is to study learning and achievement curves represented by improved performances. It seems logical to assume that motor aptitude and motor educability are aspects of motor capacity.

3

Selection and Administration of Measurements

Measurements range from highly subjective evaluations to highly objective tests. Objective measures are based largely on fact, while subjective measures are primarily a result of personal judgment. Subjective measurement, such as a teacher's evaluation of a student's character, includes some degree of objectivity, but also involves a large amount of subjective judgment. Objective measurement is based on more precise information. A measure is objective to the extent that it will produce the same results when conducted by different people under similar conditions—in other words when the subjectivity of the test administrator is eliminated. No measure in physical education is completely objective, and no measure ought to be completely subjective. Teachers should strive for a high degree of objectivity in measurement, but still realize that not all important traits can be measured objectively.

Selection Criteria

The physical education teacher is confronted with the problem of selecting good tools to be used in measurement. Successful selection of tools requires a general knowledge of measurement and of characteristics of good tests. Measurements may be selected for classifying pupils, measuring achievement, diagnosing defects, issuing grades or marks, or motivating students. Following are some important factors to consider in the selection of tests.

E 5237

Validity

Validity is the degree to which the test actually measures what it is claimed to measure. For instance, a test of strength is valid to the extent that it actually measures *strength*. The validity of a test is specific to the test, and to the reason for the test being given. Valid data reflect reality.

Concurrent or criterion-related validity is the degree of relationship between two sets of test scores. It is the amount of agreement between scores on a test and some outside criterion (rating or grades, for example).

Construct validity is the degree to which a given test compares or correlates with another test that has an established validity. This type of validity can be logical as well as statistical.

Curricular validity is present when a test deals with the material covered in a particular assigned textbook, chapter, or lecture.

Reliability

Reliability is the extent to which a measurement consistently measures the same quality each time a test is administered. Reliability means *consistency* of measurement, meaning that all persons using the procedure will achieve the same results consistently. Problems of reliability can be minimized by adopting systematic procedures of measurement, applying such procedures in practical and consistent ways, and applying the measurement to as large a group as possible. Precision is a key technique in data gathering when reliability of the test instrument is a factor.

There are several methods for determining reliability coefficients: *Test–Retest Method* in which the test is administered two times to the same group of subjects and the results are compared; *Parallel Form Method* in which the group receives two forms of a test with the same content; and *Split-Half Method* in which the test is divided into two parts, usually odd and even numbers, and the two parts are correlated.

Objectivity

As explained earlier, *objectivity* is the degree to which exact results are obtained from a measurement. Objectivity is the precision of the instruments and technique used. Since it contributes to consistency, objectivity can add or detract from the *reliability* of a measure.

Administrative Economy

Administrative economy is determined by the time and money needed to administer the test. A practical and useful test must be economical in terms of time and cost. It is difficult to say how much time and money should be devoted to the administration of any test, but in every case, before an instructor decides to use the test, the instructor should weigh the value of the results in comparison with the expenditure of money, time, and effort.

Educational Application

Educational application is the degree to which being involved in the testing experience is educational to the student and is the degree to which the test motivates the student to learn. In the selection and construction of tests, educational application should serve as an important guide. In other words the experience of taking the test should be educational. The tests used should be harmonious with and supplement the course content.

Norms

Norms are standards against which raw scores may be compared. The availability of norms may lead to the selection of one test in preference to another.

Standard Instructions

Instructions are important for the administration of standardized tests if the results are to be reliable. Hence, some good tests may be rejected because standardized instructions are not available. Instructions should be as brief, complete, and clear as possible; they should also include an example or demonstration.

In general, authorities on testing agree that, except for use in research, only valid measures that can be administered to a group of students at one time and require little equipment are highly useful in physical education. Measurements are of value only if the results can be accurately interpreted and practically applied.

Administration Techniques

Careful attention should be given to the administration of tests. Poorly administered tests can produce results which are misleading and useless to both the teacher and the students. The following guides are helpful in administering tests.

1. Select and administer a test for a specific purpose, and be certain that it is administered in such a way that it accomplishes that purpose.
2. Become familiar with the test and the procedures involved before attempting to administer it.
3. Make early arrangements for all necessary facilities and equipment, and be sure the equipment is in functional condition.
4. Determine the layout of testing stations and have needed equipment in place at the required time. The layout for testing should permit the test items to be given in correct sequence and still result in easy flow of traffic.
5. Be sure those being tested appear in appropriate clothing, especially in appropriate footwear.

6. Make early arrangements for necessary assistant leaders to help administer the test. In some cases a short period of training the assistants may be desirable.
7. Conduct the test exactly as explained in the instructions.
8. Teach the students to perform the test item correctly.
   a. State the purpose of the test item (what it measures).
   b. Give a description of the test item and the way to perform it.
   c. Demonstrate the item. (Either the teacher or a trained student may demonstrate.)
   d. Answer any questions to clarify procedure.
   e. Lead the students in the practice of items for which pretest practice is appropriate.
   f. Describe briefly the method of scoring and the way results will be interpreted and scored.
9. Have the necessary score sheets, pencils, and scoring scales available.

The test results should be interpreted and used to the advantage of the students and the program. Teachers should constantly be aware that the exactness and correctness with which they administer a test influences its reliability and therefore its validity. Measures that might have been valuable become useless when they are improperly administered or incorrectly interpreted.

Selected References

1. **Barrow, H. M.**, and **McMee, R.**: Evaluation of tests *and* Administration of Tests, in *A Practical Approach to Measurement in Physical Education*, 2nd ed. Philadelphia, Pa.: Lea & Febiger, May 1974.
2. **Baumgartner, T. A.**, and **Jackson, A.**: Reliability, validity, and objectivity, in *Measurement for Evaluation in Physical Education*. Boston, Mass.: Houghton-Mifflin, 1975.
3. **Clarke, H. H.**: Test evaluation, in *Application of Measurement to Health and Physical Education*. Englewood Cliffs, N.J.: Prentice-Hall, 1976.
4. **Johnson, Barry L.**, and **Nelson, Jack K.**: Test evaluation and construction, in *Practical Measurements for Evaluation in Physical Education*, Minneapolis, Minn.: Burgess Publishing Co., 1974.
5. **Mathews, Donald K.**: Test selection, in *Measurement in Physical Education*, 4th ed., Philadelphia, Pa.: Saunders, 1978.

Statistical
Techniques

4

Basic Statistical Methods

The use of statistical techniques permits measurement results to be more objective, provides better communication about the measurements, allows the measurements to be summarized in concise, meaningful ways, and can be used to establish reliability and validity measures.

The emphasis in this chapter is on statistical techniques that are highly useful to the educators. The chapter does not include a complete presentation of research statistical techniques.

A brief review of basic mathematical procedures is in Appendix A. Even though mathematical computations can be done with a calculator, an understanding of basic mathematical procedure is desirable in order to better understand the statistical procedures presented.

Measurement Scales

Measurement can be defined as the assignment of numbers to performances, objects, attributes of individuals, etc. according to accepted standards of measurement, for example, distance, time, or percentage. The standards are based on mathematical calculations that are standardized so that everyone using them understands their meaning.

It is valuable to organize the results of measurement into types so that proper statistical treatment can be given. The types of the measurement scales are: Nominal, ordinal, interval, and ratio. Data that are collected will fall into one of these categories.

The *nominal scale* is the most elementary scale and is used to identify persons or objects. Examples are the numbers on basketball uniforms or license plates, or divisions by sex or race. These numbers give no indication of value.

The *ordinal scale* is used with data that are ranked. The numbers are placed in order of importance, order of finish, fastest to slowest, or some other arrangement showing relationship, and are treated statistically in the ranked order in which they fall.

The *interval scale* is a very useful measurement scale, and utilizes an arbitrary zero point as on a thermometer where zero does not mean an absence of temperature.

The *ratio scale* is the most useful level of measurement. The data are ordered in equal intervals and there is an absolute zero point where there is an absence of the measurement; zero weight means no weight, zero time means no time. Measurement of time, weight, distance, can be made on ratio scales. If one child took 20 minutes to walk the track and another took 10 minutes to walk the same distance, it can be said that one child took twice as long as the other to walk the same distance.

All data can be classified as *discrete* or *continuous*. *Discrete* data are recorded in whole numbers like 1, 10, 16. The number of free throws out of 10, the number of boys in a class of 35 students, are examples of discrete data.

Continuous data can be recorded in *fractions* of whole numbers. Track, skiing, and swimming events are recorded to the hundredth of a second. Batting averages are recorded in percentages. Throwing performances can be measured in feet and inches (or fractions of inches) and weight can be measured in pounds and ounces. These are all examples of continuous data.

Describing and Presenting Data

Frequency Distributions

Anyone who has worked with test scores knows the difficulty of making meaningful interpretations from a group of unordered scores. Scores need to be presented and arranged in some meaningful fashion so that they are easy to work with and easy to interpret. One possibility is to place them in order from the highest to the lowest scores (rank order). If the number of scores is small such an arrangement is adequate, but with a large number of scores a rank-order arrangement presents an awkward situation. Therefore, a better procedure is to construct a frequency distribution. A frequency distribution is a logical arrangement of data so that large numbers of measurements can be made easier to handle.

Frequency distributions may be either simple or grouped. In a *simple frequency distribution* data are organized with all possible score values listed in order of size; the number of frequencies of each score value is then indicated. A simple frequency distribution greatly facilitates interpretation; the more frequently occurring scores stand out clearly so that the high and low scores and the total number of scores become apparent. The simple frequency distribution gives a graphic impression of the distribution of scores. Table 4-1 is an example of a simple frequency distribution.

To establish a simple frequency distribution:

1. Indicate the distribution as a table and assign it a number.
2. Give it a title which identifies it as a simple frequency distribution and describes its contents.
3. Establish three columns and label them score (x), tally (t), and frequency (f).
4. In the x column record all possible score values from the highest to the lowest score.
5. In the t column tally each score by recording a tally mark opposite that score value. ·
6. Total the tally marks for each score value and record that total in the f column.

If the scores are numerous and cover a large range, the simple frequency distribution becomes lengthy, therefore, a more compact arrangement is desirable. Such an arrangement can be accomplished by a *grouped frequency distribution*, an organization of scores with all possible score values included in equal intervals and with the score values within each interval indicated. The

TABLE 4-1 Simple Frequency Distribution of Scores Made by 50 High School Girls on the Curl-up Test (Data I)*

x (score)	t (tally)	f (frequency)
21	//	2
20	//	2
19	////	4
18	ЖТ /	6
17	ЖТ ЖТ /	11
16	ЖТ	5
15	////	4
14	////	4
13	////	4
12	/	1
11	///	3
10	/	1
9	//	2
8		0
7	/	1
		N = 50

*Data I appears in Appendix B.

grouped frequency distribution may give a better concept of the shape of the distribution of scores than a simple frequency distribution, but in a grouped distribution the identity of the individual scores is lost. A grouped frequency distribution is valuable when the scores are to be displayed in a chart or graph. Table 4-2 is an example of a grouped frequency distribution.

To construct a grouped frequency distribution:

1. Give the table a number and a descriptive title.
2. Establish three columns and label them intervals (steps), t (tally), and f (frequency).
3. Determine the range of the scores (highest score minus lowest).
4. Determine the approximate number of intervals desired (usually not more than 25 intervals nor less than 12).
5. Divide the range of scores by the desired number of intervals to determine the approximate size of the intervals.
6. Make a final decision on the number and size of intervals on the basis of convenience and purpose.
7. Record the interval limits, tally the scores, and record the frequencies.

TABLE 4-2   Grouped Frequency Distribution of Scores Made by 75 High School Boys on the Right Grip Test, Measured to the Nearest Pound, and Recorded in Intervals of 5 Units (Data II) *

Intervals	t	f
135–139	//	2
130–134	/	1
125–129	ЖНГ	5
120–124	////	4
115–119	///	3
110–114	ЖНГ ////	9
105–109	ЖНГ /	6
100–104	ЖНГ ЖНГ //	12
95–99	ЖНГ ЖНГ	10
90–94	ЖНГ //	7
85–89	ЖНГ	5
80–84	//	2
75–79	ЖНГ	5
70–74		0
65–69	/	1
60–64	///	3
		$N = 75$

*Data II appears in Appendix B.

Certain points concerning the construction and interpretation of a grouped frequency distribution are important.

1. Five, and multiples of five are preferred sizes of intervals because these numbers are easy to handle mathematically. Usually odd numbers, such as three, five, seven, are preferred because they yield a whole number as the midpoint of each interval.
2. The upper limit of one interval is always separated from the lower limit of the next higher interval by one unit of measure. The unit of measure for the data in Table 4-2 is one pound. Therefore, the step intervals are separated by one pound (60–64, 65–69, 70–74, and so on). Had the data been recorded to the nearest half pound, the step intervals would have been separated by that unit of measure (60–64.5, 65–69.5, and so on).
3. When data are recorded to the nearest unit, the real limits of a step interval extend one half unit above and one half unit below the recorded limits of the interval. For example, in Table 4-2 the recorded limits of the second and third intervals are 65–69 and 70–74, respectively. The real limits of the two intervals are 64.5–69.499 and 69.5–74.499, respectively. (74.499 represents 74.5 reduced.)

Recorded Limits (separated by one unit of measure)	Real Limits (includes all values actually represented by the interval)
75–79	74.5–79.499
70–74	69.5–74.499
65–69	64.5–69.499
60–64	59.5–64.499

4. The scores within a given interval in a grouped frequency distribution are assumed to be spread evenly over the entire interval. The midpoint of the interval is the most logical choice to represent all scores within a given interval by a single value. To compute the midpoint of the interval 100–104 in Table 4-2, the following formula should be used:

$$\text{midpoint} = \text{lower real limit of interval} + \frac{\text{upper real limit} - \text{lower real limit}}{2}$$

Hence,

$$\text{midpoint} = 99.5 + \frac{104.5 - 99.5}{2} = 102$$

Assignment 1

1. Using Data III from Appendix B, make a frequency distribution for each factor under the following conditions:

	Interval	Highest Interval
Height	1	70
Weight	5	155–159
Leg strength	20	760–779
High jump	2	60–61
100-yard run	.5	10.0–10.4*
Long jump	5	210–214

*In races the lowest time is the best (highest) score.

2. State the range for each distribution prepared under 1 above.
3. In leg strength what is the midpoint of the third step from the top?
4. In the 100-yard run what is the midpoint of the second step from the top?
5. N = the number of scores. What does N equal for weight? for high jump?

Graphical Methods

Graphs reveal the same information found in frequency distributions, but in graphs the information is conveyed pictorially. There are certain advantages of graphs over frequency distributions: (a) In some graphs the shape and characteristics of the distribution become more obvious, and (b) for people unfamiliar with the data the information in a graph is more easily understandable. Basic graphs are based on the coordinate system which involves two axes: Y, the vertical axis (ordinate); and X, the horizontal axis (abscissa).

Any point can be plotted on the coordinate system when its X and Y values are known. For example, locate point P when $X = +2$ and $Y = +2$.

The histogram, frequency polygon, and cumulative frequency curve are standard graphs. Variations of these standard forms are often used. These graphs have the following points in common:

1. In all cases the score values are recorded on the horizontal axis (abscissa), and the frequencies are represented on the vertical axis (ordinate).
2. The score values are recorded from low to high, moving from left to right.
3. When the data are grouped, the midpoint of each interval is used to

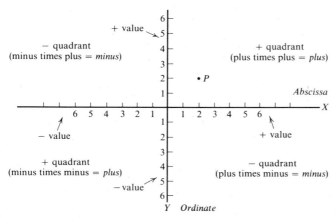

FIGURE 4-1. Coordinate system. Any point can be plotted on the coordinate system if its X and Y values are known. For example, point P is plotted when X = +2 and Y = +2.

represent all scores in the interval. Hence, all values on the horizontal scale are midpoints of intervals.

4. Each graph must carry a title and should be labeled "Figure" with a number (for example, Figure 4-1). The title is usually placed below the graph.

5. Both axes (ordinate and abscissa) are labeled.

Histogram

A histogram is a graph in which the score frequencies are represented by a series of adjacent columns. The base of each column corresponds to the size of the interval, and the height of each column is proportional to the frequencies in the interval. The middle of the column is at the midpoint of the interval, and the edges of the column represent the upper and lower real limits of the interval. Figure 4-2 is an example of the histogram.

To construct a histogram:

1. Leave a space of one-half column between the ordinate and the first column and between the last column and the end of the abscissa.

2. Be sure that all columns are exactly the same width because they represent intervals of equal size. (They need not be separate as in Figure 4-2).

3. Decide on the size for the length and height of the graph. (The height is generally about two thirds of the length.)

4. Label both the vertical and horizontal scales and assign a title describing the content of the graph.

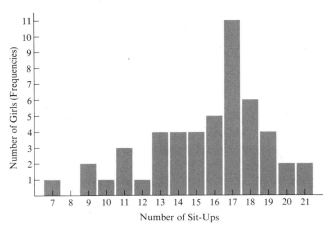

FIGURE 4-2. Histogram of scores made by 50 high school girls on the curl-up test. (See frequency distribution in Table 4-1.)

5. After establishing the vertical and horizontal scales, plot the upper and lower limits of each interval along the abscissa, plot the upper and lower limits of each interval at the height of the frequencies in that interval, and draw the necessary lines to complete the columns (see Figure 4-2).

Frequency Polygon

A polygon is a line graph in which the midpoints of the intervals are joined by straight lines at the height of the frequencies in the intervals (see Figure 4-3).

To construct a frequency polygon:

1. Place the first score along the horizontal scale at a distance of one interval from the ordinate.
2. Plot a point directly above each interval midpoint which appears on the horizontal scale and directly opposite the appropriate point along the frequency (vertical) scale. After the points have been plotted in the correct positions draw connecting lines between the points.
3. Close the graph line at both ends to a point one interval above the highest number and one interval below the lowest number on the horizontal scale.

Cumulative Frequency (Ogive) Curve

A cumulative frequency curve is made up of the total frequencies in the distribution which have been added cumulatively, beginning at the bottom of the

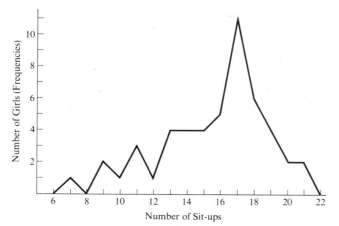

FIGURE 4-3. Frequency polygon of scores made by 50 high school girls on the curl-up test. (See frequency distribution in Table 4-1.)

column (see Table 4-3). Each cumulative frequency point is plotted at the upper limit of the step in which it falls. After being plotted, the points are connected with straight lines to form the curve. The slope of the curve indicates the concentration of scores; for example, the steeper the line the greater the concentration of scores.

TABLE 4-3 A Simple Frequency Distribution of Scores Made by 50 High School Girls on the Curl-up Test (cf column added)

x	f	cf (cumulative frequencies)
21	2	50
20	2	48
19	4	46
18	6	42
17	11	36
16	5	25
15	4	20
14	4	16
13	4	12
12	1	8
11	3	7
10	1	4
9	2	3
8	0	1
7	1	1
		$N = 50$

36

For a more meaningful curve a percentile scale may be added to the right-hand side of the graph. The scale is labeled and marked off in equal units covering a range of 0 to 100 percent. When the percentile scale is added, the curve is called an "ogive." (Percentiles are described later in this chapter.)

To construct a cumulative frequency (ogive) curve:

1. Add a cumulative frequency column to the frequency distribution (see Table 4-3).
2. Devise the *left-hand scale* to cover the range of the total number of frequencies in the distribution. (This scale is equal to the cumulative frequency (*cf*) column in a frequency distribution.) Devise the *horizontal scale* to cover the total range of scores, and the *right-hand scale* to include the complete percentile range (0–100). (The right-hand scale should correspond to the cumulative frequency scale in height and proportion.)
3. Plot a point above the upper limit of each score at the height of the cumulative frequencies of the score. Then draw lines connecting the points.
4. Label each of the scales and assign a descriptive title to the graph.

Once the cumulative frequency curve and percentile scale have been constructed, the percentile rank of any score can be determined by drawing a line vertical to the curve line and then a line horizontal to the percentile scale. The opposite procedure may be followed to find the score equal to any given percentile (see Figure 4-4).

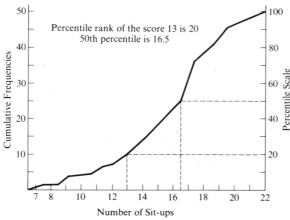

FIGURE 4-4. Combined cumulative frequency curve and percentile scale made by 50 high school girls on the curl-up test.

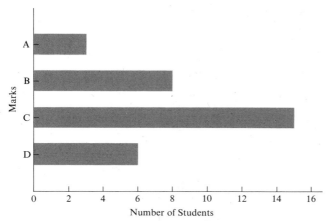

FIGURE 4-5. Horizontal bar graph of marks given to 32 students in a basketball class (A-3, B-8, C-15, D-6)

Horizontal Bar Graph

A horizontal bar graph (Figure 4-5) is a variation of a histogram. Sometimes the bars are made of figures representing the content of the graph. For instance, if the graph were about population trends, the bars might be made of figures of people.

Pie Graph

A pie graph is simply a complete circle divided into pie-shaped portions with each portion proportionate to the amount that it represents (see Figure 4-6). Each portion is usually labeled with the percentage of the whole that it represents. This type of graph is easy to read and is, therefore, often used to present information to laymen and to the masses.

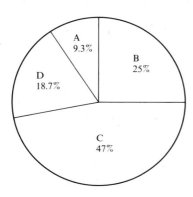

FIGURE 4-6. Pie graph of marks given to 32 students in a basketball class.

Assignment 2

1. Using the height scores in Data III from Appendix B, construct a histogram and give a verbal interpretation of what the graph tells you.
2. Using Data II as it is organized in Table 4-2, construct a frequency polygon and give a verbal interpretation of what the graph tells you.
3. Using Data II as it is organized in Table 4-2, construct an ogive curve and answer the following questions. (A *cf* column will need to be added to Table 4-2.)
   (a) Which score is at the 60th percentile? the 30th percentile?
   (b) What is the percentile rank of the score 75? of the score 115?
4. In connection with Data II from Appendix B the following ratings are given: excellent 125 and above, good 110–124, average 95–109, fair 80–94, poor 79 and below. Construct a pie graph showing the proportion of students who scored excellent, good, average, fair, and poor.

Measures of Central Tendency

Measures of central tendency are points on a scale which give a single measure that represents the whole group. The three measures of central tendency most frequently used are the mean, the median, and the mode.

The *mean* is the arithmetic average. It is the sum of the scores divided by the number of scores. The symbol for the population mean is μ. The symbol for the mean of a sample is $\overline{X}$. For purposes of clarity, the sample mean symbol will be used in this section on central tendency.

The *median* is a measure of position only. It is easy to calculate and the best representative measure of a skewed distribution, since extreme scores do not affect it. However, no further calculation may be made from it because it is a nonarithmetic measure. It is not highly stable, since it can be changed with the alteration of only a few scores (depending on which scores are altered). The symbol or abbreviation for the median is *Mdn*.

The *mode* is the most frequent score in a distribution and is easy to calculate. Yet it is extremely unstable, may be a poor representative measure of the group, and cannot be used as a basis for further calculations.

Computing the Mean

The mean may be computed by using the following formulas. In the formulas: $\overline{X}$ = mean; Σ = sum of; X = scores; N = number of scores (cases); f = frequency.

Formula A $\overline{X} = \dfrac{\Sigma X}{N}$ (To be used when data are not ordered)

Formula B $\overline{X} = \dfrac{\Sigma(fX)}{N}$ (To be used when data are ordered)

Following is an example of the application of formula A, using the unordered scores in Data I from Appendix B.

Scores

13	20	9	15	16
7	17	17	18	11
10	16	19	17	17
11	14	17	13	15
19	21	14	12	13
15	16	11	14	18
17	17	17	18	21
15	19	17	18	16
13	17	16	20	14
18	19	9	17	18

$\Sigma X = 781$
$N = 50$

$$\overline{X} = \frac{\Sigma X}{N}$$

$$= \frac{781}{50}$$

$$\overline{X} = 15.62$$

The following chart is an example of the application of formula B using a simple frequency distribution of Data I.

X	f	fX
21	2	42
20	2	40
19	4	76
18	6	108
17	11	187
16	5	80
15	4	60
14	4	56
13	4	52
12	1	12
11	3	33
10	1	10
9	2	18
8	0	0
7	1	7
N = 50		fX = 781

$$\overline{X} = \frac{\Sigma(fX)}{N}$$

$$= \frac{781}{50}$$

$$\overline{X} = 15.62$$

Assignment 3

1. Using Data III from Appendix B, and formula A, compute the mean for each of the six factors.
2. Using Data III, formula B, compute the mean for height and the high jump.
3. Using Data III, formula B, and compute the mean for strength and the 100-yard run.

Computing the Median

The median is the middle measure on a scale in which all measures have been arranged in order of their size. The median of the following scores is nine.

$$4 \quad 5 \quad 6 \quad 7 \quad 8 \quad 9 \quad 10 \quad 11 \quad 12 \quad 13 \quad 14$$
$$\uparrow$$
$$\text{median}$$

To compute the Median from a Simple Frequency Distribution:

1. Arrange the data into a simple frequency distribution.
2. Add a cumulative frequency (cf) column by successively adding the frequencies of each score beginning at the bottom.
3. Divide N by 2 and locate the step in which that number occurs in the cf column. The score in that step is the median.

Note the following example using Data I.

X	f	cf
21	2	50
20	2	48
19	4	46
18	6	42
17	11	36
16	5	25
15	4	20
14	4	16
13	4	12
12	1	8
11	3	7
10	1	4
9	2	3
8	0	1
7	1	1
	N = 50	

$$Mdn = \frac{N}{2} = \frac{50}{2} = 25\text{th score}$$

The median is the score in the step which includes the 25th score from the bottom in the cf column.

$$Mdn = 16$$

To compute the Median from a Grouped Frequency Distribution, use the any-percentile formula:

$$P = LL + \frac{np - n'}{f'} \times SI$$

where

P = desired percentile (Mdn = 50th percentile)

LL = lower real limit of the interval in which P will lie

n = number of cases

p = percentage desired

n' = number of cases included up to the lower limit of the interval in which P lies

f' = frequencies in the interval in which P lies

SI = size of the step interval

Note the following example using the any-percentile formula and Data II.

X	f	cf
135–139	2	75
130–134	1	73
125–129	5	72
120–124	4	67
115–119	3	63
110–114	9	60
105–109	6	51
100–104	12	45
95–99	10	33
90–94	7	23
85–89	5	16
80–84	2	11
75–79	5	9
70–74	0	4
65–69	1	4
60–64	3	3
	N = 75	

$$Mdn \text{ (50th percentile)} = LL + \frac{np - n'}{f'} \times SI$$

The interval in which P will lie is found by taking $n \times p$; that is, $75 \times .50 = 37.5$ (rounded to 38). The interval in which P will lie is the one corresponding to the 38th score in the *cf* column. The 38th score lies in the interval 100–104, of which the lower real limit is 99.5. Therefore,

$$Mdn = 99.5 + \frac{37.5 - 33}{12} \times 5$$

$$Mdn = 101.38$$

By use of the same formula the 10th, 20th, or any other percentile can be determined. Again, because with grouped data the identity of individual scores is lost, it must be assumed that the scores are evenly distributed within the interval in which the median is found. If the assumption is not met slight error may result.

Computing the Mode

The mode is the most frequent score in the distribution. If there are two most frequent scores, then there are two modes and the distribution is said to be bimodal. If there are three or more most frequent scores, the distribution is multimodal.

If the data are grouped, the mode is at the midpoint of the interval containing the highest number of frequencies. Because this midpoint may vary from the real mode, it is referred to as the crude mode.

Assignment 4

PROBLEMS
1. Using Data III from Appendix B, the any-percentile formula, and the groupings suggested under Assignment 1, compute the median for height and the high jump.
2. Using Data III and the groupings suggested under Assignment 1, determine the mode or modes for the 100-yard run, strength, and weight.

PRACTICE QUESTIONS
1. A physical education teacher gave a performance test to determine the number of sit-ups each student could perform. After all students were measured, the mean score was found to be 20, but the median was only 15. The teacher reasoned that, since the average student could do 20 sit-ups, 20 should be the standard number expected of all students after a short training period. He thought that 20 sit-ups would work a hardship on only a few students. What was wrong with his reasoning?
2. You gave a standardized strength test to your students and found that the median score was seriously below the national norm. The school principal asked you to do something about it. After a little thought you realized that you could raise the median considerably by concentrating on a few students. (a) Which students would you

concentrate on? (b) Which measure of central tendency would not be raised appreciably by concentrating on a few?

3. A test is given to two groups of students, A and B. The following statistics are found:

	Mean	Median
Group A	20	25
Group B	25	20

If any score above 20 is considered as good, which group has more good students in terms of this test?

4. Which is the least stable of the three measures of central tendency?

5. Which measure should be used to avoid the influence of extremely high or extremely low scores?

Measures of Variability

Variability refers to the extent of differences. The term is commonly interchanged with the words *dispersion, spread, scatter,* and *deviation.* Measures of variability are distances along the scale of scores. Except for range and equidistant percentiles a measure of variability should be thought of as a unit of distance along the scale by which any measure in the distribution may be described with a measure of *central tendency* as the reference point. By knowing measures of central tendency, one is able to visualize the concentration of scores. By knowing measures of variability, one can visualize the amount that scores spread or deviate from the central tendency.

The different measures of variability are the range, equidistant percentiles, interquartile range, semiinterquartile range, average deviation, variance, and standard deviation.

Range (R) may be expressed as the distance from the highest score to the lowest score in the distribution, for example, from 100 to 50. It may also be stated as the difference between the extreme scores (100–50; range = 50).

Equidistant percentiles are percentiles which occur on opposite sides of the median and are equal distances in terms of percentage of cases from the median. For example, the 10th and 90th percentiles are equidistant percentiles as are the 25th and 75th percentiles.

Interquartile range is the distance between Q_1 (25th percentile) and Q_3 (75th percentile).

Semiinterquartile range (Q) is half the distance between Q_1 and Q_3. It is the interquartile range divided by two.

Average (mean) deviation (AD) is the average amount by which all the scores deviate from the mean of the distribution. It is the arithmetic average of the absolute deviations.

Variance is the measure of variability based on the deviations from the mean and is the average of the squared deviations taken from the mean of the distribution.

Standard deviation is a unit along the baseline of the normal curve and is the square root of the average of the squared deviations.

Equidistant percentiles, interquartile range, and Q are based on the percentile scale. They are nonarithmetic (not affected by score values); therefore, they relate to the median, which is a nonarithmetic measure of central tendency. The average deviation, variance, and standard deviation are arithmetic measures based on score values. They relate to the mean, which is the arithmetic average of the scores, and are highly useful to the teacher, coach, and researcher when using measurements.

Coefficient of variation allows the dispersion of data that have different means and different measurement units to be compared.

Characteristics of Selected Measures

Range (R) is a nonarithmetic measure which indicates the difference between the highest and lowest scores. This measure gives the total spread of the scores and is easy to calculate. However, since it gives a limited amount of information (highest score, lowest score, and difference between the two), the range is a rough measure.

Average deviation (AD) is an arithmetic measure which is the average of the absolute deviations of the scores from the mean of the distribution. It can be used when extreme scores should be deemphasized. The average deviation is easy to calculate and understand, yet because it is not algebraically sound, this measure should not be used as a basis for further calculations.

Variance (s^2 for sample and σ^2 for population) is the average of the sum of squares. The variance is a very useful measure of how far the scores vary from the mean. The variance has the quality of being additive and is a measure of dispersion. If the range is small the variance will be small, but if the range is widely spread the variance will be large. The sumbol for the sample variance will be used in this section on measures of variability.

Standard deviation (s for sample and σ for population) is the square root of the variance. It has all of the properties of the variance, and may be preferred when the range of the distribution is very large.

Computing Average Deviation

The AD is the average amount by which all the scores deviate from the mean. The basic formula is

$$AD = \frac{\Sigma d}{N}$$

where no account is taken of $+$ and $-$ signs in the summation of deviations. For example, suppose we have seven scores: 9, 10, 13, 16, 18, 19, and 20. The mean is 15. To find the deviation of each score, we subtract the mean from the score:

X	$\overline{X}$	d
20	$-$ 15	$= +5$
19	$-$ 15	$= +4$
18	$-$ 15	$= +3$
16	$-$ 15	$= +1$
13	$-$ 15	$= -2$
10	$-$ 15	$= -5$
9	$-$ 15	$= -6$

$$\Sigma d = 26$$
(when signs are ignored)

where

$$d = X - \overline{X}$$

$$AD = \frac{\Sigma d}{N}$$

$$= \frac{26}{7}$$

$$AD = 3.71$$

To compute the AD from a simple frequency distribution, we use the formula

$$AD = \frac{\Sigma fd}{N} \quad \text{or} \quad AD = \frac{\Sigma(f \cdot d)}{N}$$

The following is an example of computing AD from a simple frequency distribution, using Data I from Appendix A.

X	f	d	fd
21	2	5.38	10.76
20	2	4.38	8.76
19	4	3.38	13.52
18	6	2.38	14.28
17	11	1.38	15.18
16	5	.38	1.90
15	4	−.62	−2.48
14	4	−1.62	−6.48
13	4	−2.62	−10.48
12	1	−3.62	−3.62
11	3	−4.62	−13.86
10	1	−5.62	−5.62
9	2	−6.62	−13.24
8	0	−7.62	0
7	1	−8.62	−8.62

$N = 50$
$\overline{X} = 15.62$

$\Sigma fd = 128.80$
(when signs are ignored)

$$AD = \frac{\Sigma fd}{N}$$

$$= \frac{128.80}{50}$$

$$AD = 2.58$$

Computing the Variance

The variance is the average of the sum of squares. It is the most often used of the measures of variability.

Formula: $$S^2 = \frac{\Sigma(X - \overline{X})^2}{N - 1}$$

The following example uses the formula (with only a few scores).

X	$(X - \overline{X})$	$(X - \overline{X})^2$
3	−1.8	3.24
10	5.2	27.04
6	1.2	1.44
7	2.2	4.84
2	−2.8	7.84
1	−3.8	14.44
4	−.8	.64
5	.2	.04
7	2.2	4.84
3	−1.8	3.24
$\Sigma X = 48$	0	67.60

$$\overline{X} = \frac{48}{10} = 4.80$$

$$S^2 = \frac{\Sigma(X - \overline{X})^2}{N - 1}$$

$$S^2 = \frac{67.60}{9}$$

$$S^2 = 7.51$$

Computing the Standard Deviation

The standard deviation is the square root of the mean of the squared deviations. It is a very reliable measure of variability.

Formula: $S = \sqrt{\dfrac{\Sigma(X - \overline{X})^2}{N - 1}}$

The following example uses the formula and the scores from the previous example for variance.

$N = 10$
$\overline{X} = 4.80$
$\Sigma(X - \overline{X})^2 = 67.60$

$$S = \sqrt{\frac{\Sigma(X - \overline{X})^2}{N - 1}}$$

$$S = \sqrt{\frac{67.60}{10 - 1}}$$

$$S = \sqrt{7.5111}$$

$$S = \quad 2.74$$

Coefficient of Variation

The coefficient of variation is used to compare the relative variations of two or more variables that have different means and standard deviations and may be in different units of measurements.

The formula is

$$C = \frac{S}{\overline{X}}$$

$C =$ coefficient of variation
$S =$ standard deviation
$\overline{X} =$ mean

If the two events being compared are the vertical jump with a mean of 12 inches and a standard deviation of 2.5 inches and the basketball throw with a mean of 75 feet and a standard deviation of 10 feet, the coefficient of variation will allow the variation of the two events to be compared.

$$C_1 = \frac{2.5}{12} = .21 \text{ or } 21\%$$
$$C_2 = \frac{10}{75} = .13 \text{ or } 13\%$$

The variation among the vertical jump scores is greater than among the basketball throw scores. This measurement is a meaningful comparison because the effect of the different units of measurement have been removed.

Assignment 5

1. Using Data III and the means found under Assignment 4, find the AD for height. Use the formula:

$$AD = \frac{\Sigma d}{N}$$

2. Find the s for leg strength and the high jump using Data III.
3. Find the s^2 for height and weight using Data III.
4. You are a high-school teacher and teach basketball to two tenth-grade classes of students. You give each class a test which presumably measures their present basketball ability. The mean score for each class is 70, but the s for one class is 6 and the other is 12. What is the significance of this difference from your point of view as a teacher? Which class would you rather teach? Why?

5

More Advanced Statistical Methods

This chapter includes the most useful information about distribution curves, percentiles, standard scales, reliability measures, comparison statistics and correlation.

Distribution Curves

A distribution is a line representing the frequencies along the scale of scores. The height of the curve at any point is proportional to the frequencies at that point. Therefore, the highest point of the curve is at the mode (most frequent score). For a clearer conception of a distribution curve, refer to the polygon in Figure 4-3. If that curve line were smoothed out, it would represent a distribution curve.

Normal Probability Curve

The normal curve is a unique bell-shaped curve that is dependent on two parameters or constraints, the mean and the standard deviation. These parameters will prevent the normal curve from being confused with other distribution curves. Normal curves always have the same proportion; however, some normal curves may be higher or lower than others and still fit the definition. Figure 5-1 illustrates the shape and characteristics of a normal distribution curve.

There are certain characteristics unique to the normal curve

1. The mean, median, and mode fall at the same point and are, therefore, equal to one another.

49

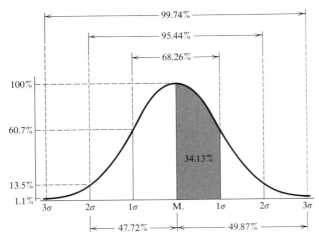

FIGURE 5-1. Characteristics of the normal curve.

2. At one S (standard deviation) from the mean in either direction the height is always 60.7 percent of the height at the mean.
3. At two S's from the mean the height is 13.5 percent of the height at the mean.
4. At three S's from the mean the height is 1.1 percent of the height at the mean.
5. The mean plus and minus one S includes 68.26 percent of the scores (34.13 percent in one direction; see Appendix D).
6. The mean plus and minus two S includes 95.44 percent of the scores (47.72 percent in one direction).
7. The mean plus and minus three S includes 99.74 percent of the scores (49.87 percent in one direction).
8. The curve is bell-shaped, bilaterally symmetrical, unimodal, and the ends of the curve approach but never touch the baseline.
9. A normal curve may be higher or lower than the one presented in Figure 4-7, but its proportions and characteristics must remain as described.

In addition the following points about the normal curve are of interest:

1. The mean plus and minus Q (interquartile range) includes the middle 50 percent of the scores.
2. The mean plus and minus AD (average deviation) includes the middle 57.5 percent of the scores.

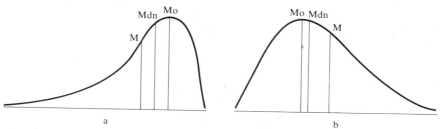

FIGURE 5-2. Skewed curves: (a) extreme skew to the left (negative); (b) moderate skew to the right (positive).

Skewed Curve

In a skewed distribution the mean, median, and mode are at different points, and the balance of the cuve is thrown to the left or right (see Figure 5-2). The degree of skewness of a distribution is measured by the formula:

$$\text{Skewness} = \frac{3(\text{mean} - \text{median})}{S^s}$$

Skewness results from too few cases, from special selection, or from a true lack of normality in the data. When the mean and median are equal, skewness = 0.

Other Shapes of Distribution Curves

In addition to the normal curve and skewed curves a distribution may take other shapes, such as those illustrated in Figure 5-3.

Assignment 7

1. Describe the following:
   a. unimodal curve
   b. bimodal curve
   c. multimodal curve
   d. bilaterally symmetrical curve
   e. bell-shaped curve
   f. normal curve
2. You give a test of cardiovascular efficiency to a group of boys and find that $\overline{X} = 72$ and $S^2 = 49$. If the distribution is near normal, give the score limits which will include approximately the middle 68 percent, 95 percent, and 100 percent of the cases. What is the approximate range of the scores?
3. From the given measures of variability describe the probable shape of distribution A; of distribution B.

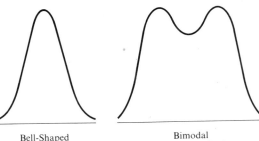
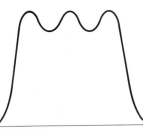

Bell-Shaped
and Unimodal

Bimodal
(two high points)

Multimodal
(more than two high points)

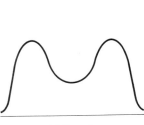
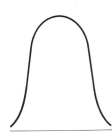

Rectangular   U-Shaped   Hairpin

FIGURE 5-3. Other shapes of curves.

A   50th percentile = 80   B $Q_3 = 35$
     95th percentile = 100 $Q_2 = 25$
      5th percentile = 20 $Q_1 = 20$

Percentiles

Percentiles and percentile rank are measures of relative status. They indicate the percent of scores below and above a given point along the scale of scores. For instance, the 30th percentile is the point where 30 percent of the scores are below and 70 percent are above. The 60th percentile is the point where 60 percent of the scores are below and 40 percent are above. The 50th percentile is the middle score and is equal to the median.

Percentiles may be found from a list of scores or from a simple or grouped frequency distribution. Finding percentiles from a simple frequency distribution is preferable because the procedure is convenient and produces no error. However, computing percentiles from grouped data may result in slight error.

Percentile rank gives approximately the same information as a percentile. If a score value is given, the percentile rank of that score may be found. For example, if, in a given distribution, a score of 56 has a percentile rank of 80, then this score is better than 80 percent of the other scores. If a percentile is given, then the score value which lies at the percentile may be determined.

To compute a percentile from a simple frequency distribution:

1. Add a cumulative frequency column to the distribution.
2. Multiplying N by the given percentile, determine the number of scores from the bottom that constitute the given percentile. (For example, $N = 50$. How many scores from the bottom is the 30th percentile? $30\% \times 50 = 15$. The 15th score is at the 30th percentile.)
3. Locate the position of that score (15th score) in the *cf* column. The score appearing opposite that number is at the given percentile.

The following are examples of how to compute a given percentile from a simple frequency distribution (Data I).

X	f	cf
21	2	50
20	2	48
19	4	46
18	6	42
17	11	36
16	5	25
15	4	20
14	4	16
13	4	12
12	1	8
11	3	7
10	1	4
9	2	3
8	0	1
7	1	1
	$N = 50$	

To find the 20th percentile.

1. $20\% \times N$ (50) = 10th score.
2. The 10th score is in the 7th step from the bottom in the *cf* column.
3. The score in the X column opposite the 10th score has a value of 13. Therefore, a score of 13 is at the 20th percentile.

To find the 70th percentile.

1. $70\% \times N$ (50) = 35th score.
2. The 35th score is in the 11th step from the bottom in the *cf* column.

3. The score in the X column opposite the 35th score has a value of 17. Therefore, a score of 17 is at the 70th percentile.

To compute percentiles from a grouped frequency distribution, use the any-percentile formula and the procedure described in the section on computing the median.

To compute the percentile rank of a given score:

1. Add a cumulative frequency column to the simple frequency distribution.
2. Determine the number of scores below the given score by finding the score in the X column and adding half of the frequencies opposite that score to the cumulative frequencies in the interval just below that score.
3. Divide the number of scores below the given score (answer from 2 above) by N and multiply by 100 to determine the percentile rank of the score.

The following is an example of how to compute a percentile rank from a simple frequency distribution.

X	f	cf
21	2	50
20	2	48
19	4	46
18	6	42
17	11	36
16	5	25
15	4	20
14	4	16
13	4	12
12	1	8
11	3	7
10	1	4
9	2	3
8	0	1
7	1	1
	N = 50	

Percentile rank (PR) of a score of 18 equals half of the frequencies opposite 18 plus the cf in the interval below 18 divided by N, then multiplied by 100. Therefore:

$$PR \text{ of } 18 = \frac{\frac{1}{2} \times 6 + 36}{50} \times 100$$
$$= \frac{3 + 36}{50} \times 100$$
$$PR \text{ of } 18 = 78$$

Deciles and Quartiles

Key percentiles in a distribution are called deciles and quartiles. They are useful as reference points along a percentile scale and as means for comparing two or more groups with each other. Deciles are indicated by D_1 (10th percentile), D_2 (20th percentile), and so on. Q_1, Q_2, Q_3 are the 25th, 50th, and 75th percentiles, respecitvely. A table of deciles or quartiles consists of a title and three columns as shown in Tables 5-1 and 5-2.

Table 5-1 provides various information. For instance, it shows that no boy gripped more than 139 pounds or less than 60 pounds. The middle 40 percent of the boys were between 94 and 110 pounds. Of these boys 50 percent did better and 50 percent did worse than 101 pounds. The interdecile differences show that the scores concentrated near the middle.

TABLE 5-1 Deciles from a Simple Frequency Distribution of Scores of 75 High-School Boys on the Right Grip Test (Data II)

Deciles	Scores*	Interdecile Differences
d_{10}	139	
		14
d_9	125	
		11
d_8	114	
		4
d_7	110	
		6
d_6	104	
		3
d_5	101	
		3
d_4	98	
		4
d_3	94	
		5
d_2	89	
		10
d_1	79	
		19
d_0	60	

*In pounds.

TABLE 5-2 Quartiles from a Simple Fre-
quency Distribution of Scores of 75 High
School Boys on the Right Grip Test (Data II)

Quartile	Grip Test* Score	Interquartile Difference
Q_4	139	
		27
Q_3	112	
		11
Q_2	101	
		10
Q_1	91	
		31
Q_0	60	

*In pounds.

The table of quartiles provides information similar to that provided by the table of deciles. It shows that no boy gripped more than 139 pounds or less than 60 pounds. Fifty percent of the boys gripped more, and 50 percent gripped less than 101 pounds.

Assignment 6

1. Using Data I and the simple frequency distribution constructed in Table 5-1 compute the following percentiles: 10, 35, 70, 95.
2. Using the same data, determine the percentile ranks of the scores 8, 11, 15, 19.
3. Using Data II and the grouped frequency distribution constructed in Table 5-2, compute the following percentiles: 25, 50, 75.

Standard Scales

To obtain a raw score is sometimes a simple matter, but to interpret the meaning and significance of the score is more difficult. For instance, if a 16-year-old boy were to do 10 dips on the parallel bars and 12 chins (pull-ups) on the high bar, a suitable standard of comparison would be necessary to determine the degree of excellence of his performance. A standard scale is often developed for a specific test to assist in the interpretation of scores and to serve as a standard against which to compare any raw score from the particular test.

A standard scale provides a technique for converting a distribution of raw scores into standard scores. It provides a measure of relative status for a raw score and thus permits a more adequate interpretation of the score. It also provides a technique for computing the averages of several different kinds of scores. Any standard scale developed from a large sample of raw scores can serve as a standard against which to compare any raw score of the same type. Thus a standard scale is used to develop norms.

One widely used scale is the percentile scale discussed previously. Although the information from this scale is easy to understand and interpret, it is relatively unstable and unreliable because the scale is nonarithmetic and may be influenced by irregularities in the distribution of scores. While percentiles are frequently averaged to secure composite measures for administrative convenience, this practice is not statistically valid.

In view of the limitations of the percentile scale, it's important to know about the z-scale and the T-scale. These scales relate to the mean and the standard deviation and are statistically more reliable than the percentiles.

z-Scores

The z-scale normally extends from -3 to $+3$. The mean of the scale $=0$, and the standard deviation $=1$. When plotted on the normal distribution curve, the z-scale appears as Figure 5-4. Thus, if a raw score were equal to the mean of the distribution, it would have a z value of 0. A score of 2 S's above the mean would have a z value of $+2$, and a score of 1S below the mean would have a z value of -1. The z score tells how many S's above or below the mean a raw score lies. A score equal to $+3$ on the z-scale would be at or near the top of the scale (excellent), whereas one equal to a z of $+3$ would be at or near the bottom of the scale (very poor). A score equal to a z of 0 would be average (at the mean).

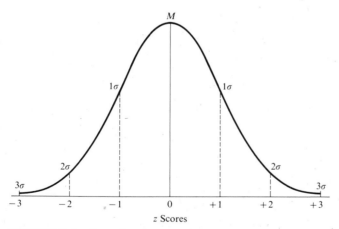

FIGURE 5-4. Z-scale plotted on a normal curve.

T-Scores

On the T-scale $\overline{X} = 50$ and $S = 10$. When plotted on a normal distribution curve, T-scale appears as Figure 5-5. If a raw score is equal to the mean of the

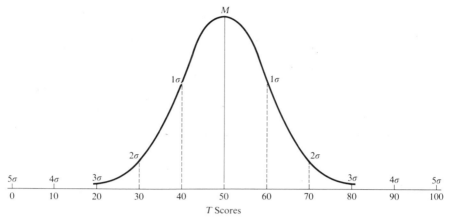

FIGURE 5-5. T-scale plotted on a normal curve.

distribution, then it has a T value of 50. A score at 2 S's above the mean would have a T value of 70, and a score at 1 S below the mean would have a T value of 40. A score with a T value of 80 would be equal to a z value of $+3$ and would be considered excellent in relation to others within the sample. A score with a T value of 20 would be equal to a z value of -3 and would be considered very poor.

Table 5-3 presents a comparison of the two types of standard scales and gives their percentile equivalent.

TABLE 5-3   A Comparison of the Standard Scales: Standard Score Values at 1, 2, and 3 S's from the Mean

	-3σ	-2σ	-1σ	M	$+1\sigma$	$+2\sigma$	$+3\sigma$
z-Scale	-3	-2	-1	0	$+1$	$+2$	$+3$
T-Scale	20	30	40	50	60	70	80
Percentile equivalent	.13	2.18	15.87	50	84.13	97.72	99.87

Computing Standard Scores

The formula for computing any standard score from a raw score is:

$$\text{standard score} = \frac{S_s(X - \overline{X})}{S} + \overline{X}_s$$

where

$S_s = S$ of the standard scale; for example, 1 for z-scale, and 10 for T-scale.
$X = $ Raw score under consideration
$\overline{X} = $ Mean of the scores
$S_X = S$ of the scores
$\overline{X}_s = $ Mean of the standard scale; for example, 0 for z-scale, and 50 for T-scale.

X
24
23
22
21
20
19
18
17
16
180
$\overline{X} = 20$
$S = 2.6$

EXAMPLE:
a. Find the z score for a raw score of 21.

$$z = \frac{1(21 - 20)}{2.6} + 0 = .385$$

b. Find the T score for a raw score of 21.

$$T = \frac{10(21 - 20)}{2.6} + 50 = 53.85$$

To develop a standard scale from a distribution of raw scores:

1. Arrange all raw score values in a column from high to low, as in a simple frequency distribution.
2. Place the mean of the standard scale opposite the mean of the raw scores.
3. Using the standard score formula, compute the standard score value of the raw score immediately above the mean and record that standard score opposite the corresponding raw score.
4. Determine the reciprocal (R) by the formula $R = \dfrac{S_s}{S}$
5. Add this reciprocal value to the result of step 3 to get the standard score

for the next higher raw score value. Continue the process for all raw scores above the mean.

6. Repeat steps 3, 4, and 5 for the score values below the mean. (For scores below the mean the reciprocal is successively added in the case of the z-scale and successively subtracted in the case of the T-scale.)

Since the mean of the distribution equals 15.62, this value is 0 on the z-scale, 50 on the T-scale. As stated in step 2 we place those values opposite the mean of the distribution. In accordance with step 3, we compute the standard score value of the raw score immediately above the mean. That score is 16. Therefore,

$$z = \frac{1(16 - 15.62)}{3.19} + 0 = .12$$

$$T = \frac{10(16 - 15.62)}{3.19} + 50 = 51.20$$

According to step 4 the reciprocal $(R) = \frac{S_s}{S}$. Hence,

$$R_z = \frac{1}{3.19} \text{ which } = .31$$

$$R_T = \frac{10}{3.19} \text{ which } = 3.13$$

As stated in step 5 we add the R value successively to the obtained standard score. After this step the portion of the standard scale above the mean is complete. The raw score 16 has a z value of .12, and a T value of 51.20. Likewise the raw score 17 has a z-value of .43, and a T value of 54.33. To complete the scales below the mean follow the instructions in step 6. For scores below the mean in the T-scale remember to successively subtract instead of add the R value.

We can now read the z, or T corresponding to any raw score in Table 5-3. For example, the z value of the score 10 is -1.74. This figure tells us that 10 is 1.74 S below the mean.

In a practical situation only one of the standard scales would be established, not two of them as done on this example. Therefore, one problem is to choose which standard scale is best for the particular situation. If a large number of students were tested on a strength test and if these scores were converted to standard scores, then the scale of standard scores could serve as a norm against which to compare the raw scores of like students on the same test.

Advantages of Specific Standard Scales

The z-scale is the simplest to calculate and the easiest to interpret if the reader understands the meaning of standard deviation. The z value identifies

TABLE 5-4 The z and T Equivalents for the Scores Made by 50 High-School Girls on the *Situp* Test (Data I)

X	z	T
21	1.67	66.85
20	1.36	63.72
19	1.05	60.59
18	.74	57.46
17	.43	54.33
16	.12	51.20
$\overline{X} = 15.62$	0	50.00
15	−.19	48.10
14	−.50	44.97
13	−.81	41.84
12	−1.12	38.71
11	−1.43	35.58
10	−1.74	32.45
9	−2.05	29.32
8	−2.36	26.19
7	−2.67	23.06

$\overline{X} = 15.62$
$S = 3.19$
$N = 50$

position in the distribution in terms of standard deviation units above or below the mean. This scale is most meaningful when the distribution approaches normality. Since it involves decimals and both negative and positive values, a z-scale may be confusing to some people.

The T-scale involves no decimals or negative values, is plotted on a 100-point scale, and is thus easy to interpret. However, it covers ten standard deviations when only six standard deviations include almost 100 percent of the cases in a normal distribution.

Increased Increment Scale

The increased increment scale is an attempt to devise a method by which performers are awarded scores proportional to the excellence of the performance. It has been recognized that as an individual approaches the limit of his present capacity in a given activity in which he is being tested, improvement becomes more difficult. The man who reduces his time in the 100-yard run from 10 seconds to 9.5 seconds has accomplished more than the man who reduces his time from 13 seconds to 12.5 seconds. The graphical representation of such a scale is a parabolic curve that moves slowly upward from the baseline and increases more rapidly as the distance between the baseline and the curve widens. An example of an increased increment scale is the one used for scoring the decathlon in track and field. Valid increasing increment scales are difficult to devise and therefore seldom used.

Rating Scales

Rating scales are useful mainly for adding accuracy to subjective judgments. Frequently rating systems are set up on 5-point scales. However, they sometimes appear on 3-, 7-, or even 10-point scales; and in some cases it may be desirable to use a scale even more refined than 10 points, such as a 100-point scale. Note these examples of rating scales.

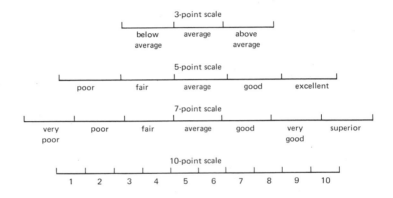

Assignment 9

1. Using the high jump scores in Data III, construct a z-scale.
2. Using the long jump scores in Data III, construct a T-scale.
3. If $X = 71$ and $S = 15$, find the z score, and T score for each of the following raw scores: 81, 100, 57.

Reliability Measures

When a test is administered to a group that represents a larger group, the smaller group is referred to as the sample and the larger group is referred to as the population. A sample will seldom truly represent the population from which it is taken; hence, a statistic derived from a sample will seldom equal the parameter (true assessment of the population). Therefore, we should usually not accept a statistic, such as the mean or standard deviation, computed from a sample for its face value but should consider it as only a statistic of a sample.

The usefulness of a statistic may depend on its proximity to the parameter. In other words the reliability or dependability of a statistic must be known to determine its significance. The amount of error in a sample statistic is estimated by sampling error procedures, which supply a description of the reliability of a statistic taken from a sample. Through these procedures the administrator can compute the standard error of the statistic and state its meaning.

Standard Error of the Mean

The standard error of the mean $(S_{\bar{x}})$ is the measure used to estimate the reliability of a mean computed from a sample of a population. If a large number of samples of the same size were drawn at random from a particular population, and if the means of the samples were formed into a distribution, then we would have a *sampling distribution of means*. If the means varied greatly from one another, then the distribution would have a large standard deviation. Conversely, if the means were near one another, the standard deviation of the sampling distribution of means would be small. If the means varied greatly, then we obviously could not place much confidence in any one of the means. Whereas, if the means were in close agreement, we could be more confident that any one mean was near the parameter. In other words the variability of the sampling distribution of means indicates the reliability of a mean taken from a sample.

The measure used to describe the reliability of a mean is the S of the sampling distribution of means. The estimated S of a sampling distribution of means is known as the *standard error of the mean*. Hence, the standard error of the mean is the standard deviation of the sampling distribution of means. The standard error is used to estimate the amount of error that may be present in the mean as a result of the chance factor in the process of random sampling. Although these errors cannot be controlled, they can be estimated; standard error formulas are designed for this purpose.

Because it is not practical to construct a sampling distribution of means for the purpose of computing the standard error of the mean, a formula has been derived which provides an estimate of the standard error. The deriviation of the formula is relatively easy to follow and is explained in several books on statistics. The formula is:

$$S_{\bar{x}} = \frac{S}{\sqrt{N}}$$

where

$S_{\bar{x}}$ = standard error of the mean
S = standard deviation of the sample scores
N = number of cases in the sample

Assume that the height measures fround in Data III from Appendix B represent a sample from a larger group of students (a population). The mean of those scores is 65.92 inches, the S is 3.30 inches, and N is 25. Place these figures in the formula

$$S_{\bar{x}} = \frac{3.30}{\sqrt{25}} = \frac{3.30}{5} = .66$$

The $S_{\bar{x}}$ of .66 indicates that if a sampling distribution of means were constructed, its S would equal .66 inches. Approximate normality of the sampling
distribution can be assumed. Recall that in a normal distribution the mean plus
and minus one $(+ls)$ includes approximately 68 percent of the scores; the
means $+2s$ includes approximately 95 percent of the scores; and the mean $+3s$
includes practically 100 percent of the scores. Since the $S_{\bar{x}}$ is an estimate of the
S of the sampling distribution, there is a 68 percent chance that the mean
obtained from the sample is within one $S_{\bar{x}}$ of the parametric mean. In other
words we can be 68 percent certain that the obtained mean deviates no more
than .66 inches $(1S_{\bar{x}})$ from the true mean. Further, we can be 95 percent
certain that the obtained mean deviates no more than 1.30 inches $(2S_{\bar{x}})$ from
the true mean. And we can be practically 100 percent certain that the obtained
mean is no more than 1.95 inches $(3S_{\bar{x}})$ away from the true mean.

A small $S_{\bar{x}}$ indicates that the obtained mean is highly reliable, whereas a
large $S_{\bar{x}}$ indicates that the obtained mean has a low level of reliability.

Standard Errors of Measures
Other Than the Mean

The reliability of statistics other than the mean may also be estimated. The
following formulas are designed for that purpose:

$$S_S = .707 \text{ times } S_{\bar{x}}$$
$$S_Q = .787 \text{ times } S_{\bar{x}}$$
$$S_{Mdn} = 1.25 \text{ times } S_{\bar{x}}$$

The standard errors of measures other than the mean are interpreted the
same as the $S_{\bar{x}}$ which was explained in the preceding section.

Standard Error of the Difference

Groups of scores are often compared according to their means or standard
deviations. On the basis of these comparisons the groups are either alike or different. The extent to which the obtained measures of difference are reliable and
the degree to which the calculated measure of difference is dependable are determined by computing and interpreting the standard error of the difference
$S_{\bar{D}}$ which is an estimate of the standard deviation of a sampling distribution
of obtained differences.

The reliability of the difference between two means $\bar{X}_1$ and $\bar{X}_2$ can be
found by computing the standard error of the difference between means. The
formula is:

$$S_{\bar{D}} = \sqrt{S^2_{\bar{X}_1} + S^2_{\bar{X}_2}}$$

remember that

$$S_{\bar{X}} = \frac{S}{\sqrt{N}}$$

Substituting:

$$S_{\bar{D}} = \sqrt{\frac{S_1^2}{N_1} + \frac{S_2^2}{N_2}}$$

Suppose we have two means taken from two comparable random samples. For group 1, $\bar{X} = 104$, $S = 9$, and $N = 100$. For group 2, $\bar{X} = 99$, $S = 10$, and $N = 100$. The obtained difference in the means equals: $(104 - 99 = 5)$. Is this difference real, or is it a result of chance error in sampling? In other words to what extent can we rely on this measure of difference? To determine reliability we compute the σ_{diff} between the two means. Substituting the correct numbers into the formula,

$$S_{\bar{X}1} = \frac{9}{\sqrt{100}} = .9$$

$$S_{\bar{X}2} = \frac{10}{\sqrt{100}} = 1.0$$

$$S_{\bar{D}} = \sqrt{(.9)^2 + (1.0)^2} = \sqrt{.81 + 1.0} = \sqrt{1.81} = 1.34$$

What does this result mean? When the obtained difference (5) is divided by the $S_{\bar{D}}$ (1.34), the result is a critical ratio (CR). The CR parallels standard deviation units of the normal curve. Therefore, if the CR were 1.0, we could be approximately 68 percent certain that the obtained difference is real. If the CR were 2, we would be approximately 95 percent certain; and if the CR were 3, we could be practically 100 percent certain that the difference is real. In this problem, the obtained difference (5) divided by the $S_{\bar{D}}$ (1.34) equals 3.73 (CR = 3.73). Therefore, we are practically 100 percent certain that the obtained difference is real and not a result of chance alone. Hence, the difference is highly reliable.

Assignment 8

1. Assume that the six sets of scores found in Data III from Appendix A represent samples from a population. Using the means and S's already obtained, find the S_x for each of the six factors. Interpret your answers.
2. Find the S_s for height and high jump scores.
3. Find the S_{mdn} for height and high jump scores.
4. Compute the S_D between the two means when the conditions are:

$\overline{X}_1 = 80, S = 5, N = 100; X_2 = 83, S = 3, N = 100.$

Then compute and interpret the critical ratio.

Comparison Statistics

When groups are to be compared to one another, either to determine how alike they are or how they differ from one another, comparison statistics are used. The two types used in this section are the Student t-test and coefficient of correlation between two groups.

Whenever two groups are to be compared, a basic hypothesis may be formed, the data are treated statistically, and the hypothesis is either accepted or rejected.

Null Hypothesis

The hypothesis that is usually formed before statistical data are collected or evaluated is a *null hypothesis*. The null hypothesis is that there is no difference between the population or the characteristics being compared, and that the mean of one group is equal to the mean of the other group $(H_0 = \overline{X}_1 = \overline{X}_2)$ when the null hypothesis is applied to the Student t statistic. A null hypothesis may be accepted or rejected as determined by the results of the statistical treatment.

Student t-Test

The word *effect*, is usually the key word used when describing research using the t-test. "What is the effect of (some specific treatment) upon the means of the two groups being compared?" The t-test is used to determine whether the difference between the means of the two groups is significant.

t-Test for Paired Samples. If the two groups are not independent but are related to each other, the t-test for paired samples formula will be used. For example, a group of students took test A and test B. Is the difference between the two test means truly different from one another? It is important to test as large a sample of students as possible in order to get a distribution that closely resembles a normal distribution. For illustration purposes, samples of 10 students will be used. The formula is:

$$t = \frac{\overline{X}_1 - \overline{X}_2}{S_{\bar{D}}}$$

$$S_{\bar{D}} = \sqrt{\frac{S^2 D}{N}}$$

$\overline{X}_1 =$ Mean of group 1
$\overline{X}_2 =$ Mean of group 2
$S_{\bar{D}} =$ Standard error of the difference
$S^2_D =$ Variance of the difference

$$S^2{}_D = \frac{\Sigma D^2 - \dfrac{(\Sigma D)^2}{N}}{N-1}$$

Children	Test A X_1	Test B X_2	D	D^2
A	7	3	4	16
B	2	2	0	0
C	6	1	5	25
D	5	1	4	16
E	4	2	2	4
F	6	3	3	9
G	3	4	-1	1
H	4	6	-2	4
I	7	5	2	4
J	2	3	-1	1
	$\Sigma X_1 = 46$	$\Sigma X_2 = 30$	$\Sigma D = 16$	$\Sigma D^2 = 80$
	$\overline{X}_1 = 4.6$	$\overline{X}_2 = 3.0$		

PROCEDURE

1. Place the data into two columns, Test A and Test B.
2. Add each column and calculate the two means
$$\overline{X}_1, \ \overline{X}_2$$
3. Subtract one column from the other (D).
4. Add the D column (ΣD).
5. Square each number in the D column (D^2).
6. Add the numbers in the D^2 column (ΣD^2).
7. Calculate the $S^2{}_D = \dfrac{\Sigma D^2 - \left(\dfrac{\Sigma D}{N}\right)^2}{N-1}$
8. Calculate the $S_{\overline{D}} = \sqrt{\dfrac{S^2{}_D}{N}}$
9. Calculate the critical ratio of $t = \dfrac{\overline{X}_1 - \overline{X}_2}{S_{\overline{D}}}$
10. Determine the d f. (d f. equals $n - 1$ of the pairs of children who took both tests).
11. Refer to Appendix E to determine the critical values 2.26 (.05) and 3.25 (.01).
12. Determine the significance of the difference (not significant).

$$S^2{}_D = \frac{80 - \frac{(16)^2}{10}}{9}$$

$$S_{\bar{D}} = \sqrt{\frac{6.04}{10}}$$

$$t = \frac{4.6 - 3.0}{.777}$$

$$= \sqrt{.604}$$

$$= \frac{1.6}{.777}$$

$$= \frac{80 - \frac{256}{10}}{9}$$

$$S_{\bar{D}} = .777$$

$$= 2.059$$

$$= \frac{80 - 25.6}{9}$$

d.f. = 9

C.V.

$$= \frac{54.4}{9}$$

.05 = 2.262

$$S^2{}_D = 6.04$$

The difference between the means of the two groups is not significant. (See Appendix E.) The children did not score significantly higher on one test than they did on the other. A null hypothesis of $H_0 - \overline{X}_1 = \overline{X}_2$ would be accepted.

t-Test for Independent Samples. When groups have been selected by randomization, and a good research design is applied, two independent groups can be tested to determine the significance of the difference between the group means on a specific measurement. One group is the control group and the other is the experimental group. The two groups do not need to be the same size. The formula is:

$$t = \frac{\overline{X}_1 - \overline{X}_2}{\sqrt{\frac{S_p^2}{N_1} + \frac{S_p^2}{N_2}}}$$

$\overline{X}_1$ = mean of group 1
$\overline{X}_2$ = mean of group 2
S_p^2 = pooled variance squared
SS_1 = sums of squares group 1
SS_2 = sums of squares group 2

$$S_p^2 = \frac{SS_1 + SS_2}{N_1 + N_2 - 2}$$

$$SS_1 = \Sigma X_1^2 - \frac{(\Sigma X_1)^2}{N_1}$$

$$SS_2 = \Sigma X_2^2 - \frac{(\Sigma X_2)^2}{N_2}$$

EXAMPLE

Experimental group [1]		Control group [2]	
X_1	X_1^2	X_2	X_2^2
2	4	4	16
5	25	8	64
3	9	3	9
1	1	2	4
6	36	4	16
4	16	1	1
7	49	2	4
$\Sigma X_1 = 28$	$\Sigma X_1^2 = 140$	6	36
$\overline{X}_1 = 4$		5	25
		4	16
		$\Sigma X_2 = 39$	$\Sigma X_2^2 = 191$
		$\overline{X}_2 = 3.9$	

PROCEDURE

1. Add the scores in each group. ΣX_1 and ΣX_2
2. Calculate the mean for each group. $\overline{X}_1$ and $\overline{X}_2$
3. Square the scores in each group. X_1^2 and X_2^2
4. Add the squares of the scores for each group. $(\Sigma X_1^2$ and $\Sigma X_2^2)$
5. Calculate the SS for each group. $(SS_1$ and $SS_2)$
6. Calculate the S_p^2
7. Calculate the t.
8. Determine the d.f. $(\text{d.f} = N_1 - 1 + N_2 = 1)$. $(6+9) = 15$
9. Refer to Appendix E to determine the critical values 2.13 (.05) and 2.95 (.01).
10. Determine the significance of the difference at the .05 level of significance.

$$SS_1 = 140 - \frac{(28)^2}{7}$$

$$140 - \frac{784}{7}$$

$$140 - 112$$

$$SS_1 = \underline{28}$$

$$SS_2 = 191 - \frac{(39)^2}{10}$$

$$191 - \frac{1521}{10}$$

$$191 - 152.1$$

$$SS_2 = \underline{38.9}$$

$$Sp^2 = \frac{28 + 38.9}{7 + 10 - 2}$$

$$\frac{66.9}{15}$$

$$Sp^2 = 4.46$$

$$t = \frac{4 - 3.9}{\sqrt{\frac{4.46}{7} + \frac{4.46}{10}}}$$

$$\frac{.1}{\sqrt{.6371 + .446}}$$

$$\frac{.1}{\sqrt{1.0831}}$$

$$\frac{.1}{1.0407}$$

$$t = .096$$
$$\text{d.f.} = 15$$
$$\text{C.V.} = 2.131$$

In the above example the difference between the two groups is not significant. See Appendix E. The treatment in the experimental group did not result in a change as indicated by the scores of the control group. A null hypothesis of $H_0 = \overline{X}_1 = \overline{X}_2$ would be accepted.

Correlation

The statistical technique known as correlation results in a coefficient (number) which expresses the relationship between two variables. The coefficient of correlation is usually designated by the symbol r. The r can range from 0 to $+1$ and from 0 to -1; hence, from -1 to $+1$. (If r is greater than 1, the computation is incorrect.) A positive correlation indicates direct relationship. A zero correlation indicates absence of relationship. A negative correlation indicates an inverse relationship.

If $r = +1$, the relationship is perfect and positive; that is, if the first variable (trait) were increased, the second variable would increase a proportional amount. For instance, the relationship of the diameter to the circumference of a circle is perfect and positive. If we were to change the diameter, we would always change the circumference by 3.1416 times that amount.

If $r = -1$, the relationship is perfect and negative; that is, as the first variable increases, the second variable decreases a proportional amount. For example, a perfect negative relationship exists between velocity and time in the 100-yard run. As velocity increases, time decreases proportionately.

When $r = 0$, there is no relationship between the variables; that is, if the first variable were changed, the second variable would not be affected in any way.

Although the coefficient of correlation is a convenient index of relationship, the degree of relationship between two variables should be interpreted with caution. A coefficient of correlation of .60, for example, does not represent exactly twice as much relationship as one of .30. The correlation should be interpreted in relation to the character and extent of the problem under investigation. In one instance an r of .50 might be considered to be quite high as a significant value, while in another instance an r of .50 might be considered to be too low. Generally a correlation of .80 is considered to be substantial, and below .40 is usually considered to be low.

Uses of Correlation

Correlation is a frequently used statistical technique to determine validity, reliability, and objectivity of tests. It also serves as a basis for construction of standard tests and for prediction of results. If a high relationship exists between two traits and one trait is measured, then the other trait can be predicted with a relatively high degree of accuracy. Measures of correlation help us to understand people and the relationships that exist among them. Correlation theory is important in some of the more advanced statistical techniques.

Pearson Product Moment Method

Two sets of corresponding scores are necessary. The raw score method is a convenient approach to compute correlation when the number of cases is relatively small, a computing machine is available, and a scattergram is not needed. The formula for the raw score method is:

$$r_{xy} = \frac{\frac{\Sigma XY}{N} - \overline{XY}}{\sqrt{\frac{\Sigma X^2}{N} - \overline{X}^2} \cdot \sqrt{\frac{\Sigma Y^2}{N} - \overline{Y}^2}}$$

The formula may also be written:

$$r_{xy} = \frac{\frac{\Sigma XY}{N} - (\overline{X}_x \cdot \overline{Y}_y)}{S_x \cdot S_y}$$

To obtain the coefficient of correlation from an unordered list of paired scores, with the use of this formula:

1. Compute the mean and standard deviation of each set of scores.
2. Multiply the two raw scores for each individual, add the products, and divide by N.
3. Multiply the mean of the X scores and the mean of the Y scores and subtract the result from the answer in step 2.
4. Divide the answer from step 3 by the product of the two standard deviations.

Table 5-5 uses the raw score formula:

$$r_{xy} = \frac{\frac{\Sigma XY}{N} - \overline{X}_x \overline{Y}_y}{S_x \cdot S_y}$$

$$= \frac{\frac{35100}{10} - (55)(63)}{(6.34)(7.50)}$$

$$= \frac{3510 - 3465}{47.55} = \frac{45.00}{47.55} = .95$$

TABLE 5-5   Scores for 10 High-School Boys in the High Jump (X Scores) and Standing Long Jump (Y Scores)

Subject	X*	Y*	XY	X²	Y²
1	60	72	4320	3600	5184
2	62	70	4340	3844	4900
3	64	68	4352	4096	4624
4	58	68	3944	3364	4624
5	48	52	2496	2304	2704
6	56	66	3696	3136	4356
7	44	50	2200	1936	2500
8	52	60	3120	2704	3600
9	48	56	2688	2304	3136
10	58	68	3944	3364	4624
$N = 10$	$\overline{X} = 55.0$	$\overline{Y} = 63.0$	$\Sigma XY = 35100$	$\Sigma X^2 = 30652$	$\Sigma Y^2 = 40252$

*Scores given in inches

where

$$S_x = \sqrt{\frac{\Sigma x^2}{N} - (\overline{X}_x)^2}$$

$$S_x = 6.34$$

$$S_y = \sqrt{\frac{\Sigma y^2}{N} - (Y_y)^2}$$

$$S_y = 7.50$$

Spearman Rho Coefficient of Correlation [Rho (P)].

When the data are originally ranked on an ordinal scale, like placement in a tournament, the spearman rho (P) coefficient of correlation can be used to get a somewhat accurate statement of relationship. The data are placed in a column with the best score at the top and the lowest score at the bottom, and then each score is ranked starting with the highest raw score being assigned rank number 1. When there are two or more scores alike, the ranks are added together, and averaged to assign each like score the same number. However, a large number of ties will render this statistic for correlation ineffective.

Raw Score Data Ordered	Rank Assignments
10	1
8	2
7	3.5
7	3.5 $3 + 4 = 7/2 = 3.5$
5	5
4	6
3	8
3	8 $7 + 8 + 9 = 24/3 = 8$
3	8
1	10

If the question were asked, "What is the relationship between the order of entering the swimming meet of 11 and 12 year old boys in the 100-yard individual medley swimming race and the order of finishing the race?" The following would be calculated from the data given:

The formula: $Rho = 1.000 - \dfrac{6\Sigma D^2}{N(N^2 - 1)}$

1.000 = perfect correlation
   6 = constant in the formula
ΣD^2 = difference squared and added
  N = number of pairs

PROCEDURE
1. Rank each set of raw data.   (Entry time and finish time)
2. Keep track of the performance of each person, and place both rank assignments opposite each name.
3. Subtract one rank from the other.   (D)
4. Square each number in the D column (D^2)
5. Add the D^2 column.   (ΣD^2)
6. Substitute the numbers into the formula.
7. Calculate the rho.   (rho = .740).

Subject	Entering Time	Entering Rank	Finish Time	Finish Rank	D	D²
DENNIS	1:11.1	1	1:13.3	4.5	3.5	12.25
ANDY	1:11.5	2	1:09.6	1	1	1
MIKE	1:20.0	3	1:10.7	3	0	0
KID	1:12.6	4	1:10.5	2	2	2
ROB	1:14.2	5	1:13.5	6.5	1.5	2.25
PHIL	1:15.2	6	1:14.7	9	3	9
RON	1:15.7	7.5	1:17.6	11	3.5	12.25
LARRY	1:15.7	7.5	1:14.0	8	.5	.25
LORIN	1:16.0	9	1:13.3	4.5	4.5	20.25
BRUCE	1:16.7	10	1:13.5	6.5	3.5	12.25
COLLIN	1:16.8	11	1:16.4	10	1	1
DREW	1:17.1	12	1:18.5	12	0	0
						74.50

$$\text{rho} = \quad \rho = 1.000 - \frac{6(\Sigma D^2)}{N(N^2 - 1)}$$

$$1.000 - \frac{6(74.50)}{12(143)}$$

$$1.000 - \frac{447}{1716}$$

$$1.000 - .26$$

$$\rho = .74$$

The correlation coefficient (r) indicates the strength of the relationship between the two variables being compared. To interpret the correlation coefficient, the *coefficient* of *alienation* should be understood. The coefficient of alienation, k, indicates the lack of relationship between the two variables.

The formulas are:

$$k = \sqrt{1 - r^2}$$
$$k^2 = 1 - r^2$$
$$k^2 + r^2 = 1.000$$

In the above example, $r = .95$

$$k = \sqrt{1 - (.95)^2} \quad \text{or} \quad \sqrt{1 - .9025}$$
$$k = \sqrt{.0975}$$
$$k^2 = .0975$$
$$k^2 + r^2 = .0975 + .9025 = 1.000$$

The closer r^2 is to 1.000, the stronger is the relationship between the variables being compared. The r^2 represents the proportions of variance in one variable that can be accounted for by the other variable. A high coefficient of correlation is needed to result in a high degree of association between the variables being compared.

The rho of .74 would be interpreted as follows:

$$k = \sqrt{1 - \text{rho}^2} \quad \text{or} \quad \sqrt{1 - .5476}$$
$$k = \sqrt{.4524}$$
$$k^2 = .4524$$
$$r^2 = .5476$$
$$k^2 + r^2 = .5476 + .4524 = 1.0000$$

The relationship and the lack of relationship are quite close together, therefore there is a moderate relationship between the order of entering the swimming event and the order of finishing the event.

Scattergrams as shown in Figure 5-6 can be prepared to illustrate the amount and type of relationship that exists between the variables being compared.

When the scores represented by tally marks tend to cluster along a line running diagonally from the lower left to the upper right on the scattergram the relationship is positive, because these quadrants are positive. The closer the tallies cluster along the diagonal line the higher is the correlation. If all the tallies fell exactly on the diagonal line, the relationship would be perfect positive. Different degrees of relationship in both positive and negative directions are shown in Figure 5-6.

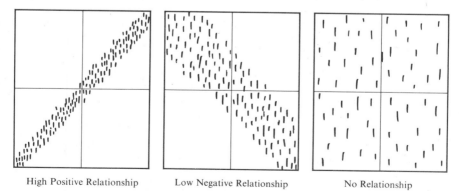

High Positive Relationship   Low Negative Relationship   No Relationship

FIGURE 5-6. Tally-mark patterns on scattergrams illustrating amount and type of relationship.

Assignment 10

1. Using the following data, complete the columns in the table and compute *r* with the raw score formula.

Subject	X	Y	XY	X²	Y²
1	65	56			
2	66	51			
3	68	55			
4	67	47			
5	69	54			
6	66	48			
7	62	49			
8	69	52			
9	68	47			
10	60	46			

2. Using the raw score means and standard deviations already obtained from Data III in Appendix B, compute the correlations between height and weight, and height and high jump.

3. Compute the rho from the following data.

Person	Tennis Tournament Ranking	Score on Strategy
A	3.5	16
B	2	20
C	1	25
D	7	18
E	6	16
F	5	10
G	8	12
H	3.5	19

Fitness
Measurements

6

Muscular Strength and
Endurance Tests

Strength is defined as the ability of the body, or a segment of it, to apply force. Strength has often been considered as the contractile force of a muscle or group of muscles. But the definition of strength and the methods used to measure it indicate that strength is a combination of (1) the combined contractile forces of the muscles causing the movement, (2) the mechanical ratio of the particular body levers involved, and (3) the ability to coordinate the agonistic muscles into one unified force working with the antagonistic and stabilizer muscles.

Strength is dependent on the force with which each contributing muscle can contract. As the contractile forces of the contributing muscles increase, strength increases. In addition strength depends on the relative length of the body levers and the positions of muscle attachments to these levers. Mechanical ratio changes as a body segment moves through its range of motion, causing strength to differ at various positions. This is known as the strength curve.

The definition of strength implies its importance in athletic performance. Even though nearly all movements are performed against some resistance, athletes perform against greater resistance than usual. For example, in the shot put, discus throw, pole vault, various gymnastic movements, jumping, running, swimming, and working against an opponent, the body segments exert maximum force. If all else remains equal, greater strength often results in better success; in fact some prominent physical educators have claimed that strength is the most important single contributor.

In addition to being an important trait by itself strength is a factor in several other traits which influence motor performance. Strength is an element in power. Expressed in a simple formula, power = force × velocity. Increased strength results in more force; hence strength contributes to power.

Strength is also a factor in muscular endurance, the ability of the muscles to resist fatigue while doing work. Suppose a person were to move a given resistance through a particular range of motion 100 times. If this individual's strength were increased 50 percent, he or she would then be able to move (provided resistance is constant) through the range of motion with greater ease; hence he or she would be able to repeat the movement considerably more than 100 times. This example illustrates how strength can contribute to muscular endurance.

Through experimentation we have learned that strength can best be increased by applying the basic principles of strength *overload* and *progressive resistance*. The principle of strength *overload* simply means that if muscles are contracted regularly against resistance heavier than they are accustomed to, they will respond by increasing in strength. If they are not loaded beyond their usual levels, muscles will gain only the strength resulting from normal growth. The principle of *progressive resistance* means that as the muscles become stronger the loads against which they contract must progressively be increased in order to continue to apply overload.

Any form of exercise which applies heavier than usual resistance to muscle contractions will stimulate an increase in strength. For example, hard manual labor or vigorous athletic performance; specific exercises against body weight, as in pull-ups or dips; exercises against external movable resistance, such as weight-training equipment; and muscle tensions against a fixed object or another body part are all strength-building stimuli.

Types of Strength

There are two types of strength: static (isometric) and dynamic (isotonic). Static strength is the ability to apply force at a particular position without moving through the range of motion. It involves the isometric muscle contractions involved in pulling against a fixed object, a cable tensiometer, or a back and leg lift dynamometer. Dynamic strength is the ability to apply force through the range of motion. It involves the isotonic muscle contractions demonstrated in pull-ups or dips on the parallel bars. Dynamic strength is used more in athletics, but the two types of strength are closely related. Static strength can be measured more accurately than dynamic strength.

Since strength is so important in vigorous performance, it is essential to identify the lack of strength and to attempt to correct the condition. For this reason strength tests have been devised.

Some Instruments for Measuring Strength

The *back* and *leg* lift *dynamometer*, the hand dynamometer, and the cable tensiometer are instruments designed specifically to measure strength.

The back and leg lift dynamometer is a meter with a chain and bar attached, mounted on a platform. A performer, holding the bar, stands on the platform and applies force upward. The meter indicates in pounds amount of force exerted. This instrument measures the strength of the leg muscles or back muscles, depending on how the force is applied.

The *hand dynamometer* tests right- and left-hand grip strength. With attachments it is useful for measuring strength of the arm and shoulder abductor and adductor muscles.

The *cable tensiometer* tests the strength of numerous muscle groups. With the use of a well-designed testing table this instrument, attached to almost any segment of the body, measures the strength of that segment (see Figure 6-1).

FIGURE 6-1. Strength testing table, especially designed for use of tensiometer.

Recently several *isokinetic strength machines* have been developed, and some of them are designed to measure strength through the range of motion. These are very useful for testing dynamic strength (see Figure 6-2).

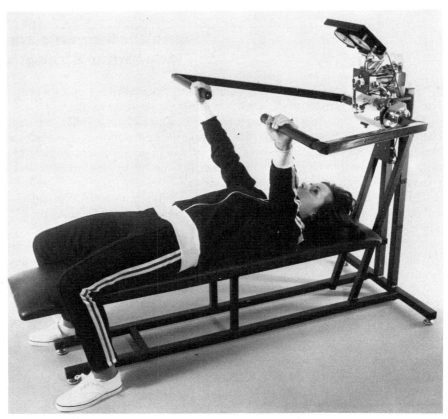

FIGURE 6-2. Isokinetic strength device which has the capacity for measuring strength through the range of motion. (Courtesy of Lumex Corporation.)

Static Strength Tests

Static strength tests, the most accurate measures of strength, are useful in school programs. However, they have two limitations: static tests measure strength at only one angle despite the variance of strength at different angles through the range of motion. In addition static strength is a less valid indicator of ability to perform motor skills than is dynamic strength.

Leg Lift Test

This test measures the strength of the leg extensor muscles; the results indicate total leg strength. A leg lift dynamometer with a belt attachment is the

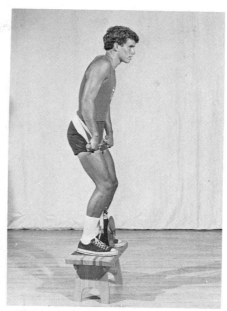

FIGURE 6-3.   Leg lift static strength test using dynomometer.

only equipment necessary. About 25 students can be tested in a 40-minute period.

Procedure: The student holds the bar with both hands (palms down) so that the bar rests at the juncture of his thighs and trunk. The student maintains this position while the belt is fastened to the handle and adjusted to the body. The student then takes position on the dynamometer platform so that the pull will be directly upward. Bending the knees slightly, he or she holds this position while the chain length is adjusted (see Figure 6-2). At a signal from the leader the student exerts a maximum force upward by extending the legs, at the same time keeping the arms and back straight, the head erect, and the chest high.

Scoring: Each student takes two trials: the better of the lifts is recorded to the nearest pound. Achievement scales (norms) are not available for this test; therefore the examiner must interpret scores by comparing the scores of the different students or by comparing the scores of the same student taken at different times. ·

Back Lift Test

This test measures the strength of the back extensor muscles. It requires the same amount of time and the same equipment as the leg lift test, without the use of the belt.

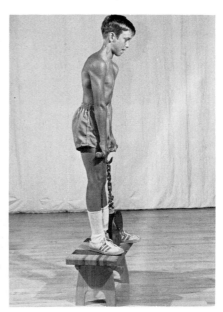

FIGURE 6-4. Back lift static strength test.

Procedure: The student stands in position on the dynamometer platform. When the chain length has been properly adjusted, he or she bends forward and grasps the bar firmly with one palm upward and one palm downward, keeping the legs straight, the feet flat on the platform, the head up, and the eyes straight forward (see Figure 6-4). At a signal from the leader the student lifts steadily with maximum force.

Scoring: The same method is used as for the leg lift test.

Hand Grip Test

This test measures the grip strength of the right and left hands. The only equipment needed is a hand grip dynamometer. About 30 students can be tested in a 40-minute period.

Procedure: The student places the grip dynamometer in the palm of the right hand (with the dial toward the palm) so that the convex edge is between the first and second joints of the fingers and the rounded edge is against the base of the hand. The student bends the elbow slightly and raises the arm upward; he or she then moves the arm forward and downward, gripping with maximum force. At the same time the student is careful not to touch the body or any object. He or she then repeats the test using the left hand.

Scoring: Each student has two trials with each hand. The better of the grips is recorded.

Arm Abduction Test

This test measures the strength of the arm abductor and shoulder girdle protractor muscles. It requires a hand grip dynamometer with push and pull attachments. Thirty students can be tested in a 40-minute period.

Procedure: With the dynamometer in front of the chest and with the dial facing outward, the student grasps the handles with both hands. On a signal from the leader the student pulls steadily outward with both hands, applying maximum force.

Scoring: The same method is used as for the leg lift test.

Arm Adduction Test

This test measures the strength of the arm adductor and shoulder girdle retractor muscles. It requires the same equipment and the same amount of time as the arm abduction test.

Procedure: The student, in the same position as in the arm abduction test, grasps the handles of the dynamometer with both hands and pushes them toward each other with maximum force.

Scoring: The method is the same as for the leg lift test.

Cable Tensiometer Tests

The cable tensiometer accurately measures the static strength of almost any body segment, provided the tests are administered correctly.

After experimenting for several years, H. Harrison Clarke (2) identified 38 different muscle groups that can be tested by use of the cable tensiometer. Physical educators, with their background and insight into muscular actions, can identify the muscle groups they want to test and the angle at which they want the test applied.

Procedure: The student is placed in the desired testing position. Then one end of the tensiometer cable is attached to the body segment to be tested and the other end to a fixed object. The tensiometer is placed on the cable and the amount of force applied by the segment is then measured. For measures of this type to be accurate the body must be in a stable position to allow for the application of maximum force by the body segment (see Figures 6-5 and 6-6).

Scoring: Test scores that are to be compared must be obtained at the same angle of pull. For example, a comparison of the scores of two students on the elbow flexion test would not be valid if one student were tested with the elbow

FIGURE 6-5.   Test of elbow flexion static strength using tensiometer.

at a 90-degree angle and the other student with the elbow at a 120-degree angle.

Dynamic Strength Tests

Pure dynamic strength is difficult to measure. Maximum lifts with weight training equipment provide some useful results. This approach is not totally satisfactory because a certain amount of experimentation is necessary to determine the maximum weight that can be lifted once. When it is determined, the maximum weight represents the dynamic strength score for that particular movement. Figures 6-7 through 6-11 are some examples of useful lifts for testing dynamic strength of major muscle groups. Any weight training exercise can be used as a test of dynamic strength. Also, as mentioned earlier, certain isokinetic strength machines have an attachment which registers the amount of strength throughout the range of motion. (See Figure 6-2.)

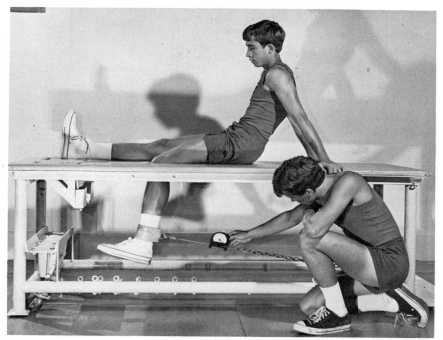

FIGURE 6-6. **Test of knee extension static strength, using tensiometer.**

Dynamic Strength–Endurance Tests

Often movements against one's body weight, such as pull-ups, have been used as measures of dynamic strength. Such tests do not measure pure strength but rather a combination of strength and endurance. Any test calling for repetitions of a movement (such as a maximum number of pull-ups) combines strength with endurance. A pure strength test involves only a single maximum muscle contraction; a second maximum contraction in succession will likely be less intense than the first one, and a third contraction will be even less than the second.

The extent to which strength or endurance is the primary factor in a particular strength–endurance test depends on the number of times a person can perform the movement. If a student is able to perform only one pull-up, then his strength rather than his endurance is measured. A failure to do even one pull-up results from insufficient strength, not from a lack of endurance. On the other hand, if a student performs 25 pull-ups, then the test measures endurance primarily rather than pure strength. Although a student must be very strong to do 25 pull-ups, the test measures primarily endurance rather than strength.

FIGURE 6-7.   Leg press test (dynamic).

Many muscular strength–endurance tests are simple to administer and require limited space and little or no special test equipment. These tests are reasonably good indicators of general ability to perform in athletics. They also provide an immediate sense of achievement for students as they see themselves accomplish work.

Dips on Parallel Bars

This test measures strength and endurance of the elbow extensor, shoulder flexor, and shoulder girdle depressor muscles. With the use of a testing station at each end of the apparatus about 60 students can be tested in 40 minutes.

Procedure: The student stands at the end of the parallel bars (adjusted to the proper height and width), grasps one bar in each hand, and jumps to the front support position, keeping the arms straight. Lowering the body until the angle

FIGURE 6-8.   Bench press test (dynamic).

FIGURE 6-9. Two arm curl test (dynamic).

at the elbows is a right angle (90 degrees) or less (see Figure 6-12), the student executes the bar dip as many times as possible without jerking or kicking.

Scoring: The jump to the support position counts one and each additional dip properly executed counts 1. Improperly executed dips count ½.

Floor Push-Ups

This test measures strength and endurance of the elbow extensor and shoulder flexor muscles. Because the trunk must be held straight throughout the exercise, extreme weakness of the hip flexor and abdominal muscles may also be detected with this test. The test can be administered to several students at one time, with a counter for each student.

Procedure: The student lies down facing the floor, with the body straight, the arms bent, and the hands flat on the floor beneath the shoulders (see Figure 6-13). From this position the student pushes upward to a straight arm position and then lowers the body to touch the counter's hand which is placed palm

FIGURE 6-10. Sit-up test with weight.

down under the chest. The student should keep the body rigid throughout, touching only the hands and toes to the floor. The student repeats the action as many times as possible.

Scoring: The total number of push-ups correctly done in succession is counted.

Modified Push-Ups

This test is the same as the floor push-up test, with modifications to suit the abilities of weaker performers.

Procedure: The student grasps the outer edges of a bench (15 inches high and 15 inches long) at the nearest corners (see Figure 6-14). In the front leaning rest position the student performs push-ups as described in the floor push-

FIGURE 6-11. Partial squat test.

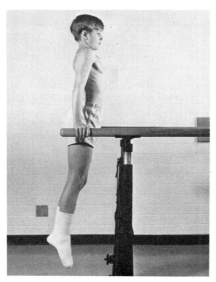 

FIGURE 6-12. Parallel bar dips.

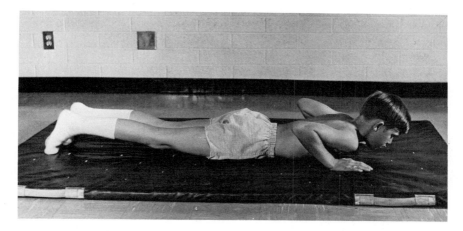

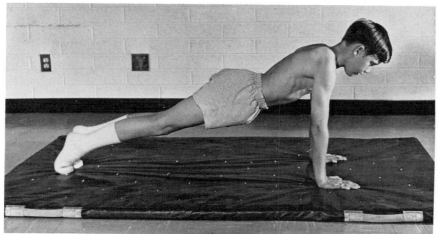

FIGURE 6-13. Push-ups.

up test. The knee push-up (see Figure 6-15) is another version of a modified push-up.

Scoring: The method is the same as for the floor push-up test. However, achievement scales are not available.

Pull-Ups

This test measures the strength and endurance of the elbow, wrist, and finger flexors; the shoulder extensors; and the shoulder girdle depressor muscles. A high horizontal bar is the only equipment required. About 40 students can be tested in 40 minutes at each station.

FIGURE 6-14. Modified push-ups (bench).

Procedure:. The student takes a straight-arm hang position (hands directly above shoulders) on the horizontal bar with the body fully extended. Using the forward grip (palm forward), the student raises the body until he or she can place the chin over the bar without kicking or swinging. The student then lowers his body to the original position. The procedure is repeated as many times as possible.

FIGURE 6-15. Modified push-ups (knee).

Scoring: The score is the total number of pull-ups correctly performed in succession. Pull-ups done incorrectly count half.

Modified Pull-Ups

This test is the same as the pull-up test, with modifications to suit the abilities of weaker performers. The bar is adjusted to a height equal to the base of the student's sternum, when the student is standing erect.

Procedure: The student grasps the bar with a forward grip (palms forward) and slides the feet under the bar until the arms are straight and the angle between arms and trunk is 90 degrees (see Figure 6-16). Keeping the body straight and rigid, the student executes as many pull-ups as possible, bringing the chin over the bar each time.

Scoring: The method is the same as for the regular pull-up test. However, achievement scales are not available.

Rope Climb

This test measures the strength and endurance of the fingers, wrist, and elbow flexors; the shoulder extensors; and the shoulder girdle depressor muscles. A stopwatch and a suspended rope not less than 1½ inches or more than 2 inches in diameter are necessary. About 40 students can be tested in 40 minutes at one station.

Procedure: From a standing position the student grasps the rope. At the signal she or he climbs the rope, using both hands and feet, until one hand reaches the 20-foot mark.

Scoring: The student is allowed two trials; the examiner records the better time to the nearest tenth of a second.

FIGURE 6-16. Modified pull-ups (low bar).

FIGURE 6-17. Body curl.

Sit-Ups

This test measures the strength and endurance of the trunk and hip flexor muscles. If the students are arranged into pairs to count for each other and to check each other's performance, a large number of students can be tested in a short time. The counter sits on the performer's legs midway between the knees and ankles and holds the feet down by applying force at the ankles.

Procedure: The student lies in a supine position with the hands clasped behind the head. Keeping the knees straight, the student comes to a sitting position and touches one elbow to the opposite knee and then the other elbow to the alternate side. Returning to the supine position, the student repeats the movement as many times as possible.

Scoring: The score is the number of complete sit-ups the student performs correctly.

Body Curls

This test is used to measure strength and endurance of the abdominal muscles. The body curl is the same as the sit-up except that the performer's knees are elevated, the feet are placed flat on the floor, and the hands are clasped behind the head (see Figure 6-17). Achievement scales are not available.

Squat Jumps

This test measures strength and endurance of the leg and foot extensor muscles. It requires no special equipment. If students are arranged into pairs to serve as counters and checkers for each other, a large number can be tested in a short time.

Procedure: The student takes a standing position with one foot 12 to 15 inches forward of the other foot and his hands clasped behind his head. He jumps upward just high enough to exchange positions of his feet and, upon landing, dips to a half squat position. Resuming the standing position, he repeats the jump, exchanging positions of the feet, and continues this procedure as many times as possible.

Scoring: The score is the number of jumps the student correctly executes in succession. Achievement scales are not available.

Static Strength–Endurance Tests

If certain muscles are contracted against the body weight and held in position as long as possible, their endurance can be tested. The following simple tests measure the strength–endurance of the major muscle groups. Except for the flexed arm hang test achievement scales are not available.

Flexed Arm Hang

The height of the horizontal bar should be adjusted so that it is approximately equal to the student's standing height. The student should use a palms forward grasp. With the assistance of two spotters, one in front and one in back, the student raises off the floor to a position where the chin is above the bar, the elbows are flexed, and the chest is close to the bar. He holds this position as long as possible.

The stopwatch is started as soon as the student takes the correct hanging position. The watch is stopped at three points: when the student touches his chin to the bar, when the student tilts his head backward to keep his chin above the bar, and when the student lets his chin fall below the level of the bar. The length of time the student holds the hanging position is recorded in seconds to the nearest second.

Half-Flexed Arm Hang

The test measures the strength–endurance of arm and shoulder muscles. The student grasps a horizontal bar as if he or she were going to perform a pull-up. The student pulls herself or himself upward until the angle at the elbows is 90 degrees and holds this position as long as possible. The longer he or she holds the position, the greater is the ability of the arm and shoulder muscles to resist fatigue when contracted against the weight of the body. The score is the length of time the student can hold the position, measured to the nearest second.

Straight Arm Hang

This test is performed the same as the half-flexed arm hang test, except that the student's arms are fully extended.

Leg Raise and Hold

This test measures the ability of the abdominal and hip flexor muscles to hold against the weight of the legs and feet. Lying on the back with hands clasped behind the head, feet together, and legs straight, the student raises both feet 4 inches above the floor and holds this position as long as possible.

Chest Raise and Hold

This test measures the ability of the back and neck extensors to hold against the weight of the upper body. The student assumes a prone position with hands clasped behind the head and elbows held horizontally. Another student sits on the performing student's lower legs. By contracting the back and neck extensor muscles, the performer raises the chest from the floor and holds this position as long as possible.

Sit and Hold

This test measures the ability of the knee extensor (thigh) muscles to hold against the body weight. With the back and head flat against a wall the student lowers the body and moves the feet away from the wall until right angles form at the hip and knee joints (sitting position). The student holds this position as long as possible.

Strength Test Batteries

Each test measures the strength of only one body region. A battery of tests consists of several test items and may, therefore, be a much better indicator of total body strength. Usually the scores of the several items are combined to give the total score for the battery.

Larson Muscular Strength Test

Leonard Larson (6) designed this test to measure dynamic strength. The test consists of pull-ups and dips, which measure a combination of strength and endurance, and the vertical jump, which mainly measures explosive power. All three test items depend heavily on strength, but none measures pure strength. With a chinning bar, parallel bars, and a vertical jump board, about 30 students can be tested in a 40-minute period.

Procedure: All students should perform the tests in the following sequence:

1. Pull-ups: See description on page 93.
2. Vertical jump: See description on page 139.
3. Dips: See description on page 88.

Scoring: The number of pull-ups, the height of the vertical jump to the nearest half inch, and the number of dips are the raw scores. Achievement scales for high school boys and college men were printed in *The Physical Educator* (1).

Rogers Strength Test

This test of total body strength consists of seven items, some of which measure pure strength while others test strength and endurance (8). Necessary equipment are an adjustable horizontal bar, parallel bars, back and leg lift dynamometer, hand grip dynamometer, push-up bench, height and weight measuring equipment, and a wet spirometer. With all testing stations operating simultaneously, about 20 students can be tested in a 40-minute period.

Procedure: All students should perform the items of the test in the sequence in which they are listed. Age, height, and weight should be measured and recorded to the nearest month, half inch, and pound, respectively.

1. Hand grips (right and left): See description on page 84. Record the scores for both the right and left hands.
2. Back lift: See description on page 83.
3. Leg lift: See description on page 82.
4. Pull-ups: See description on page 93.
5. Push-ups: See description on page 90.
6. Lung capacity: There is no evidence that this item relates to strength in any significant way. But since lung capacity was included in the original test, the item must be retained if the established norms are to be useful. This aspect of the test measures the amount of air that can be expelled from the lungs in one breath. The student inhales as much air as possible; then he places his mouth over the sterilized mouthpiece

and expels as much air into the spirometer as possible. The score is recorded in cubic inches.

Scoring: There are two steps in scoring this test: computing arm strength and determining the strength index (*SI*).

$$\text{arm strength} = \text{pull-ups} + \text{push-ups} \times \left(\frac{\text{weight}}{10} + \text{height} - 60 \right)$$

The student's weight is recorded in pounds and his height in inches. If the student is 60 inches or less in height, the minus 60 phase of the formula is eliminated.

Strength index (*SI*)
= arm strength + right grip + left grip + back lift + leg lift + lung capacity

The student's strength index may be compared to *SI* norms (8).

Frederick Rogers (8) proposed that a person's physical fitness could be measured by the following formula:

$$\text{physical fitness index } (PFI) = \frac{\text{achieved } SI}{\text{normal } SI} \times 100$$

The physical fitness index is discussed in more detail in Chapter 9.

Kraus–Weber Test of Minimal Strength

The Kraus–Weber tests (4, 5) were constructed from clinical experience over a period of 18 years. The six test items included in the battery are considered the most valid of a large number of tests administered under clinical situations. These diagnostic tests are designed to identify students age 6 through 18, whose strength is below minimal level. However, they are only screening tests to detect cases of subnormal strength and are not valid measures of maximum strength. To pass each item the student must make the maximum score, without having done warm-up exercises prior to the test.

Test 1 measures minimal strength of the abdominal and hip flexor muscles. The student lies on the back with the legs straight and together and the hands clasped behind the neck (see Figure 6-18). With a partner holding down the feet the person tries to roll up to a sitting position. Twisting of the trunk or absence of the rolling action indicates weak abdominal muscles. If he or she cannot raise the shoulders, the student scores zero. If the examiner must help him or her half-way to the sitting position, the student scores five. If he or she performs the sit-up correctly and unaided, the student scores 10.

Test 2 measures minimal strength of the abdominal muscles. From a supine position with knees elevated to release the hip flexor muscles from action, feet

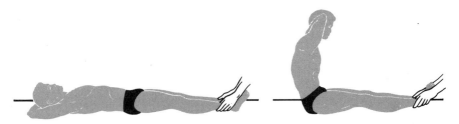

FIGURE 6-18.   Kraus-Weber Test 1.

held down, and hands behind the neck, the student rolls up to a sitting position (see Figure 6-19). He is scored the same as for Test 1.

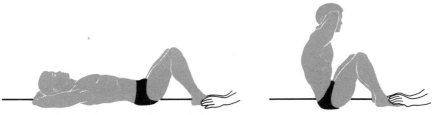

FIGURE 6-19.   Kraus-Weber Test 2.

Test 3 measures minimal strength of the hip flexor and lower abdominal muscles. From a supine position with legs straight and hands behind the neck, the student lifts the feet 10 inches above the surface and holds this position for 10 seconds (see Figure 6-20). The student scores one point for each second he holds the position; the maximum he or she can score is 10.

Test 4 measures minimal strength of the upper back muscles. The student lies in a prone position with a pillow under the hips and lower abdomen. With a partner holding the feet the student raises the chest, shoulders, and head from the surface and holds this position for 10 seconds (see Figure 6-21). Scoring is the same as for Test 3.

Test 5 measures minimal strength of the lower back. The student takes the same position as in Test 4, except that he or she places the forearms on the sur-

**FIGURE 6-20.
Kraus-Weber Test 3.**

TABLE 6-1 Results of the Kraus–Weber Test Administered to Children of the United States and European Countries (4)

	Percent			
	Austrian	Italian	Swiss	American
Number tested	678	1036	.1156	4264
Failure	9.5	8.0	8.8	57.9
Incidence of failure	9.7	8.5	8.9	80.0

face with the hands under the face. With a partner holding down the trunk the student raises the legs and feet above the surface, keeping the knees straight, and holds this position for 10 seconds (see Figure 6-22). Scoring is the same as for Test 3.

Test 6 measures the flexibility of the hamstring and lower back muscles. The student removes shoes and stands erect with feet together. Keeping the knees straight he or she bends slowly forward until he or she touches the floor with the fingertips. The student holds this position without bobbing for three seconds (see Figure 6-23). If the student touches the floor he or she passes the test.

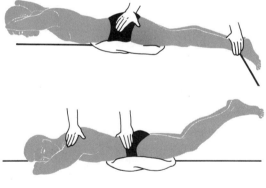

FIGURE 6-21. Kraus-Weber Test 4.

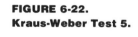

FIGURE 6-22. Kraus-Weber Test 5.

FIGURE 6-23. Kraus-Weber Test 6.

If the student does not touch the floor he or she receives a minus score of one for each inch between the floor and the fingertips.

The Kraus–Weber test has caused much excitement and controversy because it has been used as the testing instrument in a number of studies in which school children of the United States have been compared with children of other countries. The United States children have fared poorly in the comparisons, as illustrated in Table 6-1. As a result this test has been effective in stimulating greater efforts toward physical fitness of our young people.

Precautions in the Interpretation of Strength Test Results

A strength score is not usually meaningful unless it is interpreted in view of the following facts: Larger people must be stronger than smaller people to perform at the same level; hence raw scores by people of different sizes cannot logically be compared. For people of the same size men are normally stronger than women. When body size is equal, young adults (ages 20–25) are normally stronger than younger or older people. Mesomorphs (with heavy musculature) are normally stronger for their size than ectomorphs or endomorphs, and ectomorphs are usually stronger for their size than endomorphs. Thus, to be meaningful, strength tests must be interpreted relative to age, sex, size, and body type.

Selected References

1. **Bookwalter, K. W.**: Achievements Scales in Strength Tests for Secondary School Boys and College Men, *The Physical Educator*, 11:130–141, 1942.
2. **Clark, H. H.**: *A Manual: Cable-Tension Strength Tests.* Chicopee, Mass., Brown-Murphy Co., 1953.
3. **Johnson, B. L., et al.**: A comparison of concentric and eccentric muscle training. *Med. Sci. Sports* 8:35–38, 1976.
4. **Kraus, H., and Hirschland, R. P.**, Minimum muscular fitness tests in school children. *Research Quarterly* 25:177–188, 1954.
5. **Kraus, H., and Hirschland, R. P.**, Muscular fitness and orthopedic disability. *New York State Journal of Medicine*, 54:212–215, 1954.
6. **Larson, L. A.**: A factor and validity analysis of strength variables and tests with a test combination of chinning, dipping, and vertical jump. *Research Quarterly*, 11(4), 1940.
7. **Linford, A. G., and Rarick, L.**: The effect of knee angle on the measurement of leg strength of college males. *Research Quarterly*, 39:582, 1968.
8. **Rogers, F. R.**: *Physical Capacity Tests in the Administration of Physical Education.* New York: Bureau of Publications, Teacher's College, Columbia University, 1926.

7

Tests of Circulorespiratory Endurance

The trait that enables a person to continue a vigorous activity over a period of time is referred to as endurance. It is the ability to resist fatigue and to recover quickly after fatigue. Circulorespiratory endurance (which encompasses cardiovascular endurance) is the ability of the individual's circulatory and respiratory systems to resist fatigue while they effectively support vigorous muscular activity.

Importance of Endurance

Physiologists agree that the main limitation in most endurance performances is the supply of oxygen to the working muscles. The circulorespiratory system is directly responsible for supplying oxygen to the tissues and to remove carbon dioxide and other waste products. Therefore circulorespiratory endurance is essential to prolonged vigorous exercise. When endurance gives way to fatigue as a result of exercise, several elements important to good performance diminish: strength, coordination, timing, speed of movement, reaction time, and alertness.

Endurance of the circulorespiratory system is increased by applying overload. In this case overload means exercising until the heart rate and the rate and depth of breathing increase a significant amount. Endurance can be increased by regular participation in sustained activity, such as jogging, basketball, soccer, cycling, swimming, etc. But the most effective method for increasing endurance is interval training, which consists of several bouts of vigorous exercise with a brief recovery period following each bout.

Interval training for endurance makes good sense from the physiological point of view because the prime objective of an endurance training program is to expose the person to the greatest work load before the onset of fatigue. Research shows that when work is done continuously, a work level which can be tolerated for an hour with the interval training technique will bring about exhaustion in nine minutes. Thus the total work accomplished before fatigue is much greater when the interval training technique is used instead of the continuous training method. This greater output results in a stronger endurance stimulus.

The interval training technique is used extensively for swimmers and distance runners and can be used successfully in activities such as wrestling, baseball, basketball, and court and field games.

Circulorespiratory Tests

The measurement of circulorespiratory endurance has proved difficult because endurance can be measured accurately only if the organism is worked to complete fatigue—neither a feasible nor a prudent practice. As a substitute, tests estimating endurance have been devised, but they do not always furnish highly accurate results. At best they are only indicators of endurance. This word of caution is not to imply that the tests are not useful; they are valuable as screening devices to identify extreme weakness in endurance, and they serve as an endurance indicator for the performer. With wise use and interpretation these tests serve a worthwhile purpose in school programs.

Circulorespiratory tests measure the durability and efficiency of the circulatory and respiratory systems. In other words they measure the ability of these systems to carry on their functions under strenuous demands. Circulorespiratory tests are usually based on the variables of pulse rate and blood pressure. Supposedly the amount of change in these variables, as a result of a given amount of work, indicates the condition of the total circulorespiratory system. The condition of the circulorespiratory system is generally a good indicator of endurance of the total body.

Measuring Pulse Rate and Blood Pressure

Certain circulorespiratory tests should be administered and interpreted cautiously because rest, food intake, body position, activity, time of day, and emotional changes may alter pulse rate and blood pressure.

Pulse Rate. The average pulse rate of adults in general is 72 beats per minute, with a range of about 35 to 110 beats per minute. Children and elderly people have faster pulse rates. On the average, men have slower pulse rates

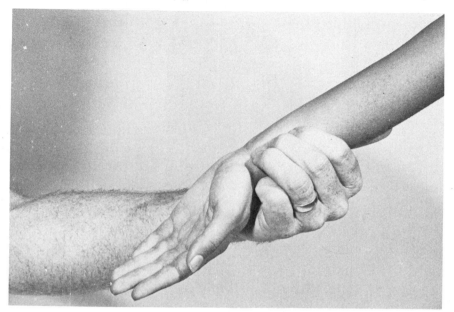

FIGURE 7-1. Pulse rate taken at the wrist.

than women, and well-conditioned people have slower pulse rates than poorly conditioned people. Pulse rate can best be measured by lightly pressing the middle finger against the axillary artery in the wrist (see Figure 7-1) or against the carotid artery in the neck (see Figure 7-2). The beat should be counted for 30 seconds; then the number of beats multiplied by 2 to give the pulse rate per minute.

Blood Pressure. The measurement of systolic and diastolic blood pressure is relatively simple with the use of a sphygmomanometer and a stethoscope; however, like most testing, such measurement requires considerable practice for proficiency.

The tester wraps the cuff of the sphygmomanometer around the bare arm above the elbow of the person being tested. With the earphones of the stethoscope in the ears the tester places the bell of the stethoscope on the brachial artery just above the hollow of the elbow of the person being tested and pumps up the cuff until the artery collapses and no pulse beat is heard (see Figure 7-3). Then the tester slowly releases pressure and watches the gauge or mercury column. When the first sound of the pulse is heard, the tester notes the reading in millimeters of mercury at that instant. This reading is the systolic pressure. The tester continues slowly to release pressure until a dull, weak beat is perceived. At that instant the tester notes the pressure in millimeters of mercury.

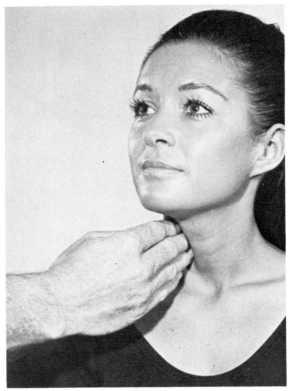

FIGURE 7-2. Pulse rate taken at the neck.

This reading represents the diastolic pressure. The tester records the measures, with the systolic pressure first and then the diastolic pressure. A typical reading might be 120/80.

Cooper Twelve Minute Run–Walk Test

Kenneth Cooper (4) did the basic research for this test with United States Air Force personnel. He and his wife conducted subsequent research utilizing the same test for women (5). The research showed the importance of such vigorous activities as running, swimming, cycling, fast walking, handball, basketball, and squash in the development of circulorespiratory endurance. Cooper developed the 12-minute run–walk test and scale as a simple method of self-evaluation of circulorespiratory fitness. A validity coefficient of .90 has been reported when maximum oxygen uptake was used as the criterion. Using the test–retest method, a reliability of .94 has been reported.

TABLE 7-1 12-Minute Run Walk—Scoring Scale

Men Distance Covered	Fitness Level	Women Distance Covered
Less than 1 mile	Very Poor	Less than .95 miles
1–1.25 miles	Poor	.96–1.15 miles
1.26–1.50 miles	Fair	1.16–1.35 miles
1.51–1.75	Good	1.36–1.65 miles
More than 1.75 miles	Excellent	More than 1.65 miles

Procedure: The test consists of running, or running and walking, as far as possible in 12 minutes. The route can be measured by running around a standard length track, or by using an automobile odometer to measure the distance.

Scoring: The score is the total distance covered in 12 minutes. The score may be interpreted by applying it to the following scale:

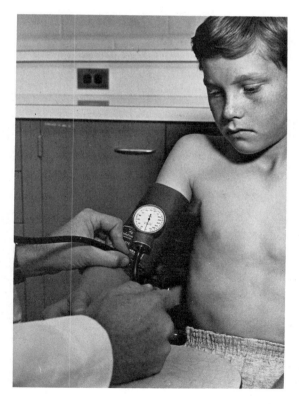

FIGURE 7-3. The measurement of blood pressure.

Doolittle and Bigbee (7) report a reliability of .90 when the 12 minute run walk test was correlated with oxygen intake for adolescent boys. Maksurd and Coutts report similar results.

600-Yard Run Walk

This test (16) measures a combination of running speed and endurance. It requires a track or large field, a starting pistol or whistle, and a stopwatch to time each contestant. Several students can perform the test at once. Often one watch is used to time more than one student by reading the times as each student crosses the finish line. Validity and reliability of the test have not been established, but various research appears to be indicating coefficients of .90 on test retest reliability. Moneham and Gutin report a validity correlation of .82 between the run–walk test and a 2-count step test performed by ninth grade girls.

Harvard Step Test

The Harvard step test (3) measures the ability of adults to perform hard muscular work. The test consists of the student's stepping up and down on a bench in the prescribed manner for a period of 5 minutes. There must be one examiner for each student being tested. The examiner stands close to the student to make sure the student performs the test correctly. Scoring is based on the student's pulse rate taken at prescribed times after exercise, combined with the length of time that the student performs. A stopwatch and bench or platform 20 inches high are necessary. If a group of students is to be tested, a wall clock with a sweep second hand may be preferred. With the necessary number of benches and leaders several students can be tested every 10 minutes. The test may be administered in slightly less than 10 minutes if the rapid form of scoring is used. Testing more than 20 students at one time is not recommended. Ratings of validity and reliability have not been established.

Procedure: The student stands facing the bench and at the starting signal begins the exercise (see Figure 7-4). He or she places one foot on the bench, then steps up and places the other foot beside the first one. The student straightens the back and legs to an erect standing position, then immediately steps down again, one foot at a time, leading with the foot that stepped up first. The student continues to step up and down in this manner, keeping time with the cadence of 30 steps per minute, which is counted aloud as, Up, 2, 3, 4, Up, 2, 3, 4, and so on. He or she may change the lead foot if one leg tires. The student continues this procedure until he or she is halted at the end of five minutes or until he or she can continue no longer; he or she then turns around and sits quietly on the bench.

Forty-five seconds after the end of the exercise, the examiner locates the pulse and prepares to count. The count starts at exactly 1 minute after exercise

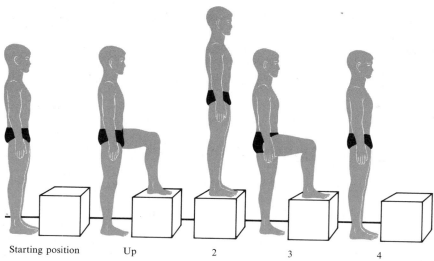

Starting position   Up   2   3   4

FIGURE 7-4. Harvard Step Test.

and continues for ½ minute. (If the student did not last 5 minutes, the count starts 1 minute from the time he or she terminated the exercise.) Locating the pulse in advance, the examiner again counts for 30 seconds, beginning at 2 minutes after exercise, and again at 3 minutes after exercise. The examiner records each count.

After hard exercise, it is easier to count the pulse at the subclavian artery or the carotid artery than at the wrist. The subclavian artery can be located by holding the fingers vertically and placing them alongside the neck just in back of the clavical bone. The carotid artery can be located by placing the fingers horizontally and pressing on the front of the neck alongside the trachea.

Scoring: The formula for computing the final score is:

$$\text{Score} = \frac{\text{duration of exercise in seconds} \times 100}{2 \text{ times the sum of the 3 pulse counts}}$$

The Harvard step test was modified by Skubic and Hodgkins (*13*) to be used for girls and women to measure levels of physical fitness. They indicate that a 3 minute test, using an 18 inch bench and a stepping rate of 24 steps per minute has a reliability of .82 and a validity of .78 and clearly differentiates females who are highly active, moderately active, and sedentary active.

The score is then interpreted according to the following scale:

Excellent Condition	90 and above
Good	80–89
High Average	65–79
Low Average	55–64
Poor Condition	54 and below

To illustrate, if a person finished 5 minutes (maximum length) of exercise and if his three pulse counts were 90, 80, 70, then his score would be:

$$\frac{300 \text{ seconds} \times 100}{2 \times (90 + 80 + 70)} = 62.5$$

A score of 62.5 is rated low average.

To simplify calculations, a scoring scale has been computed which gives the scores for those students who continue for 5 minutes. To use the scale, the examiner simply totals the number of heart beats counted during the three 30-second periods and reads the score opposite that number. For example, for the man whose three pulse counts were 90, 80, 70, the examiner would find the sum of the counts (240) and, using the scoring scale in table 7-2, look for the score opposite the sum (62).

A rapid form for scoring the Harvard step test has been developed based on the duration of exercise and a single pulse count taken from 1 to 1½ minutes after exercise. The formula:

$$\text{Score} = \frac{\text{duration of exercise in seconds} \times 100}{5.5 \times \text{pulse count}}$$

The scores for the rapid form may be interpreted as follows:

Poor condition	49 and below
Average condition	50–80
Good condition	81 and above

Fairbanks Submaximal Test

The Fairbanks (8) submaximal text is based on heart rate after exercise to estimate the amount of oxygen the body is using. The test was developed for those who do not get much exercise, but can be used by anyone who would like to measure his or her fitness progress. A flat walking course about 100 feet long should be located. The temperature should be moderate, not above 80 degrees. Rest 10 minutes before the test, then record the pulse at the wrist. Begin walking the 100-foot course, turning in a semicircle at the ends using a normal, brisk walking pace. Monitor the walking speed to cover the 100 feet in 15 or 16 seconds. After 5 minutes of walking, come to a standstill and take the

TABLE 7-2 Achievement Scales for the Harvard Step Test*

Duration of Effort (Minutes)	Total Heart Beats 1½ Minutes in Recovery											
	40– 44	45– 49	50– 54	55– 59	60– 64	65– 69	70– 74	75– 79	80– 84	85– 89	90– 94	95– 99
	Score (Arbitrary Units)											
0 – ½	6	6	5	5	4	4	4	4	3	3	3	3
½–1	19	17	16	14	13	12	11	11	10	9	9	8
1 –1½	32	29	26	24	22	20	19	18	17	16	15	14
1½–2	45	41	38	34	31	29	27	25	23	22	21	20
2 –2½	58	52	47	43	40	36	34	32	30	28	27	25
2½–3	71	64	58	53	48	45	42	39	37	34	33	31
3 –3½	84	75	68	62	57	53	49	46	43	41	39	37
3½–4	97	87	79	72	66	61	57	53	50	47	45	42
4 –4½	110	98	89	82	75	70	65	61	57	54	51	48
4½–5	123	110	100	91	84	77	72	68	63	60	57	54
5	129	116	105	96	88	82	76	71	67	63	60	56

*From *Physiological Measurements of Metabolic Function in Man* by Consolazio, Johnson, and Pecora. Copyright 1963. Reprinted by permission of McGraw-Hill Book Company.

pulse during the first 10 seconds of the body's recovery from the exercise. Figure the maximum amount of oxygen the body would use during heavy exercise by multiplying 0.06198 times the body weight in pounds, 0.4564 times the recovery heart rate in beats per minute and 0.0867 times the resting heart rate in beats per minute. Add the resulting figures, then subtract the total from 111.6. The answer will be the number of millileters of oxygen the body uses per kilogram per minute at maximum work. If the result is less than 29 the fitness is very poor; if it is 30–39, the fitness is poor; 40–49 is average; 50–59 is good; and above 60 is excellent.

Balke Treadmill Test

The Balke (2) treadmill test consists of walking 3.5 miles per hour on a motor drum treadmill on which the slope increases each minute. The score is the length of time the subject walks to reach a heart rate of 180 beats per minute.

Astrand and Rhyming Nomogram

In their test (1) the nomogram is used. It is designed to calculate an individual's maximal attainable oxygen intake from heart rate and oxygen intake or work level reached during a test with a submaximal rate of work. A step test, a treadmill test, or a cycle test can be chosen.

Ohio State University Step Test

The Ohio State University Step test (9) is a submaximal test of cardiovascular fitness for men age 18 years and over, and was developed by Kurucz, Fox, and

Mathews in 1969. The OSU test comprises 18 innings of bench stepping, each of 50 seconds duration. In each inning, the subject steps for 30 seconds and rests for 20 seconds; during each rest period, he counts his own pulse for 10 seconds, between 5 and 15 seconds. The test is terminated when the pulse rate reaches 25 beats (150 beats per minute) or when the subject completes the entire 18 innings. The individual's score is the number of innings completed. The stepping consists of three consecutive phases as follows:

Phase 1: six innings, 15-inch bench, 24 steps per minute.
Phase 2: six innings, 15-inch bench, 30 steps per minute.
Phase 3: six innings, 20-inch bench, 30 steps per minute.

The test–retest reliability coefficient was .94. A validity correlation of .94 was obtained between the OSU and the Balke treadmill test.

Selected References

1. Astrand, P. U. and Ryhming, I.: "A Nomogram for calculation of aerobic capacity from pulse rate during submaximal work." *Journal of Applied Physiology* 1955, 2, 218.
2. Balke, B., Grillo, G. P., Konecci, E. B., and Luft, U. C.: "Work capacity after blood donation, *Journal of Applied Physiology* 7: 231: 1954.
3. Brouha, L.: The step test: A simple method of measuring physical fitness for muscular work in young men. *Research Quarterly*, 14, 1943.
4. Cooper, K. H.: *The New Aerobics*, New York: M. Evans and Co., 1970.
5. Cooper, M. and Cooper, K. H.: *Aerobics for Women*, New York, M. Evans and Co., 1972.
6. DeVries, H. A.: *Physiology of Exercise*, 2nd ed. (Dubuque, Iowa: William C. Brown Co., 1974.
7. Doolittle, T. L., and Bigbee, R.: The twelve-minute run–walk: A test of cardiorespiratory fitness of adolescent boys. *Res. Q.* 39, 1968.
8. Fairbanks, J. G.: Submaximal walking test: prediction of Max VO_2 Physical Fitness in Adult Males. Unpublished Dissertation Brigham Young University, 1978.
9. Kurucz, R. S., Fox, E. L. and Mathews, D. K.: Construction of a submaximal cardiovascular step test, *Research Quarterly* 40(1):115, March 1969.
10. Maksud, M. G. and Coutts, K. D.: Application of this Cooper Twelve Minute Run-Walk Test to young males. *Res. Q.* 42(1), 1971.
11. Manahan, J. E. and Gutin, B.: The one-minute step test as a measure of 600-year run performance. *Research Quarterly*, 42:2, 1972.
12. Scheuer, J., and Tipton, C. M.: Cardiovascular adaptation to physical training. *Am. Rev. Physiol.* 39:221–225, 1977.
13. Skubic, V. and Hodgkins, J.: Cardiovascular Efficiency Test for girls and women. *Research Quarterly* 34(2), 1963.
14. Sloan, A. W.: A modified Harvard step test for women. *Journal of Applied Physiology*, 14, 1959.

15. **Witten, C.**: Construction of a submaximal cardiovascular step test for college women, *Research Quarterly*, 44(1), 1973.
16. *Youth Fitness Test Manual*. American Alliance for Health, Physical Education and Recreation, 1975.

8

Measures of Flexibility

Adequate flexibility allows for a full range of motion in the joints and is often limited by the amount of extensibility of the muscles, tendons, and ligaments. Other factors such as relative length of body segments, or amount of body fat may also affect flexibility. One of the most frequent cause of improper or inefficient movement is poor flexibility.

Importance of Flexibility

Flexibility is important in all types of motor performance, and is easily observed in such activities as modern dance, ballet, gymnastics, diving, swimming, hurdling, and high jumping. In these activities the body must be unusually flexible to assume certain positions which determine good form.

Flexibility can be increased by regular stretching of the muscles and connective tissues that surround the joints. Flexibility is increased best by (1) moving slowly through the particular movement until a mild *stretch pain* is felt, (2) holding this position for 5 to 10 seconds while consciously relaxing the muscles involved, (3) then stretching a little farther, thus increasing the extensibility of the muscles and connective tissues. Five to 10 repetitions daily of this kind of exercise will improve flexibility.

Flexibility Tests

The tests presented here are practical tests of flexibility that can be administered by the teacher with little assistance by other people and with minimal equipment. The tests measure flexibility in the specific regions of the body that rely on optimum flexibility for good performance. Although validity and reliability coefficients for these tests have not been determined, the tests are obviously measures of flexibility and can be used as such. It is important to remember that flexibility is specific, and a high degree of flexibility in one or two movements is not a reliable indication total body flexibility.

Forward Bend of Trunk

This test measures flexion of the trunk and hips. Most of the movement occurs in the lower spine and hip joints. A small measuring tape is the only equipment needed. About 40 students can be tested in a 40-minute period.

Procedure: The student sits on a table or on the floor with the feet flat against the wall, hip width apart, and the legs straight and rigid. He or she bends the trunk forward and downward as far as possible, reaching the hands toward the heels of the feet (see Figure 8-1). As the student holds this position, the examiner measures the vertical distance from the table to the top of the student's sternum (suprasternal notch).

Scoring: The score is the distance measured, to the nearest quarter inch. As flexibility increases the measured distance will become shorter. Because achievement scales are not available, the measurement is meaningful only when compared to measurements of other students or to measurements of the same student on different occasions. If the examiner needs another indication

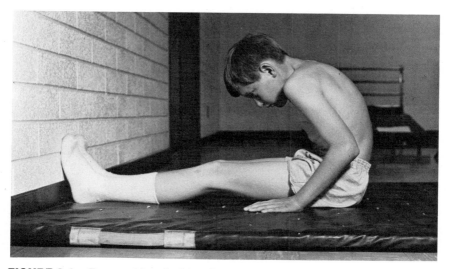

FIGURE 8-1. Forward bend of trunk test.

of flexibility, he or she may determine how near the student can come to touching the heels with the fingers.

Upward–Backward Movement of Arms

This test measures flexibility of the shoulders and shoulder girdles. The equipment and time required are the same as that for the forward bend of trunk test, with the addition of a stick 2 feet long.

Procedure: The student lies in a prone position on a table with the chin touching the table and the arms reaching forward directly in front of the shoulders. He or she holds the stick horizontally with both hands. Keeping the elbows and wrists straight and the chin on the table, he or she raises the arms upward as far as possible (see Figure 8-2).

Scoring: The examiner measures the vertical distance from the bottom of the stick to the table. For interpretation the student's score is compared with the scores of other students or with the scores of the same student on different occasions.

Sideward–Backward Movement of Arms

This test measures flexibility of the same body region as the upward–backward movement of arm test, except that the movement is in a different direction.

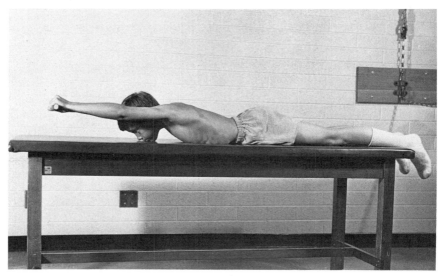

FIGURE 8-2.   Upward-backward arm movement test.

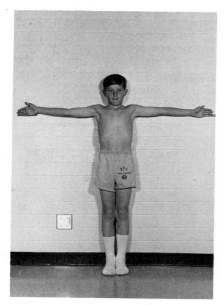

FIGURE 8-3. Sideward–backward arm movement test.

Procedure: To perform the test the student stands with the back against a wall, places the palms forward, and raises the arms until they are horizontal. Keeping the arms horizontal and the fifth finger of each hand in contact with the wall, he or she moves the back forward, away from the wall, as far as possible (see Figure 8-3).

Scoring: The examiner measures the horizontal distance, to the nearest quarter inch, from the wall to the spine at arm level. The examiner should interpret scores as described for the forward bend of trunk test.

Plantar–Dorsal Flexion of Foot

This test measures flexibility in the ankle and foot regions. A paper pad, a pencil, and a protractor are necessary.

Procedure: The student sits on a table with the legs straight and together. Keeping the heels and backs of the knees on the table, he or she plantar flexes the foot as far as possible. With a pad of paper placed in a vertical position at the inside of the foot, the examiner places a dot on the paper at the end of the toenail of the great toe. The student then dorsi flexes the foot as far as possible, and the examiner places a second dot on the paper in a similar manner. Finally the student relaxes the ankle, and the examiner places a third dot on the paper where the ankle bends at the top of the instep (see Figure 8-4).

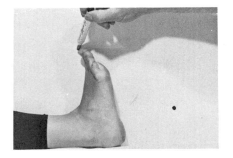
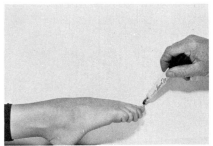
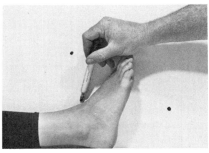

FIGURE 8-4. Plantar–dorsal flexion test.

Scoring: The examiner removes the pad and draws lines from the third dot to each of the other two dots. Using a protractor or goniometer, he or she measures the angle of each of the lines from the horizontal and interprets the scores as described for the forward bend of trunk test.

Trunk Extension

This test measures trunk extension. A small measuring tape is the only equipment necessary to test 40 students in 40 minutes.

Procedure: The student takes a prone position on a table or the floor with the hands clasped together near the small of the back. With a partner pressing downward on the back of the legs, the student lifts the chest from the floor as high as possible (see Figure 8-5).

Scoring: For the raw score the examiner measures the distance, to the nearest quarter inch, from the suprasternal notch to the floor. For the final score, which is more meaningful, the examiner multiplies the raw score by 100 and divides the product by trunk length measured in inches.

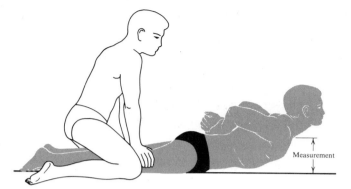

FIGURE 8-5. Trunk extension test.

FIGURE 8-6. Bridge up test.

Bridge Up

This test measures the student's ability to extend the back and hips and to reach backward with the arms, under force. Only a tape measure is needed to test about 40 students in a 40-minute period.

Procedure: From a supine position on the floor or mat the student extends the hips upward by arching the back and walks on the hands and feet, keeping them as close together as possible (see Figure 8-6).

Scoring: The examiner measures the distance between the fingertips and the heels to the nearest quarter inch. The lesser the distance, the better the score.

Observation Measures of Flexibility

Figures 8-7 and 8-11 illustrate observation measures of flexibility.

FIGURE 8-7. Normal flexibility of the neck allows the chin to move close to the upper chest.

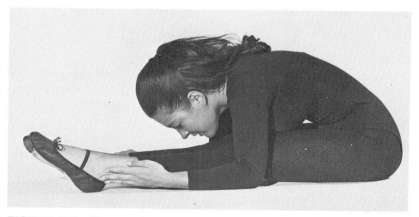

FIGURE 8-8. Normal flexibility in the hips and lower back allows flexion to about 135 degrees in the young adult.

FIGURE 8-9. Normal flexibility of the hamstring muscles allows straight leg raising from a back-lying position to 90 degrees.

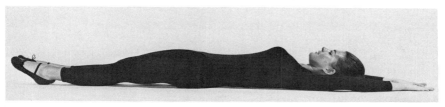

FIGURE 8-10. Normal flexibility of the chest muscles allows the arms to be flexed at the shoulders to 180 degrees.

FIGURE 8-11. Normal flexibility in the back with the knees bent allows the face to meet the knees.

Selected References

1. **Barney, V. S., Hirst, C. C.,** and **Jensen, Clayne R.**: *Conditioning Exercises*, 3rd ed. St. Louis, Mo.: Mosby, 1974.
2. **Broer, M.,** and **Galles, N.**: Importance of relationship between various body measurements in performance of the toe-touch test. Res. Q. 29:262, 1958.
3. **DeVries, H.**: Evaluation of static stretching procedures for improvement of flexibility. *Research Quarterly*, 33:222–29, 1962.
4. **Hutchins, G. Lee**: The relationship of selected strength and flexibility variables to the anteroposterior posture of college women. *Research Quarterly*, 36, 1965.
5. **Laubach, L. L.,** and **McConville, J. T.**: Relationships between flexibility, anthropometry and the somatotype of college man. *Research Quarterly*, 37:241, 1966.
6. **Laubach, L. L.,** and **McConville, J. T.**: Muscle strength, flexibility and body size of adult males. *Research Quarterly*, 37:384, 1966.
7. **Massey, B. H.,** and **Chaudet, N. L.**: Effects of systematic heavy resistance exercises on range of joint movement in young male adults. *Res. Q.* 27:41, 1956.
8. **Tyrance, H. J.**: Relationship of extreme body types to ranges of flexibility. *Research Quarterly*, 29:248, 1958.

9

Fitness Test Batteries

A person's total fitness is the ability to function in overt and covert activities. Part of total fitness is the ability to perform in vigorous motor activities. This phase of fitness, often referred to as motor fitness (or physical fitness), consists of a number of individual traits. The extent to which a person possesses such traits as strength, endurance, flexibility, power, agility, and speed determines fitness for motor performance. In efforts to develop motor fitness emphasis is usually placed on strength, endurance, and flexibility.

When a person is fit, the various systems of the body are well conditioned so that each system can do its part toward effective performance. Fitness serves as a general base for excellence in performance, but it does not include all essentials. An excellent performer in a particular activity must possess, in addition to motor fitness, the specific skills that are part of that activity.

Motor Fitness Tests

Several tests to measure motor fitness have been developed in recent years. These tests measure a person's ability to exhibit motor traits basic to good performance. Each test consists of several items that are combined to form one measure of motor fitness. An increase in the score on one item of a test will result in an increase in the score for the whole test.

AAHPER Fitness Test

The American Alliance for Health, Physical Education and Recreation promotes and has revised the youth fitness project. (1) One result was the construction of a seven-item test to measure the general fitness of youth. The seven

125

items in the test are: pull-ups, sit-ups, 40-yard shuttle run, 50-yard run, standing long jump, softball throw for distance, and 600-yard run–walk.

The test should be administered during two class periods: Pull-ups, sit-ups, standing long jump, and shuttle run should be tested in the first period; 50-yard run, softball throw for distance, and 600-yard run–walk should be tested in the second period. With the battery of tests spread over two class periods and test items administered simultaneously, 40 students can be tested in two 40-minute periods. Validity and reliability rating have not been established for the test.

Procedure. The test items should be administered in the order in which they are described.

1. *Pull-ups.* See description on page 93. Some may do the flexed arm hang (see page 95).
2. *Sit-Ups.* See description on page 97. One point is allowed for each completed sit-up to a maximum of 50 points for girls and 100 points for boys.
3. *Standing Long Jump.* See description on page 140.
4. *Shuttle Run.* See description on page 148.
5. *50-Yard Run.* This event measures sprinting speed and is therefore an indication of power. The test is conducted as a standard 50-yard run and is timed to the nearest tenth of a second.
6. *Softball Throw for Distance.* See description on page 140.
7. *600-Yard Run–Walk.* See description on page 108.

Scoring. Two sets of scoring scales are printed in the AAHPER *Youth Fitness Test Manual.* (1) One set of scales is based on age and the other one on the Neilson–Cozens Age–Height–Weight Classification Plan.

Youth Fitness Test

In 1961 the President's Council on Youth Fitness designed this test for screening purposes (17). It consists of three items primarily to measure strength and agility. One subject can be tested in 10 minutes. With three stations operating simultaneously, 30 students can be tested in a 40-minute period. Validity and reliability coefficients for the test have not been established.

Procedure: Each test item is scored as *pass* or *fail*.

1. *Pull-Ups.* See description on page 93, and page 95 (modified).
2. *Sit-Ups.* See description on page 97.
3. *Squat Thrusts.* See description on page 146.

Scoring: To pass each test item, a student must perform the exercise the number of times indicated in the following table:

TABLE 9-1 Passing Standards for Youth Fitness Screening Test

Exercise	Girls Ages 10–17	Boys Ages 10–13	Boys Ages 14–15	Boys Ages 16–17
Pull-ups	8 modified	1	2	3
Sit-ups	10	14	14	14
Squat thrusts	3	4	4	4

Division of Girls' and Women's Sports (DGWS) Test

The DGWS, a division of the American Association of Health, Physical Education and Recreation, selected eight test items to compose a motor fitness test for high school girls. The test is also useful for college women. The standing long jump, basketball throw and agility run were selected to measure general athletic ability. Sit-ups, push-ups, and pull-ups were selected to measure strength. The 10-second squat thrust test was included as a measure of agility, and the 30-second squat thrust test was selected to measure endurance. Validity and reliability ratings have not been established for the test. The committee that prepared the test recommends that if all eight items cannot be administered, the battery may be shortened to the standing long jump, the basketball throw, the agility run or 10-second squat thrust, the sit-up, and the push-up or pull-up.

Procedure. The items may be taken in any order provided the agility run is separated from the squat thrust test and the pull-up and push-up tests are separated. The following order is recommended:

1. *Basketball Throw.* Marks should be placed on the floor at five-foot intervals from the restraining line. The only equipment necessary is a regulation basketball. The student stands one step behind the restraining line and throws the ball as far as possible using any throwing method she desires. If necessary she may take one approach step. The score is the distance from the restraining line to the spot where the ball first strikes the floor. The better distance of two trials is recorded to the nearest foot.
2. *Agility run.* Same as the shuttle run in the AAHPER Fitness Test. See description on page 148.
3. *Push-Ups (modified).* See description on page 91.
4. *Standing Long Jump.* See description on page 140.
5. *Squat Thrusts (10 seconds).* See description on page 126.
6. *Sit-Ups.* See description on page 97.
7. *Pull-Ups.* A pull-up bar (or one side of a parallel bar) is placed three

FIGURE 9-1.   Pull ups for the DGWS test.

and one-half feet above the floor. The student grasps the bar using a re-
verse grip (palms up) and moves under the bar until her shoulders are
directly underneath. Her arms should be straight; her body should be
straight from the shoulders to the knees; and her knees should be bent
almost to a right angle with her feet flat on the floor (see Figure 9-1).
Keeping her trunk straight, she pulls up from this position until her
chest touches the bar. She does as many pull-ups in succession as possible.

8. *Squat Thrust* (30 *seconds*). See description of squat thrusts for 10 seconds on page 126.

Scoring.   The standard scores for the individual items may be averaged to
obtain a standard score for the total test.

Jumping, Chinning, Running (JCR) Test

This test (*11*) measures the student's ability to perform fundamental athletic
activities such as jumping (J), chinning (C), running (R), and changing direction. It consists of three items: vertical jump, pull-ups (chins), and a 100-yard
shuttle run. Validity coefficients of .90 and .81 were obtained when scores on
the test were compared with scores on 19 and 25 general athletic ability test
items. Reliability ratings are not available. One student can complete the test
in 5 minutes. Using two jump boards, two chinning bars, and four running
lanes, approximately 50 students can be tested in a 40-minute period.

Procedure.   The test items should be administered in the following order:

1. *Vertical Jump.* See description on page 134.
2. *Pull-ups* (*Chins*). See description on page 93.
3. *Shuttle Run.* A stopwatch for each lane and a shuttle run area as illustrated in Figure 9.2 are needed. This test measures running speed and agility (the ability to change direction rapidly). The student stands inside the starting line with one foot on or touching the backboard. On the signal to start the student runs back and forth between the turning blocks, making five complete round trips. The examiner should keep the runner informed of the number of laps completed. The student's score is the time taken to complete the run, measured to the nearest half second.

Scoring.   The height of the vertical jump in inches, number of pull-ups, and shuttle-run time are the raw scores.

Rogers' Physical Fitness Index (PFI)

The *PFI* relates to Rogers' strength test (see page 100). This index has been used extensively in research and as a screening test to identify students who are low in fitness. The PFI expresses a relationship between a person's achieved

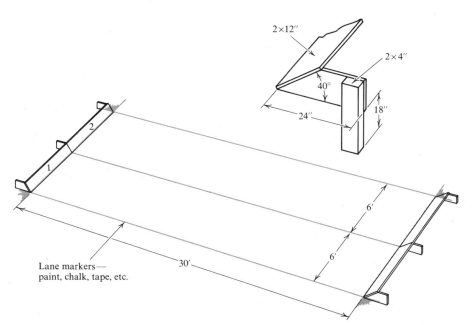

FIGURE 9-2. Shuttle run floor plan for JCR Test. If a structure of this type is not available the run can be done back and forth between two lines 30 feet apart marked on the gym floor or grass.

strength index (*SI*) score (see Rogers' strength test) and strength norm. The *PFI* is computed by use of the following formula:

$$PFI = \frac{\text{achieved strength index}}{\text{normal strength index}} \times 100$$

If a person's *SI* were equal to the norm for his or her age and weight, the *PFI* would be equal to 100. A PFI of 100 is average; therefore a score below 100 is below average and a score above 100 is above average.

In addition to the tests already described several other fitness tests have been constructed. These tests are not used extensively throughout the nation, but they are useful in certain locales.

California Physical Performance Test

This test (4) is for boys and girls ages 10 to 18. The test items are the standing long jump, the knee-bent sit-up for 1 minute, the side step for 10 seconds, chair push ups, pull-ups (for girls who cannot perform one regular pull-up, the flexed arm hang is substituted), and the jog–walk (this is scored as the number of 100-yard distances covered in 6 minutes). Percentile tables are available.

Indiana Motor Fitness Test for High School and College Men

This test (3) includes four indexes.[1]

Motor Fitness Index I = (chins + push-ups) × (vertical jump)
Motor Fitness Index II = (chins + push-ups) × (standing long jump)
Motor Fitness Index III = (straddle chins + push-ups) × (vertical jump)
Motor Fitness Index IV = (straddle chins + push-ups) × (standing long jump)

Indiana Physical Fitness Tests for High School Boys and Girls

These tests (12, 13) are based on an age–height–weight classification and each test includes four test items: straddle chins, squat thrust (20 seconds), push-ups, and vertical jump.[2]

[1] A copy of the complete test, including achievement scales, may be obtained from the Indiana State Department of Public Instruction in Indianapolis.
[2] A copy of the complete test, including achievement scales, may be obtained from the Indiana State Department of Public Instruction in Indianapolis.

New York State Physical Fitness Test.[3]

The New York State Physical Fitness test (8) was revised in 1968. The test is presented in two forms—the total test and a screening test. The total test consists of test components of the following kinds: posture, accuracy, strength, agility, speed, balance, and endurance. The screening test consists of: side step for 10 seconds; straight knee sit-ups for one minute; shuttle-run (15-yard traverse), with the distance depending on grade in school; and squat thrust for 30 to 60 seconds, depending on sex and grade in school. Achievement scales and percentile ranks are available for boys and girls grades 4 through 12.

Oregon Motor Fitness Test[4]

State fitness tests (10) were developed through cooperation with the University of Oregon and Oregon State University in the early 1960s. For girls, the test items are: flexed arm hang; standing long jump; and bent-knee sit-ups. The test items for boys are: standing long jump; floor push-ups; and straight leg sit-ups. The junior and senior test items are: the vertical jump; pull-ups; and 160-yard shuttle run.

Texas Physical Fitness-Motor Ability Test[5]

The Texas Physical Fitness Program (16) is a program of tests and awards to help teachers of grades 4–12 to diagnose the physical weaknesses of students, identify students with acceptable levels of fitness and motivate all students to achieve excellence in physical fitness as they strive for self-improvement. The test items are: chin-ups; dips; timed bent-leg sit-ups; 12-minute run–walk; 1.5 mile run; running speed; shuttle run; zigzag run; vertical jump; and standing long jump. Scoring methods and achievement standards are available, along with the test descriptions and instructions from the Texas Physical Fitness Educational Foundation.

Army Physical Fitness Tests

The following three test batteries were authorized for use by Army personnel to measure physical fitness. *Army Minimum Physical Fitness Test:* squat bender or squat stretch; push-ups; sit-ups or body twist; leg over leg spreader; squat thrusts or "mountain climber", and stationary run or half-mile run. *Physical Combat Proficiency Test:* 40-yard crawl, horizontal ladder travel by hands; dodge run and jump; 150-yard man carry; and one-mile run. *Airborne Trainee Physical Fitness Test:* pull-ups; knee bender; floor push-ups; knee-bent sit-ups; and one-mile run.

[3] A manual for teachers of physical education is available from the State Department of Education, Division of Health, Physical Education and Recreation, Albany, New York.
[4] Department of Public Instruction, Salem, Oregon.
[5] Texas Physical Fitness Educational Foundation, P.O. Box 4505, Austin, Texas 78765.

Marine Corps Physical Fitness Tests

The Marine Corps in 1971 established a motor fitness test, for women between 18 and 38 years and for men between the ages of 17 and 44 years. The test items for women Marines are: 80-yard shuttle run; knee push-ups; bent knee sit-ups; vertical jump and 600-yard run–walk. The test items for male Marines are: pull-ups, bent-knee sit-ups; and three-mile run. The tests are on a pass or fail standard.

United States Military, Naval and Coast Guard Academies Physical Fitness Test

The test for the cadets at the United States Naval Academy is: one-mile run, chins, bent-knee sit-ups, and bar dips. The Coast Guard Academy test items are: pull-ups, bent-knee sit-ups for 2 minutes; standing long jump; and 300-yard shuttle run (60 yard distance), and the 12-minute run. The test at the Military Academy is: pull-ups, standing long jump; basketball distance throw from the knees, and 300-yard shuttle run (25 yard distance).

AAU Physical Fitness and Proficiency Test

This test (2) is designed for all boys and girls within the age limits. There are no registration fees required for the awards of proficiency for this test. The test consists of: bent-knee sit-ups; push-ups; modified push-ups for girls; standing long jump; walk or run indoor course or outdoor course; and the following elective events: pull-ups (modified pull-ups for girls); sprints; running high jump; and shuttle run. There are different standards for performance for each sex and for six age groups. Awards and certificates for achievement are available from the AAU.

Peabody Test of Physical Fitness

This test (9) was designed for use by classroom teachers in the assessment of physical fitness of elementary school children. The test items include: ball bouncing; Burpee; shuttle run; and volleyball throw. The scores are recorded in percentiles, and norms for different age groups and for both sexes are available.

Dauer and Pangrazi Physical Fitness Test for Children

The test is in two parts: (1) A screening test of (a) flexed arm hang for girls and pull-ups for boys, (b) sit ups, (c) squat thrusts. (2) Revision of the President's Council of Physical Fitness and Sports test to include: (a) flexed arm hang for girls and pullups for boys, (b) situps, (c) standing long jump, (d) 50-yard or 50-meter dash, (e) mile run/walk or 1600 meter run/walk.

Standards for each test are available with classifications of excellent, good, satisfactory, and poor for ages 9, 10, 11, and 12.

Some Precautions

As educators, it is important that we be aware of current research concerning various items that are often included in tests. Some test items appear to have been traditionally included in test because other items are not useable due to special equipment requirements. The most often used items that have come under criticism by kinesiologists are:

1. *Sit-ups.* The bent leg sit-up (body curl) is done with the iliopsoas muscles shortened, and therefore appears to be a better exercise for testing abdominal strength than is the sit-up done with the legs extended.
2. *Squat Jumps.* Squat jumps are included in some of the tests presented. The National Federation of State High School Activity Associations and the Committee on the Medical Aspects of Sports of the American Medical Association has recommended that full squat jumps be avoided and half squats be substituted.
3. *Pull-ups, Push-ups, Sit-ups, and Dips.* Specific instructions should be followed when these items are included in tests. This is so because these items can be performed in slightly different variations, and these potential inconsistencies can influence the results. Some examples are: (1) pull-ups can be done with the palms forward or the palms back, (2) the sit-up can be done with legs straight, partially bent or completely bent, and (3) push-ups and bar dips can be done with various degrees of completeness. When scores are to be compared to other scores or to standards, consistency of how the item is performed is of utmost importance.

Selected References

1. *AAHPER Youth Fitness Test Manual*, rev. ed. Washington D.C: American Alliance for Health, Physical Education and Recreation, 1975.
2. **Amateur Athletic Union,** 3400 West 86th Street, Indianapolis, Indiana 46268.
3. **Bookwalter, K. W.,** and **Bookwalter, C. W.:** *A Measure of Motor Fitness for College.* Bulletin of the School for Education, Indiana University, 1953, *19*, (2).
4. *California Physical Performance Tests*, Sacramento, Calif.: State Department of Education, Bureau of Health Education, Physical Education, and Recreation, 1962.
5. **Dauer, V. P.,** and **Panarazi, R. P.:** *Dynamic Physical Education for Elementary School Children* Minneapolis, Minn.: Burgess Publishing Co., 1979.
6. **Franklin, C. C.** and **Lehsten, N. G.:** "Indiana physical fitness tests for the elementary level (grades 4–8). *The Physical Educator*, 5(3), 1948.
7. *Motor Fitness Test for Oregon Schools.* Salem, Ore.: State Department of Education, 1962.

8. *New York State Physical Fitness Test: A Manual for Teachers of Physical Education.* Albany, N.Y.: State Department of Education, Division of Health, Physical Education and Recreation, 1958.
9. **Norris, R. C.**: The Peabody Test of Physical Fitness. George Peabody College for Teachers, Nashville, Tenn. 37203.
10. *Oregon State Motor Fitness Test.* Department of Public Instruction, Salem, Oregon.
11. **Phillips, B. E.**: The JCR test. *Research Quarterly,* 18:12–29, 1947.
12. *Physical Fitness Manual for High School Boys.* Indianapolis, Ind.: Department of Public Instruction, Bulletin No. 136, **1944.**
13. *Physical Fitness Manual for High School Girls.* Indianapolis, Ind.: Department of Public Instruction, Bulletin No. 137 (revised), 1944.
14. *Physical Fitness Manual for the U.S. Navy,* Bureau of Naval Personnel, Training Division, Physical Section, 1943, ch. 4.
15. *Physical Fitness Research Digest.* Series 5, No. 1, January 1975. President's Council of Physical Fitness and Sports, Washington D.C., Edited by H. Harrison Clarke.
16. **Texas Physical Fitness Foundation,** P.O. Box 4505, Austin, Texas 78765.
17. *Youth Physical Fitness Manual.* Washington, D.C.: President's Council on Youth Fitness. Superintendent of Documents, U.S. Government Print Office, July 1961.

IV

Motor
Performance
Tests

10

Measures of Power

Muscular power, often referred to as explosive power, is a combination of speed and strength. Power is the ability to apply force at a rapid rate and is typically demonstrated in the long jump or the shot put. The individual uses the muscles to apply strong force at a rapid rate to give the body or the object momentum. In the form,

power = force × velocity

A person can be unusually strong and still not be very powerful. Also he or she may be able to move with great speed but lack the strength to move rapidly against resistance. However, if a person has sufficient strength combined with rapid speed, then the person is powerful.

Importance of Power

Muscular power is important in vigorous performances because it determines how hard a person can hit, how far he-she can throw, how high he-she can jump, and to some extent how fast he-she can run or swim. Certain performers are described as power athletes: the player who kicks the football into the end zone; hits the home run in baseball; makes a long golf drive; tosses the shot, discus, or javelin a long distance; outjumps the opponent in basketball or volleyball; or drives through the line in football. In addition, in running, which involves a series of body projections, power affects an individual's running speed, which is basic to many athletic performances.

There are various ways to increase power: by increasing strength without

137

sacrificing speed, by increasing speed of movement without sacrificing strength, and by increasing both speed and strength. Usually the approach with the greatest potential is to increase strength. Weight lifting against heavy resistance is the most expedient method. Speed can also be increased a limited amount as a result of training. Both speed and force can be stressed by applying strong force through rapid motion.

Tests of Power

Tests of power ordinarily take three forms: ability to project one's body, ability to project an object, and ability to strike or kick forcefully. Power is specific to the muscles involved in any selected movement. For the measurement of power to be accurate, those performers being tested should be taught the particular skill and should then be given adequate practice periods. Where the skill is complex or relatively unfamiliar, this procedure is very important. For example, with some basic instruction and a limited amount of practice most people can improve considerably in a throwing event or a jumping event. The Margaria–Kalamen Test is probably the best measure of power which can feasibly be used in connection with an instructional program. Its one disadvantage is that some fairly specialized equipment is required. The other tests included in this chapter are practical and useful, but their validity is questionable even though validity coefficients have been calculated for most of them. Even though these tests are quite unsophisticated, they have been included because they are relatively easy to administer, practical in terms of time, space, and equipment, and they do produce quite meaningful results. The term *face validity* will be used to indicate that the specific test has no statistical validity measure, and that the test does require specific power for the performance of the activity.

Margaria–Kalamen Power Test

The Margaria–Kalaman test (4) is designed for high school and college males, but can be used for women students of those same ages. The original test by Margaria has been modified by Kalamen. The subject begins by standing 6 meters in front of a series of standard 8-inch steps. On command he runs as quickly as possible up the stairs. A microswitch embedded in a mat is placed on the third step and activates a timer when the subject steps on the mat. A second switch is placed on the ninth step. This switch causes deactivation of the timer when hit. The elapsed time represents the time required to move the body weight the vertical distance between the third and ninth steps. The formula for computing power output is:

$$\text{Power} = \frac{\text{Body weight (kg)} \times \text{vertical distance (meters)}}{\text{Elapsed time (seconds)}}$$

Vertical Jump (Jump and Reach)

The vertical jump test was first reported by Dudley A. Sargent in 1921 and is therefore often referred to as the Sargent jump test. It is also known as the jump and reach test as well as the vertical jump test.

This test measures explosive power of the extensor muscles of the legs and feet and the toe flexors. A validity coefficient of .78 has been reported when the test was correlated with four power events in track and field. A reliability coefficient of .93 has been reported. With a vertical jump board and a yardstick, about 30 students can be tested in 40 minutes at each station.

Procedure: The student faces the wall with both feet flat on the floor, toes touching the wall. He then reaches as high as possible with either hand and makes a chalk mark on the jump board (chalkboard). From the desired jump position, with the preferred side to the wall, he jumps as high as possible and at the peak of the jumping makes another chalk mark above the first one (see Figure 10-1). After each test the chalk marks should be erased.

Scoring: The final score is the best of three jumps measured to the nearest half inch. The measurement is the distance between the two marks.

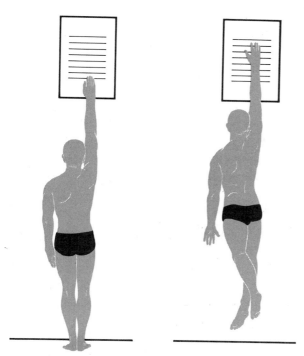

FIGURE 10-1.   Vertical jumping test.

Standing Long Jump

This test measures about the same qualities as the vertical jump test and requires about the same amount of time. A validity coefficient of .61 was obtained when the test was compared to pure power. A reliability coefficient of .96 has been established. Each testing station requires a yardstick, a take-off mark on the floor, and for measurement purposes additional marks at 6 and 9 feet in front of the take-off mark. The marks may be made with masking tape. About 30 students can be tested in 40 minutes at each station.

Procedure: The student stands with his feet a comfortable distance apart and his toes just behind the take-off mark. He crouches, leans forward, swings his arms backward, and then jumps horizontally as far as possible, jumping from both feet and landing on both feet (see Figure 10-2).

Scoring: The best of three jumps is measured to the nearest inch. The measurement is taken from the back of the take-off mark to the nearest point where the student touches the floor at the completion of the jump.

Softball Throw for Distance

This throwing test measures power of the total body with emphasis on the upper extremities. Its validity and reliability are accepted at face value. Each testing station needs two or more softballs, 12 inches in circumference, and a steel measuring tape. On the field should be a restraining line, behind which the throw is made, and additional lines, placed 100 feet and 150 feet beyond the restraining line, for measurement purposes. About 25 students can be tested at each station in a 40-minute period.

Procedure: The student stands the desired distance behind the restraining line, up to a maximum of 15 feet. Using the typical baseball throwing approach, he moves up to the line and throws the ball as far as possible with the overarm throwing technique, being careful not to cross over the restraining line.

Scoring: The student is allowed three trials; the best throw is recorded to the nearest foot. Measurement is taken from the back of the restraining line to the spot where the ball first strikes the ground.

Shot Put

This test for boys and men measures total body power. Its validity and reliability are accepted at face value. The test requires a shot (8 pounds for junior high school boys and girls, 12 pounds for high school boys, 8 pounds for high school girls, and 16 pounds for college men), and 8 pounds 13 ounces (4 kilo) for college women, a shot-put ring 7 feet in diameter, and a steel measuring

FIGURE 10-2. Standing long jump test.

tape 50 feet long. About 20 students can be tested at each station in a 40-minute period.

Procedure: The student holds the shot on four fingers and thumb, and the hand near the top and front portion of the shoulder. The student starts near the back edge of the ring with the back toward the direction of the put. Using the typical shot-putting technique, the student moves across the ring and thrusts the shot as far as possible.

Scoring: The student is allowed three trials; the best put is recorded to the nearest inch. Measurement is taken from inside the front of the ring to the nearest mark made by the fall of the shot.

Football Punt

This test for boys and men measures kicking power. Its validity and reliability are accepted at face value. Two regulation footballs and a steel measuring tape are needed at each testing station. On the field should be a restraining line, behind which the punt is performed, and additional lines, placed 50 feet and 100 feet beyond the restraining line, for measurement purposes. About 25 students can be tested at each station in 40 minutes.

Procedure: The student stands the desired distance behind the restraining line. He approaches the line and punts the ball as far as possible, being careful not to cross over the restraining line (see Figure 10-3).

Scoring: The student is allowed three trials; the best punt is recorded to the nearest foot. Measurement is taken from the back of the restraining line to the spot where the ball first strikes the ground. Achievement scales are not available.

FIGURE 10-3. Football punt test.

Bar Snap

This test measures the power of the arms and shoulders. Its validity and reliability are accepted at face value. With a chinning bar set at a height of 4 feet and 6 inches about 30 students can be tested in 40 minutes at each station.

Procedure: The student stands close to the bar and grasps it with both hands using the forward grip (palms forward). The body and arms should be straight with feet closer than the shoulders to the vertical plane of the bar. Taking off from both feet, the student jumps upward slightly and then flexes the hips so that the insteps of the feet come close to the bar. As his flexed body swings under the bar, the student shoots the feet upward, arches the back, and with the arms thrusts the body as far as possible in the horizontal direction, landing on the feet (see Figure 10-4).

Scoring: The distance is measured along the floor from directly below the bar to the place where the feet contact the floor nearest the bar. The student is allowed three trials; the best jump is recorded.

Other Muscular Power Tests

In addition to the aforementioned tests there are the basketball throw for distance, the football pass for distance, and the running long jump. Achievement scales for these events are not available.

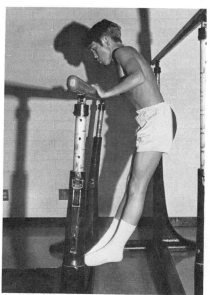

FIGURE 10-4. Bar snap test.

Selected References

1. **Considine, W. J.,** and **Sullivan, W. J.:** Relationship of selected tests of leg strength and leg power on college men. *Research Quarterly,* 4:4, 1973.
2. **Gray, R. K., Start, K. B.,** and **Glencross, D. J.:** A test of leg power. *Research Quarterly,* 33:44–50, 1962.
3. **Gray, R. K.,** and others: A useful modification of the vertical power jump. *Research Quarterly,* 33:230–35, 1962.
4. **Margaria, R., Agheno, Piero,** and **Rovelli, E.:** *Applied Physiology,* 21:1662–1664, September 1966.
5. **McClements, L. E.:** Power relative to strength of leg and thigh muscles. *Research Quarterly,* 37:71, 1966.

11

Measures of Agility

Agility is the ability to change the direction of the body or its parts rapidly. It is dependent primarily on strength, reaction time, speed of movement, and specific muscle coordinations. People with great agility have been said to be less accident prone because of their ability to make quick adjustments in body position and direction of movement.

Importance of Agility

In court games such as basketball, tennis, badminton, and volleyball and in field games such as soccer, football, speedball, and baseball, fast starts and stops and quick changes in direction are fundamental to good performances. Gymnastics and diving depend largely upon rapid body movements and quick changes in positions. Skiing, skating, and certain forms of dance require rapid adjustments in position and quick changes in direction. However, such activities as track events and swimming do not depend on agility to any large degree.

Agility in specific movements can be increased if the movements are practiced extensively so that the coordinations involved are improved. Strength is a contributing factor to agility. If strength is increased, the agility will increase in movements involving heavy resistance such as rapid stopping and starting, or other movements involving the force of inertia which keeps the body in motion in the same direction, such as dodging. The other factors which influence agility—speed of movement and reaction time—may be increased by practicing fast movements.

Agility Tests

Agility tests are especially useful for classifying students into homogeneous groups for instruction in field and court games, skating, skiing, and other types of performance requiring quick changes in direction or position. Most agility tests involve running maneuverability, or quick changes in body position.

Squat Thrust

The 10-second squat thrust test was first reported by Royal H. Burpee and is often referred to as the Burpee Test. The test measures agility of the total body. Validity and reliability coefficients of .55 and .92, respectively, have been established. The only equipment needed is a stopwatch. A large number of students can be tested in a short time if they are arranged into pairs to count for each other and to check each other's performance.

Procedure: The student takes a standing position. On the signal he or she moves to a squatting position, then to a front leaning rest position, back to a squatting position, and finally to the erect standing position. In the standing and front leaning rest positions the body should be straight (see Figure 11-1). In the squatting position the hands should touch the floor. The movement is repeated as rapidly as possible for 10 seconds.

Scoring: Each completed squat thrust counts 1 point and every quarter movement counts ¼ point. For example, if a student finished four complete squat thrusts and started the fifth but reached only the squat position on the way down, the score would be 4¼ points. If he or she reached the front leaning rest position, the score would be 4½ points. If he or she returned to the squatting position from the front leaning rest position, the score would be 4¾ points. The best of three trials is recorded as the final score. Achievement scales are not available.

Dodging Run

The dodging run (4) is a running test of total body agility which has proved to be among the better agility tests. Validity and reliability coefficients of .82 and .93, respectively, have been established. Four hurdles and a stopwatch are necessary at each station; about 30 students can be tested at one station in 40 minutes.

Procedure: The instructor places a starting line 3-feet long on the floor. He or she then places a hurdle 15 feet in front of the starting line, a second hurdle 6 feet beyond the first hurdle, a third hurdle 6 feet beyond the second hurdle, and a fourth hurdle 6 feet beyond the third hurdle. The hurdles should be

Starting position

1

2

3

4

FIGURE 11-1.   Squat thrust test.

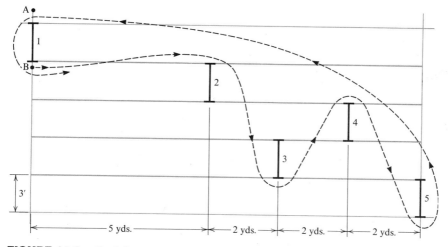

FIGURE 11-2.   Dodging run test.

staggered as shown in Figure 11-2. On the signal the student starts running and follows the course indicated by arrows on the dotted lines. He or she runs the course two complete times before stopping.

Scoring: The score is the time required to run the course two times, measured to the nearest tenth of a second. Achievement scales are not available.

Shuttle Run (Agility Run or Potato Race)

The shuttle run (1) measures total body agility. Validity and reliability are accepted at face value. Equipment required at each testing station includes two small wooden blocks or suitable substitutes and a stopwatch. About 30 students can be tested in a 40-minute period.

Procedure: The instructor places two small blocks of wood 30 feet from the starting point. At the signal the student starts from behind the starting line, retrieves one of the blocks, and places it behind the starting line. He or she then retrieves the second block and sprints back across the starting line. If two stopwatches are available, two students can compete against each other.

Scoring: The student is allowed two trials, with a short rest between trials. If the student commits an error, he or she should stop immediately and start again at the beginning. The score is the time required to complete the course correctly, recorded to the nearest tenth of a second. The time for the better run is recorded.

Right-Boomerang Test

This test (4) measures running agility. Validity coefficients of .82 for boys and .72 for girls and reliability coefficients of .93 for boys and .92 for girls have been established. The equipment needed is a jumping standard or similar object placed at the center point four Indian clubs or other such object for the outside points, and a stopwatch. About 25 students can be tested at each station in 40 minutes.

Procedure: The student stands at the starting line. At the signal he or she runs to the center point, turns 90 degrees to the left, and continues through the remainder of the course as rapidly as possible (see Figure 11-3).

Scoring: The time for the better run is recorded to the nearest tenth of a second. Achievement scales are not available.

Sidestep Test

This test is a modification of H. D. Edgren's test (2); it measures the speed with which the person can change direction moving sideward. A stopwatch is the only equipment needed. Forty students can be tested in 40 minutes.

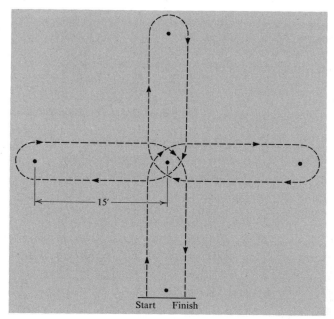

FIGURE 11-3.   Right boomerang course.

Procedure: The instructor places three parallel lines 5 feet apart on the floor. The student straddles the middle line. On the signal he or she sidesteps to the right until the right foot crosses over the line to the right; then he or she sidesteps to the left until the left foot crosses over the line to the left (see Figure 11-4). These movements are repeated as rapidly as possible for 20 seconds.

Scoring: Each time the performer crosses over the center line he scores 1 point. Current achievement scales are not available.

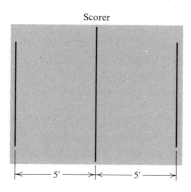

FIGURE 11-4.   Sidestep test floor plan.

Other Agility Tests

In addition to the tests described in this chapter the following are also useful tests of agility: 40-yard maze run (4), loop-the-loop run (4), zigzag run (4), quadrant jump (3), and LSU agility test (3).

Selected References

1. **American Association for Health, Physical Education and Recreation:** *Youth Fitness Test Manual*, 1961.
2. **Edgren, H. D.:** An experiment in testing ability and progress in basketball, *Research Quarterly* III, 1, March 1932, p. 159.
3. **Johnson, Barry L.,** and **Nelson, Jack K.:** *Practical Measurements for Evaluation in Physical Education.* Minneapolis, Minn.: Burgess Publishing Co., 1969, pp. 100–14.
4. **McCloy, Charles H.,** and **Young, Norma D.:** *Tests and Measurements in Physical Education*, 3rd ed. New York: Appleton-Century-Crofts, 1954, p. 80.
5. **Seils, L. G.:** Agility-performance and physical growth. *Research Quarterly*, 22:244, 1951.

12

Measures of Reaction Time and Speed

Reaction time, response time, and running speed are three factors to consider in determining speed in performance.

Reaction time is the time lapse between an external stimulus and the initial response to that stimulus. It is extremely important in all performances requiring quick responses. It has special significance in events in which individuals must defend against each other and thereby respond to each other's movements. A performer who reacts slowly is left behind at the start of a running event. A person with slow reactions is ineffective in defensive efforts against a person with faster reactions. Slow reactions also hinder offensive play because the performer is not able to employ the necessary quickness.

Response time is determined by reaction time and movement time. The relative speed of contraction of different muscles varies greatly among individuals. For example, person A may have faster leg actions while person B has faster arm actions. Moreover, person A's arm extensor muscles may contract relatively fast while the arm flexors contract slowly. In other words, speed varies with individual body movements. Although a person is a slow runner, he or she may have fast arm and finger movements or vice versa. Speed of response of the body as a hole or in part is important in a variety of performances; it determines how quickly a performer can respond completely and correctly to a given situation.

Running speed is not only an athletic event itself, but it is also an important factor in numerous other sports. Running speed and maneuverability are important in almost all court and field games. It can make the difference in whether a performer is able to gain an advantage over his opponent.

There is evidence that reaction time in specific movements will improve as a result of extensive practice of those movements. For example, practice of starting to a pistol shot will result in faster reactions to that stimulus. Also dedicated practice of responding to an opponent's moves will result in quick reactions of that kind.

Running speed is determined by the length of stride and frequency (speed) of stride. To increase running speed, the student must increase one or both of these factors. Length of stride is dependent primarily on leg length and the power of the stride. Leg speed (frequency) is dependent mostly on speed of muscle contractions and neuromuscular coordination (skill) in running.

Tests of Reaction Time

Nelson Finger and Foot Reaction Tests

These tests (7) are designed to measure how quickly a person reacts to a visual stimulus. They are equally useful for boys and girls of any age group. The tests have not been validated, probably because there is no suitable criterion measure against which to compare them. Their validity is accepted at face value. Reliability coefficients of .89 for the hand test and .85 for the foot test have been produced for the test-retest method. A Nelson reaction timer, a desk chair or a table and chair are needed; however a yardstick made of hard wood may be substitutes for the Nelson reaction timer. About 15 students can be tested on each test in a 40-minute period.

Procedure for the finger reaction test: The student sits on the chair with the forearm and hand resting comfortably on the edge of the desk. He or she holds the index finger and thumb about 2 inches apart and beyond the edge of the

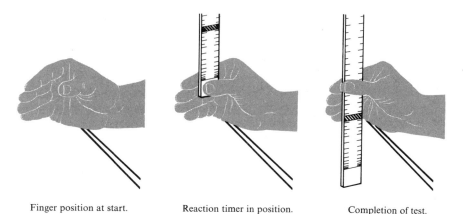

Finger position at start.   Reaction timer in position.   Completion of test.

FIGURE 12-1. Nelson finger reaction test.

desk (see Figure 12-1). The thumb and index finger should be in a horizontal position, and the baseline of the reaction timer should be even with the upper surface of the thumb. Ready to grip the reaction timer when it is released, the student looks directly at the concentration zone, a black shaded area. On the command "ready" the test administrator releases the reaction timer and the student grasps it, as quickly as possible, with the thumb and index finger. The student has 20 trials.

Scoring: The score for each trial is the number at the upper edge of the thumb. The score is recorded in hundredths of a second. The five slowest and five fastest trials are discarded, and an average of the middle 10 trials is recorded as the score.

Procedure for the foot reaction test: The student sits on a table or bench about 1 inch from a wall. With shoe removed, the student positions the foot so that the ball of the foot is about 1 inch from the wall with the heel resting on the edge of the table about 3 inches from the wall. The test administrator holds the reaction timer next to the wall so that it hangs between the wall and the student's foot, with the baseline at the end of the big toe (see Figure 12-2). The student looks directly at the concentration zone, and when the administrator drops the timer, the student presses the stick against the wall as quickly as possible with the ball of the foot.

Scoring: The student is scored the same as for the finger reaction test.

Hand and Arm Reaction Test

This test (7) is designed to measure the hand and arm reaction time. It is suitable for both boys and girls of any age group. A Nelson reaction timer (or a yardstick), a table and a chair are needed. About 15 students can be tested in 40 minutes.

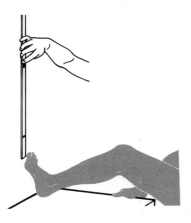

FIGURE 12-2. Nelson foot reaction test.

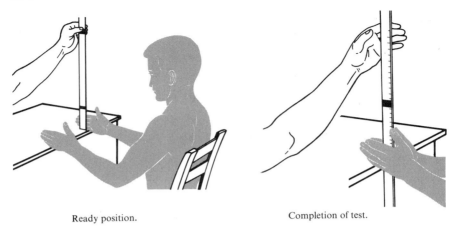

Ready position.   Completion of test.

FIGURE 12-3.   Hand and arm reaction test.

Procedure: The student sits at the table, as illustrated in Figure 12-3, with hands 1 foot apart and the ends of the little fingers on the table. He or she looks directly at the concentration zone on the reaction timer, and when the administrator drops the timer, he or she slaps the hands together on the timer as quickly as possible.

Scoring: The student is scored the same as for the finger reaction test.

Tests of Response Time

Four-Way Alternate Response Test

This test (5) is designed to measure how quickly a person can complete a response to a signal to move in a given direction. Its validity and reliability have not been established; however, because of the nature of the test they can be accepted at face value. The test is suitable for both boys and girls of any age group. A floor area should be marked according to Figure 12-4. Only a stopwatch is needed to test about 20 students in 40 minutes.

Procedure: The student stands at point X on the floor and concentrates on the right hand of the test administrator standing at point Y on the floor. After giving the preparatory command "ready," the test administrator makes an obvious movement with his hand in one of four directions. On the signal the student moves in the designated direction as rapidly as possible and crosses over the line 5 yards from point X. Hence if the tester were to move his or her hand up, the student would move forward across the line. If the tester were to move his or her hand down, the student would move backward. If the tester were to

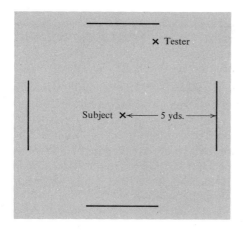

FIGURE 12-4. Floor area for four-way alternate response test.

move the hand to either side, the student would move in the direction of the tester's motion. The student is given 20 trials, five in each direction. The trials in the different directions may come in any order the tester chooses.

Scoring: The tester holds a stopwatch which he starts at the beginning of each hand movement. The watch is stopped when the student crosses the correct line, and records the time to the nearest tenth of a second. The score is the total of the times on all 20 trials. Achievement scales are not available.

Two-Way Alternate Response Test

This test (8) is the same as the four-way alternate response test except the student is required to respond to either the right or the left. Ten trials are given, five to each side. The score is the total time for the 10 trials.

Hand and Arm ResponseTest

This test (5) is designed to measure how quickly the student can respond with his arm and hands. Its validity and reliability are accepted at face value. The test may be used with men and women of any age group. Equipment needed is the same as that for the hand and arm reaction test. About 15 students can be tested in 40 minutes.

Procedure: The procedure is the same as that for the hand and arm reaction test except the student's hands are placed on the table three feet apart instead of one foot apart. This additional distance places emphasis on both reaction time and speed of movement time and therefore indicates response time.

Scoring: The student is scored the same as for the hand and arm reaction test.

Tests of Speed

Sprint for Speed Test

This test is to measure a person's ability to run a prescribed distance (50 yards or 100 yards) in the shortest time possible. Necessary equipment includes a starting pistol or a whistle and as many stopwatches as there are contestants in each heat. Four to six students can be tested at one time if enough watches and timers are available. Timers should be trained to time correctly. Students should receive thorough instruction on correct starting techniques and should be allowed adequate practice. Starting blocks should be used if they are available, and practice using the blocks should be allowed.

Procedure: On the starter's command the student takes the "on-the-mark" position. On the second command he moves to the "set" position. On the starting signal (pistol shot or whistle) he sprints as fast as possible to the finish line.

Scoring: A student's score is the time, measured to the nearest tenth of a second, that lapses between the starting signal and the time the student crosses the finish line.

Running Maneuverability Test

Chapter 11 describes tests that measure a person's ability to maneuver while running. Among the better tests of running maneuverability are the dodging run, the shuttle run, and the right-boomerang run.

Selected References

1. **Gibson, D. A.**: Effect of a Special Training Program for Sprint Starting on Reflex Time, Reaction Time and Sargent Jump. Microcarded master's thesis, Springfield College, 1961.
2. **Gottshall, D. R.**: The Effects of Two Training Programs on Reflex Time, Reaction Time and the Level of Physical Fitness. Microcarded master's thesis, Springfield College, 1962.
3. **Henry, F. M.**: Reaction time-movement time correlations. *Perceptual and Motor Skills,* 12, 1961.
4. **Howell, M. L.**: Influence of emotional tension on speed of reaction and movement." *Research Quarterly,* 1953, 24.
5. **Jensen, C. R.**: Practical Measurements of Reaction Time, Response Time and Speed. Unpublished study, Brigham Young University.
6. **Nelson, F. B.**: *The Nelson Reaction Timer.* Instructional leaflet, 1965. P.O. Box 51987, Lafayette, Louisiana.

7. **Nelson, J. K.**: Development of a Practical Performance Test Combining Reaction Time, Speed of Movement and Choice of Response. Unpublished study, Louisiana State University.
8. **Smith, L. E.**: Effect of muscular stretch, tension, and relaxation upon the reaction time and speed of movement of a supported limb. *Research Quarterly, 35,* 1964.

13

Measures of Balance and Kinesthetic Perception

Balance and kinesthetic perception are quite different from each other. However, perception is an important contributor to balance. Tests of balance and tests of perception are combined into one chapter more for convenience than for any other reason.

Balance is involved to some degree with all motor performances, and some performances depend heavily upon balance. Among them are certain gymnastic events such as balance beam, floor exercise, and dismounts from various apparatus; Diving, rebound tumbling, and some forms of dancing also require unusual amounts of balance. Stability (firmness of balance) is of special importance in all body contact sports such as wrestling, football, rugby, and soccer and in some other sports such as basketball and hockey. In an off-balance stance a performer is in a poor position to respond to the act of an opponent, to perform an act requiring accuracy, and to resist force or apply force in any direction except the direction in which he or she is off-balance. In many cases increased balance will result in improved performances.

Kinesthetic perception is important to both balance and accuracy. In certain activities an individual is at a disadvantage if unable to judge accurately the position of the body parts or the amount of force applied by the muscles. A high degree of kinesthetic sense results in better coordination and a more accurate "touch."

Balance in certain positions is strongly dependent on strength because the supporting muscles must be able to hold the weight and the body parts firmly in position. Therefore in some cases balance will improve a limited amount as

158

a result of increased strength. Agility, reaction time, and neuromuscular coordinations also contribute to balance.

The best way a person can improve is through extensive practice of balancing in the particular position. In balance, as in many other aspects of performance, correct practice makes perfect.

In addition to agility, reaction, coordination, and strength, kinesthetic perception contributes to balance. Perception will increase with extensive and varied use of the neuromuscular system.

Static Balance Tests

Balance is defined as the ability to remain in equilibrium. When the body is in equilibrium, an even adjustment exists among all opposing forces, and the body remains balanced. The state of equilibrium may be stable or precarious. A balance center located in the inner ear, the kinesthetic sense, and the eyes all play important roles in maintaining balance.

For an individual to maintain balance in any stationary position the center of gravity must remain over the base of support. Whenever the center of gravity moves outside the supporting base, the body is off-balance in that direction. This fact applies to all body positions, including upright, inverted (hands forming the base of support), and three-, four-, or six-point positions. If the center of gravity moves outside the base of support, the individual must make a quick adjustment to regain balance. He or she may move or enlarge the base, or shift a body part to return the center of gravity to a position over the base. After making the adjustment the performer is more stable and less susceptible to another loss of balance if the center of gravity is lowered.

Balance tests are either static or dynamic. Static tests measure ability to remain in balance in a stationary position, while dynamic tests measure ability to remain in balance while in motion. The two types of balance tests are arranged according to their difficulty. These tests can be given to a large number of students in a 40-minute period if the students are arranged in pairs so they can score each other.

The following tests of static balance are useful in educational programs. The term, face validity, will be used to indicate that the test has no statistical validity measures, and that the test does require specific balance for the performance of the activity.

Upright Static Tests

The objective of these tests is to measure the individual's ability to balance in a stationary, upright position while standing on a small base.

Stork Stand (Foot). This test (3) has produced a reliability coefficient of .85 when the test–retest method was employed. Its validity is accepted at face

FIGURE 13-1. Stork stand balance test.

value. To perform the test the student stands on the flat foot of the dominant leg and places the other foot on the inside of the supporting knee. He or she then puts the hands on the hips and holds this position as long as possible. The student is scored on the length of time, in seconds, that he or she is able to maintain balance. (See Figure 13-1.) The best of three trials is recorded.

Stork Stand (Toes). The student performs this test as the previous test except she or he balances on the ball of the foot instead of on the whole foot. This test has produced a reliability coefficient of .87 with the test–retest method. Its validity is accepted at face value.

Bass Stick Test (Lengthwise). This test (1) has produced a reliability coefficient of .90. Its validity is accepted at face value. Necessary equipment is a stick 1 inch wide and 12 inches long, a stopwatch, and adhesive tape to fasten the stick to the floor. To perform the test the student places the ball of the dominant foot lengthwise on the stick and lifts the opposite foot from the floor main-

FIGURE 13-2. Bass stick test (length-wise).

taining balance in that position as long as possible (see Figure 13-2). The test is performed three times on the right leg and three times on the left leg. The score is the total time, in seconds, for all six trials.

Bass Stick Test (Crosswise). The student performs this test (1) the same as the previous test except he or she places the foot crosswise to the stick and balances on the ball of the foot (see Figure 13-3).

Inverted Static Tests

The objective of these tests is to measure the performer's ability to remain in balance while in the inverted position.

Tripod Test. From a squat position the student places the hands shoulder width part with the fingers pointing straight ahead. He or she then leans forward bending at the elbows and places the backs of the knees against and slightly above the outside of the elbows. He or she continues to lean forward until the feet come off the floor with the forehead resting on the mat (see Fig-

FIGURE 13-3. Bass stick test (crosswise).

FIGURE 13-4. Tripod test.

ure 13-4). Balancing in this position as long as possible, the student is scored on the length of time balance is maintained, measured to the nearest second. Three trials are permitted.

Tip-Up Test. This test is the same as the tripod test except the student does not rest the head on the mat, but instead balances on both hands with the face several inches above the floor (see Figure 13-5).

FIGURE 13-5. Tip up test.

Head and Hand Balance. The student puts the forehead on the mat several inches in front of the hands. He or she kicks upward, one foot at a time and maintains balance, keeping the back slightly arched, legs straight and together, and toes pointed. With the body weight primarily on the hands and some weight on the forehead, the student balances in this position for as long as possible (see Figure 13-6). The score is the best time of three trials recorded to the nearest second. To get out of this position the student pushes with the hands, ducks the head, and rolls forward, or he or she steps down one foot at a time.

FIGURE 13-6. Head and hand balance.

Head and Forearm Balance. The student places the forearms on the mat and brings the hands close enough together for the thumbs and forefingers to form a cup for the head. He or she then puts the head in the cup and kicks upward one foot at a time, balancing in this position for as many seconds as possible (see Figure 13-7). The score is the best time of three trials.

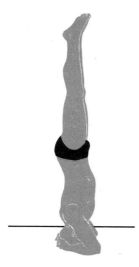

FIGURE 13-7.   Head and forearm balance.

Two-Hand Balance.   The student bends forward and places the hands on the mat about shoulder width part. He or she leans the shoulders over the hands and places one foot ahead of the other. Then swinging the rear foot upward as the front foot pushes from the mat, a balanced position is maintained with the feet overhead for as many seconds as possible (see Figure 13-8). The score is the best time of three trials.

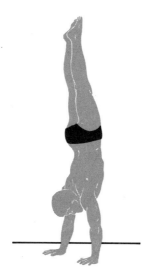

FIGURE 13-8.   Two-hand balance.

One-Hand Balance. The student performs the same as for the two-hand balance test, except he or she balances on one hand instead of on two. He or she moves into the one-hand balance from the two-hand balance position (see Figure 13-9). He or she is scored the same as for the two-hand balance test.

FIGURE 13-9. One-hand balance.

Dynamic Balance Tests

The following dynamic balance tests have proved useful in school programs.

Upright Dynamic Tests

The objective of these tests is to measure how well the performer can balance while in motion in an upright position.

Balance Beam Walk. A regulation balance beam is the only equipment needed for this test. Starting from the standing position on one end of the beam, the student walks slowly the full length of the beam, pauses for 5 seconds, turns around, and walks back to the starting position (see Figure 13-10). He or she is allowed three trials and is scored either "pass" or "fail." (For a more difficult test a balance beam 2 inches wide and 12 feet long may be used.)

Johnson Modification of the Bass Test of Dynamic Balance (5). Validity of this test is accepted at face value. With the test-retest method it produced a reliability coefficient of .75. A stopwatch, masking tape, and a yardstick are needed. The floor plan is according to Figure 13-11.

FIGURE 13-10. Balance beam walk.

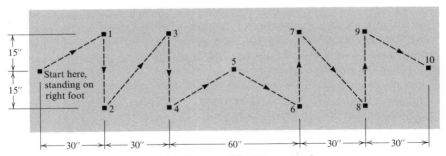

FIGURE 13-11. Floor plan for the modified bass test.

To perform the test the student stands with the right foot on the starting mark. He or she then leaps to the first tape mark and lands on the left foot, balancing on the ball of the foot as long as possible up to 5 seconds. Then he or she leaps to the next tape mark, landing on the right foot and balancing again for 5 seconds. He or she continues this procedure, balancing on each tape mark as long as possible up to 5 seconds.

The student scores 5 points each time he or she lands successfully on the tape mark, plus 2 points for each second he or she balances on the mark up to 5 seconds. Thus the student could score 10 points for each mark with a total of 100 points possible for the test. However, he or she could lose 5 points for an improper landing from the leap if any of the following errors are committed:

1. Failure to stop upon landing.
2. Failure to keep the heel or any part of the body other than the ball of the supporting foot from touching the floor.
3. Failure to cover the mark completely with the ball of the foot.

(The student is allowed to reposition for the 5-second balance on the ball of the foot after making a landing error.)

In addition the student sacrifices the remaining points at the rate of 1 point per second if he or she commits any of the following errors prior to the completion of the 5 seconds:

1. Failure to keep any part of the body other than the ball of the supporting foot from touching the floor.
2. Failure to hold the foot steady while in the balance position.

(When he or she loses balance, the student must step back on the proper mark and then leap to the next mark.)

Modified Sideward Leap Test (9).   The validity of this test is accepted at face value. The original (unmodified) test has produced reliability coefficients ranging from .66 to .88 at different age levels. The floor plan is according to Figure 13-12.

The student starts the test by standing on one foot on spot X. He or she leaps to spot A, landing on the same foot, and balances in that position for 5 seconds. Then the student leaps to either spot B or spot C and balances for 5 seconds. He or she repeats the test four times, twice to each side.

The student can earn up to 20 points on each trial for a total score of 80 points. The student is awarded 5 points for landing correctly on spot A, 5 points for balancing 5 seconds or spot A, 5 points for landing correctly on either spot B or spot C, and 5 points for balancing 5 seconds on spot B or spot C.

Inverted Dynamic Tests

The objective of these tests is to measure how well the performer can balance while in motion in an inverted position.

Tip-Up Walk Test.   This test is the same as the tip-up test previously described in this chapter, except the student walks on the hands while in the tip-up position. The score is the number of feet walked before losing balance.

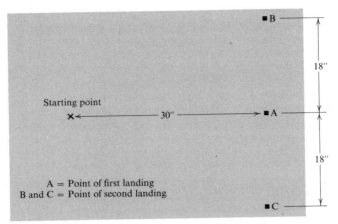

FIGURE 13-12.   Modified sideward leap test.

Hand Walk Test.   This test is the same as the two-hand balance test, except the student walks on the hands as far as possible. The score is the number of feet he or she walks before losing balance.

Tests of Kinesthetic Perception

Kinesthetic perception is the sense that gives us an awareness of the body and its parts in space so that we can cause desired movements without using our five basic senses of smell, taste, touch, sight, and hearing; hence it is sometimes referred to as the sixth sense or the muscle sense. With this sixth sense we are aware of muscle contractions—the degree of contraction and the force of the contraction.

Tests of kinesthetic perception are designed to measure our ability to judge the positions and movements of our body parts without the use of the five basic senses. Hence these tests measure the effectiveness of the "sixth" sense."

Distance Perception Jump

The distance perception jump test (8) was designed to measure the ability of the performer to perceive the distance jumped without the use of the eyes, by concentrating on the feel of the jump. Validity and reliability of the test are accepted at face value. The test is useful for both sexes, age 10 through college age. A measuring tape, blindfolds, chalk, and marking tape are needed to test about 30 students in 40 minutes at each station.

Procedure: Two lines are placed on the floor 24 inches apart as illustrated in Figure 13-13. The student stands at the starting line and visually reviews the

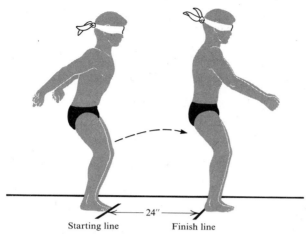

24″

Starting line   Finish line

FIGURE 13-13. Distance perception jump.

situation. Then he or she closes the eyes, pauses for 5 seconds, and jumps from the starting position trying to judge the distance of the jump so that the heels land on the target line (see Figure 13-13).

Scoring: The number of inches the student jumps between the target line and the heel farthest from the line is measured to the nearest quarter inch. The student has two trials, and the score is the total inches measured for the two trials.

Pedestrial Tests of Distance and Vertical Space

The purpose in these tests (*10*) is to measure the ability of the performer to position the feet without the use of the eyes. Validity and reliability of the test are accepted at face value. The tests are useful for both sexes from age 10 through college age. With the same equipment as for the distance perception test and a 12-inch ruler about 30 students can be tested in 40 minutes at each station.

Procedure for the test of distance: With eyes closed or with a blindfold placed over the eyes, the student tries to spread the heels so the inside of the heels are 12 inches apart; at the same time he or she concentrates on the length of a 12-inch ruler and attempts to place the heels the correct distance from each other (see Figure 13-14).

Scoring: The student has three trials, and the score for each trial is the distance that the heels deviate from the preferred distance of 12 inches, measured to the nearest quarter inch. The final score is the total of the scores on the three trials.

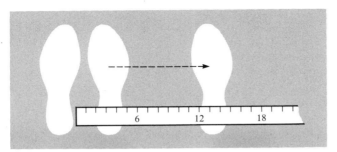

FIGURE 13-14.   Pedestrial test of size.

Procedure for the vertical space test: While blindfolded the student attempts to place the bottom edge of the shoe sole of one foot on top and parallel with a line drawn on a wall 14 inches above the floor (see Figure 13-15).

Scoring: The student has three trials, and the score for each trial is the far-thest distance that the sole of the foot deviates from the line, measured to the nearest quarter inch. The final score is the total scores of the three trials.

The purpose in these tests (*10*) is to measure the kinesthetic ability to deter-mine specific positions along horizontal and vertical lines. The tests are suit-able for both sexes age 10 through college age. With a measuring tape, yard-stick, blindfolds, and marking tape about 25 students can be tested in 40 minutes at each station.

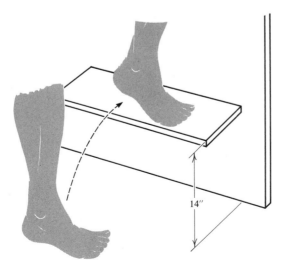

FIGURE 13-15.   Pedestrial test of vertical space.

Procedure for horizontal space test: Figure 13-16 illustrates the physical arrangement for this test. The yardstick is placed on the wall so that it is at approximately eye level while the student is in the sitting position. The student sits on the chair facing the yardstick and attempts to establish mentally a sense of its position. Then while blindfolded and without a practice trial he or she attempts to point the index finger of the right hand to the mark on the yardstick indicated by the instructor.

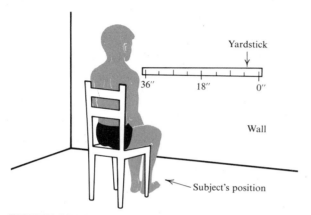

FIGURE 13-16. Horizontal space test.

Scoring: The score is the deviation from the desired mark, measured to the nearest quarter inch. The final score is the total of the deviations on three trials.

Procedure for the vertical space test: Figure 13-17 illustrates the arrangement for this test. The yardstick is placed so that the 16-inch mark is about eye level for the student while sitting. The student sits on the chair facing the yardstick and attempts to establish mentally a sense of its position. Then while blindfolded and without a practice trial he or she points the index finger of the right hand to the point indicated by the instructor.

Scoring: The score procedure is the same as for the horizontal space test.

Basketball Foul Shot Test

The purpose of this test (4) is to measure the performer's ability to shoot foul shots accurately without using the eyes. In other words, the test measures kinesthetic perception in connection with foul shooting. Twenty-five students can be tested in 40 minutes at each station. The equipment includes a basketball standard, basketball, and blindfold at each testing station.

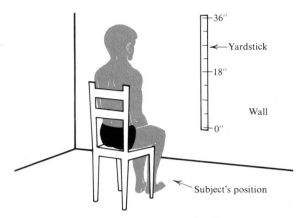

FIGURE 13-17. Vertical space test.

Procedure: The student stands at the foul line and shoots three trials shots. Then without moving from the line the student blindfolds (her)himself and shoots five additional shots.

Scoring: The student is scored for each shot as follows: 3 points if the ball goes through the hoop; 2 points if it strikes the hoop but fails to go through; 1 point if it strikes the backboard but misses the hoop; 0 points if it misses the backboard and the hoop. The final score is the total for the five trials.

Ball Throw Test

The purpose of this test (4) is to measure the performer's ability to throw a ball a specified distance without using his eyes. In other words, the test measures kinesthetic perception as it relates to throwing. Figure 13-18 illustrates the physical arrangement. Equipment needed is a softball and blindfold at each testing station. Thirty students can be tested in 40 minutes at each station.

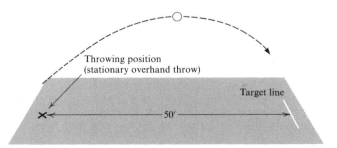

FIGURE 13-18. Ball throw test of kinesthetic perception.

Procedure: The student stands on the starting line in a throwing position and reviews the situation carefully, trying to develop a sense of the distance to the target line. Then, while blindfolded, he or she attempts to throw a softball in such a way that it lands on the target line.

Scoring: The student is allowed three trials, and the score for each trial is the distance the ball misses the target line, measured to the nearest foot. The final score is the total of the scores for three trials.

Bass Kinesthetic Stick Tests (Lengthwise and Crosswise)

These tests (*11*) measure kinesthetic perception as it relates to balance. The tests are performed the same as the Bass stick tests (lengthwise and crosswise) described earlier in this chapter, except in this case the performer is blindfolded. The student is allowed three trials; the score for each trial is the number of seconds balance is maintained, measured to the nearest second. The final score is the sum of the scores for the three trials.

Tests of Perception for Children With Special Needs

Educators, pyschologists, and medical authorities have developed evaluation techniques to be used with children who, for one reason or another, have displayed special learning problems. These tests often have had no statistical treatment and are only diagnostic of a child's performance on the specific test instrument. The results of the tests are a part of a professional work-up evaluation done by a team of professionals so that individualized programs can be designed for each child.

Kephard Test of Perceptual Motor Skills

Newell C. Kephart includes in his test of perceptual–motor evaluation 11 test skills. The gross motor items included are: (1) walking board—(low balance board) forward, backward, and sideward; (2) jumping—both feet, left foot, right foot, skip and hopping rhythms; (3) stepping stones—a patterned course for right and left discrimination; (4) Kraus–Weber Test as described elsewhere in this text. Evaluation techniques are included, but there is no evidence of the reliability or the validity of the techniques.

Cratty Six Category Gross Motor Test

The test includes six skills and two levels of performance. The six skills are: (1) body perception; (2) gross agility; (3) balance; (4) locomotor agility; (5) ball throwing; (6) ball tracking. Level two includes the same skills on a more difficult level. Means and standard deviations have been determined and a correlation matrix is presented.

The Purdue Perceptual Motor Survey

This test includes gross motor items of (1) the walking board (balance beam), (2) jumping, and (3) Kraus–Weber Test items. Instructions for administering the test are included and reliability and validity measures are cited in the test manual.

Selected References

1. **Bass, R. I.**: An analysis of the components of tests of semi-circular canal function and of static and dynamic balance. *Research Quarterly*, 10, 1939.
2. **Cratty, B. J.**, and **Sister M. M. Martin**: *Perceptual–Motor Efficiency in Children.* Philadelphia, Pa.: Lea and Febiger, 1969.
3. **Jensen, C. R.**: Unpublished Studies of Tests of Balance, Brigham Young University, 1970.
4. **Jensen, C. R.**: Unpublished Studies of Tests of Kinesthetic Perception, Brigham Young University, 1970.
5. **Johnson, B. L.**, and **Leach, J.**: A Modification of the Bass Test of Dynamic Balance. Unpublished study, East Texas State University, 1968.
6. **Kephart, N. C.**: *The Slow Learner in the Classroom*, Columbus, Ohio: Charles E. Merrill Publishing Co., 1960.
7. **Roach, E. G.** and **Kephart, N. C.**: *The Purdue Perceptual-Motor Survey*, Columbus, Ohio: Charles E. Merrill Publishing Co., 1966.
8. **Scott, M. G.**: Measurement of kinesthesis. *Res. Q.*, 26, 1955.
9. **Scott, M. G.**, and **French, E.**: *Measurement and Evaluation in Physical Education.* Dubuque, Iowa: W. C. Brown Co., 1959.
10. **Wiebe, Vernon R.**: A Study of Tests of Kinesthesis. Unpublished master's thesis, State University of Iowa, 1951.
11. **Young, Olive G.**: A study of kinesthesis in relation to selected movements, *Research Quarterly*, 16, 1945.

14

Measures of Neuromuscular Skills

An individual's skill is the ability to perform a series of movements smoothly and efficiently, using all the muscles—agonists, antagonists, neutralizers, and stabilizers—in correct coordination. In other terms skill is the ability to use the right muscles with the exact force necessary to perform the desired movements in the correct sequence and timing. Skill is competence in the performance.

Performance in any activity includes several specific skills. For example, basketball requires skill in jumping, shooting, running, throwing, catching, and dribbling. In soccer a player must be able to dribble, pass, screen, dodge, and kick effectively. A person must learn the skills specific to a particular activity in order to become effective. The development of specific skills is a paramount concern in physical education and athletics.

A person improves his or her skill by determining the correct mechanics and incorporating them into the performance. The individual must practice a specific skill correctly until the pattern of movement becomes naturally smooth and efficient. In addition to such practice the performer may increase skill by better judgment of speed, distance, and time and by better insight into the environmental circumstances related to the performance.

Skill tests are used to measure specific skills which are essential to a particular activity. Once estimates of skill have been obtained this information can serve as a basis for determining the rate of student progress for classifying students into groups for instruction and competition, and selecting content of instruction.

In addition to the tests described in this chapter, actual performances in competition can serve as a useful measure of skill. In fact this is the best test of anyone's performance ability.

Archery

Hyde Archery Test

Edith Hyde (34) constructed standards of archery performance for college women in the Columbia Round. The Columbia Round, a standard event in archery, consists of 24 arrows shot at 50 yards, 24 arrows shot at 40 yards, and 24 arrows shot at 30 yards. The achievement scales which Hyde developed consist of three parts:

1. A scale for evaluating achievement in the first Columbia Round. This scale is used to evaluate the student's total score made in the first round after a minimum of practice, which might include 120 arrows shot at each distance—30, 40, and 50 yards.
2. A scale for evaluating the student's score made in the final Columbia Round after an undetermined amount of practice in the event. It is best used toward the end of the archery season or at the end of an archery course.
3. A scale consisting of three separate sections for evaluating the student's achievement at each of the distances (50, 40, and 30 yards) included in the round.

Procedure: The progress of beginning as well as advanced female students may be evaluated using the Columbia Round directions:

The student shoots the arrows in ends of six arrows each. She is allowed only one practice end for each distance and must shoot 24 arrows at each distance. She does not have to complete the entire test or round in one day but should finish at least one distance (24 arrows) each session.

Scoring: A standard 48-inch target face is used. The target has a gold center worth 9 points, an adjacent red circle worth 7 points, a blue circle worth 5 points, a black circle worth 3 points, and an outside white circle worth 1 point. The center of the gold circle is 4 feet from the ground. The student is given the higher value in scoring an arrow which cuts two colors. If an arrow goes completely through the target or if it bounces off the target, she receives an arbitrary score of 5 points for that arrow.

Other Archery Tests

In addition to the forenamed test, the following are useful measures of archery skills: Reliability of Archery Achievement (73) and the American Alliance for Health, Physical Education and Recreation Archery Test (1).

Badminton

Lockhart–McPherson Badminton Volleying Test

The Lockhart–McPherson Volleying test (44) measures the badminton playing ability of college women. It may also be used effectively to classify college men and high school girls and boys for instruction and measurement of progress in skill development. As a test of badminton skill it has produced validity coefficients on two different occasions of .72 and .60. It has a reliability coefficient of .90.

A stopwatch, badminton racket, indoor shuttlecock (bird), and unobstructed wall space at least 10 feet by 10 feet are necessary. (If sufficient wall space is available, several students can be tested simultaneously.) One scorer is needed for each student being tested. Two to three minutes are required to administer the test to one person.

Procedure: A net line is marked on the wall at a height of 5 feet. A starting line is marked on the floor 6 feet 6 inches from the wall, and a restraining line is marked parallel to the starting line and 3 feet from the wall. The student stands behind the starting line. On the signal "go" she puts the shuttlecock into play against the wall with an underhand stroke, volleying the bird against the wall as many times as possible in 30 seconds. For a volley to count, the shuttlecock must strike the wall on or above the net line. The student may move up to the restraining line after serving the shuttlecock, but if she crosses the restraining line, the hit will not count. If she loses control of the shuttlecock, she should pick it up as quickly as possible and put it into play again with an underhand stroke from behind the starting line.

Scoring: The student has three trials, with each trial 30 seconds in length. The combined number of good hits during the three trials is the final score. A score may be interpreted in comparison with scores made by other students or with scores made by the same student on different occasions. The following scale rates college women:

Rating	Test Score
Superior	126 and up
Good	90–125
Average	62–89
Poor	40–61
Inferior	39 and below

French Short Serve Test

This test (61) measures a student's ability to serve accurately and low in badminton. The test was originally designed for college women, but it may be used effectively for college men and high school boys and girls. A validity coefficient of .66 was reported with tournament rankings as the criterion measure. Reliability coefficients ranging from .51 to .89 have been obtained on different occasions.

A clothesline rope long enough to stretch between two net standards, a badminton racquet, and at least five shuttlecocks are needed at each testing station. Marks are placed on the badminton court as illustrated in Figure 18-2. About 10 students can be tested in 40 minutes at each station.

Procedure: The student stands in the service court diagonally opposite the target (see Figure 14-1). She or he takes 20 serves either consecutively or in groups of 10 trying on each serve to send the shuttlecock between the net and the rope, which is 2 feet above the net, into zone 5, near the intersection of the center line and the short service line.

Scoring: The zones are given point values of 5, 4, 3, 2, and 1, as indicated in Figure 18-2. The value of the area in which the serve hits is recorded as the score for that serve. A serve that does not pass between the net and the rope

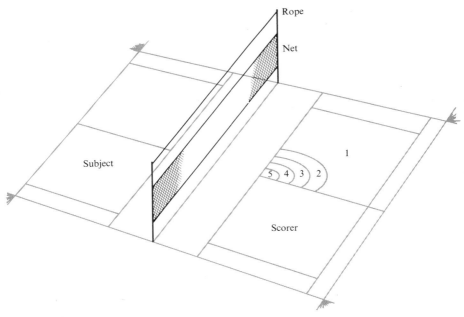

FIGURE 14-1.   French short serve floor plan.

counts zero; a serve that does not land in one of the five designated zones counts zero; and a serve that lands on one of the division lines counts the higher value. If the shuttlecock hits the rope, the trial does not count, and the serve is taken again. The final score is the total of the values made on the 20 serves.

Scott-Fox Long Serve Test

This test (61) measures the student's ability to serve high and deep into the court in badminton. It is useful for college men and women and high school boys and girls. The test has a validity coefficient of .54 when compared to the subjective judgments of badminton experts. Reliability coefficients of .68 and .77 have been obtained.

Each testing area needs a racquet, at least five shuttlecocks, a rope, and two extra standards from which the rope can be stretched across the court at a height of 8 feet and a distance of 14 feet from the net. Floor markings are placed on the court as illustrated in Figure 14-2. Ten students can be tested in 40 minutes at each station.

Procedure: The student stands in the service court diagonally opposite the target and serves the shuttlecock over the rope and into the corner of the court containing the target. He or she is allowed a total of 20 trials.

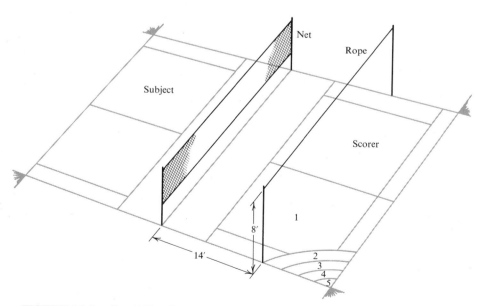

FIGURE 14-2. Scott-Fox long serve test floor plan.

Scoring: A score corresponding to the number of the zone in which the shuttlecock lands is given for each serve. The final score is the sum of the scores for the 20 different serves. A serve that does not pass over the rope or one that falls outside the five zones is scored zero. Only legal serves count as trials.

French Clear Test

This test (26) measures a student's ability to perform the clear shot in badminton. It was originally designed for college women but can be used for college men and high school boys and girls. The test has produced a validity coefficient of .60 when correlated with tournament rankings. Its reliability rating is .96.

Each testing station needs a racquet, five shuttlecocks, a rope, and an extra set of standards from which the rope can be stretched across the court at a height of 8 feet and a distance of 14 feet from the net. The court is marked as illustrated in Figure 14.3. About 10 students can be tested in 40 minutes at each station.

Procedure: The student stands behind the short service line on the court opposite the target. An experienced player serves the shuttlecock to the student who stands between two marks on the court. The student attempts to return the shuttlecock using a clear shot that goes over the rope and lands near the end line. This procedure is repeated for 20 trials. The serve to the student should

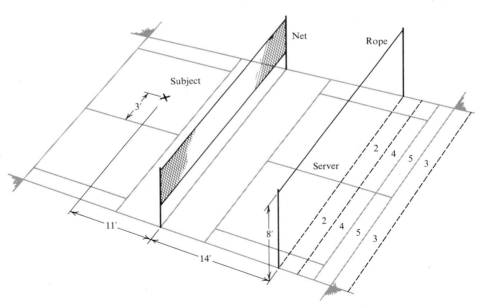

FIGURE 14-3. French clear test floor plan.

fall between the two marks; if it is too short, too long, or falls outside the two marks, she or he should not return it. Only those serves that are played count as trials.

Scoring: The score for each trial is determined by the number of the zones in which the shuttle lands. The total score is the sum of the scores for the 20 trials. If the shuttlecock fails to pass over the rope, or if it lands outside the scoring areas, it counts zero.

Other Badminton Tests

There are other tests of skill in badminton in addition to those described here: the French–Stalter badminton test for college women (26), the Miller wall volley test (49), and test of game sense (66).

Genevie Dexter (21) checklist to rate performance in badminton

Student's Name _____ Date _____ Rated by _____

Directions: Check appropriate items as you watch the student play badminton.

Desirable Performance	*Undesirable Performance*
_____ Grips racket correctly	_____ Fails to look at shuttlecock
_____ Keeps eyes on shuttlecock	_____ Strokes with stiff wrist or elbow
_____ Uses wrist snap	_____ Fails to return to good court position after stroking
_____ Sends short serves low over net	
_____ Sends high clear within three feet of back line	_____ Runs around shuttlecock to avoid backhand shots
_____ Places shots strategically	_____ Uses drive strokes excessively
_____ Starts strokes with same preliminary movements	_____ Returns most shots to center of opponent's court
_____ Uses variety of shots and a change of pace	_____ Fails to use a variety of strokes
	_____ Gives away direction and type of shot to be made
_____ Displays good footwork	
_____ Uses effectively a doubles system of teamwork	_____ Starts late and moves slowly
	_____ Gives no indication of definite partnership play in doubles

---

Basketball

Stroup Basketball Test

This test (65) measures basketball playing ability of college men and high school boys. According to Stroup a high correlation exists between scores on this test and basketball playing ability in the game situation.

A regulation basketball standard, three basketballs, seven Indian clubs (or substitute markers), a running area 100 feet long, a solid wall against which a basketball may be bounced, and three stopwatches are necessary for each testing area. If one testing station is used for each test item, about 20 students can be tested in a 40-minute period.

Procedure: The test consists of three items to be performed as follows:

1. Standing at any position on the court, the student shoots as many baskets as possible in one minute. He must retrieve the ball himself after each shot. He is scored 1 point for each basket; his final score is the total number of points.
2. Standing behind a line 6 feet from the wall, the student passes the ball against the wall as many times as possible in one minute. A pass is not counted if the student bats the ball instead of catching it or if he steps over the restraining line as he makes the pass. His score is the number of legal passes he makes in one minute.
3. The student dribbles the ball as he zigzags alternately to the left and right of seven Indian clubs placed in a line 15 feet apart for a 90 foot distance. He circles the end club each time and continues dribbling for one minute. A miss is counted if he knocks over a club, or if the club is not passed on the proper side. His score is the number of clubs he passes properly within the time limit. The starting line is 15 feet from the first Indian club.

Scoring: The raw scores for the three phases are converted to standard scores which may be averaged to obtain a final standard score.

Leilich Basketball Test

This battery of tests (42) was designed for college women but is also appropriate for high school girls. Its purpose is to measure general basketball playing ability. The battery resulted from a factor analysis study covering all basketball tests available at the time. The factors included in the analysis were basketball motor ability, speed, accuracy in ball handling, speed in passing, and accuracy in goal shooting. Validity and reliability of the test have not been determined. When all stations operate simultaneously, about 25 students can be tested in 40 minutes.

Procedure: The three individual test items are conducted as follows:

1. *Bounce and Shoot.* This test measures agility, ball handling ability, and speed and accuracy of shooting. Two marks are placed on the floor 18 feet from a basket is illustrated in Figure 14-4. Two basketballs are placed on two chairs adjacent to the two marks. On the starting signal the student picks up the ball from chair A, bounces the ball once as he or she moves toward the basket, and then shoots. The student catches the ball on the rebound and passes it to the person standing behind chair A. Then he or she runs to chair B and repeats the procedure until he has completed 10 shots. The student is allowed three trials and is scored on the best of these for accuracy and speed. His accuracy

score is the total number of points he accumulates from his shots: 2 points for each basket, 1 point for hitting the rim but missing the basket, and no points for missing the rim and basket. The speed score is the total number of seconds he takes to complete the test.

2. *Half-Minute Shooting.* This test measures accuracy and speed of shooting. The student stands near the basket, holding a basketball. On the signal he or she begins shooting and continues shooting for 30 seconds from any position on the floor. The score is the number of baskets he makes in 30 seconds. The student is allowed two trials, and the better trial is the final score.

3. *Push Pass.* This test measures speed and accuracy of passing. Figure 14-4, illustrates the arrangement for the test. The student stands behind the restraining line and passes the ball to the target using a two-hand push pass. The student repeats this passing as many times as possible in a 30-second period. The student must keep both feet behind the restraining line when he or she passes the ball but may move forward of the restraining line to retrieve the ball. A ball that hits inside a given circle is scored by the value of that circle. A ball that strikes a line scores the higher value. The student is allowed two trials, and the better trial is recorded as the final score.

Scoring: Each of the three tests is scored separately.

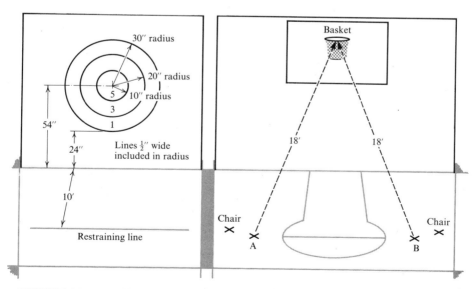

FIGURE 14-4.   Leilich basketball test floor plan.

Other Basketball Tests

In addition to the tests already described, the following are also useful measures of basketball skill: Achievement levels for women (50) Knox basketball test for high school boys (39), LSU basketball test (53) factor analysis of skill tests (33), and American Alliance for Health, Physical Education and Recreation basketball test for boys and for girls (2), (3).

Bowling

There have been no actual bowling skill tests reported. Performance in the game itself is the best measure of bowling skill. However, some interesting and useful norms have been developed and may be found in the Phillips–Summers bowling achievement scales for college women (56) and the Martin bowling norms for college men and women (45). Spot bowling is evaluated by Olson and Liba (55).

Field Hockey

Friedel Field Hockey Test

This test (27) measures ball control and maneuverability of high school girls. The test is also useful for college women. It has a validity coefficient of .87 when correlated with the Schmithals–French hockey achievement test (Schmithals and French 1940). A reliability coefficient of .90 has been produced.

A field at least 30 yards long and 15 yards wide is needed as a testing area. (Several testing areas are recommended.) With a trained assistant who knows how to roll the ball into play the teacher can test five students at each station in a 40-minute period.

Procedure: The field arrangement should be according to Figure 14-5. An assistant to the teacher throws a ball either from the right or left corner, aiming toward the target area. (If it is not accurately aimed, the ball should be rolled again.) The student stands behind the starting line holding her hockey stick. On the signal she runs toward the target area to receive the ball which the assistant has rolled from one of the corners. Controlling the ball, the student passes the restraining line on the way to the end line. At the end line she turns around and drives the ball back to the starting line, keeping it within the 10-yard lane. She may follow the ball to drive it a second time if necessary. The student has 20 trials, 10 from each side.

Scoring: Each trial is timed from the beginning signal until the ball crosses the starting line on the return trip. The final score is the student's total times for the 20 trials.

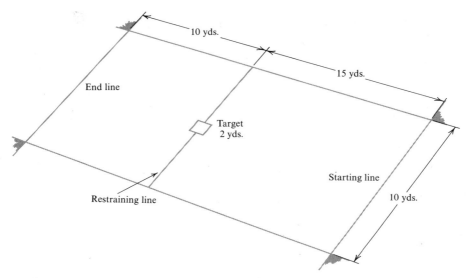

FIGURE 14-5. Friedel hockey test floor plan.

In addition to the aforementioned tests, the Schmithals–French Field Hockey Test for College. Women (60) is a useful test of skill in field hockey.

Football

There has been little done toward the development of objective skill tests in football. The only current work in this area is the AAHPER football skill test (4). In addition the Borleske touch football test for college men (8) and the Brace (9) football achievement test for college men may prove useful.

Golf

Clevett Golf Putting Test

This test (16) measures golf putting accuracy. It is useful for either men or women of practically any age.

A smooth carpet 20 feet long and 27 inches wide is marked as illustrated in Figure 14-6. Each zone is nine inches square; square 10 represents the hole. A putter and at least 10 golf balls are required. Validity and reliability of the test have not been determined. About 25 students can be tested at each station in 40 minutes.

Procedure: The student stands at the starting mark, which is approximately 15 feet from the hole and attempts to putt the ball into square 10. He or she is allowed 10 trials.

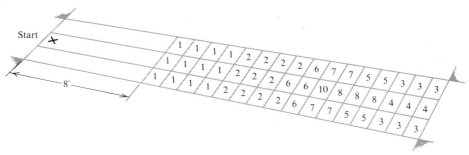

FIGURE 14-6.   Clevett golf putting test floor plan.

Nelson Golf Pitching Test

This test (52) measures the ability of the golfer to use the short irons in pitching close to the pin, and it is suitable for men and women of practically any age. It has produced a validity coefficient of .86 when compared to judges' ratings and .79 when compared to golf scores. A reliability coefficient of .83 has been obtained with the test–retest method.

A target should be marked on the field as shown in Figure 14-7. The inner circle of the target is 6 feet in diameter, and from the center of the target the radius of each circle is five feet wider than the radius of the previous circle. Hence diameters are 6, 16, 26, 36, 46, 56, and 66 feet. The target is divided into equal quadrants. A restraining line is marked 20 yards from the flag, and

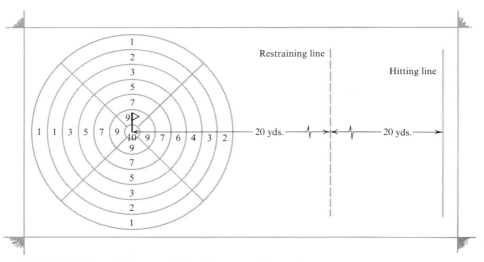

FIGURE 14-7.   Nelson golf pitching test floor plan.

the hitting line is marked 40 yards from the flag. (As many as four stations can be set up around one flag.) The numbers for the particular sectors of the circle are shown in Figure 14-7. About 15 students can be tested at each station in a 40-minute period.

Procedure: The student stands behind the hitting line with the appropriate club (usually an 8 iron, a 9 iron or a wedge) and at least 13 balls. He or she is allowed three practice balls and then has 10 official trials, trying to knock each ball as close to the flag as possible. A legal ball must be airborne until it passes the restraining line. Each swing is counted regardless of how far the ball goes or how poorly the ball was hit.

Scoring: The scorer stands close to the flag and records the value of each hit. The point value of the area in which the ball comes to rest is the recorded score. A ball resting on a line is given the higher point value. The score is the total point value for the 10 trials.

Other Golf Tests

In addition to the Clevett golf putting test and the Nelson golf pitching test, the following tests are also useful measures of golf skills:

Cochrane indoor golf skills test (17) McKee golf test (47), Vanderhoof golf test (67), Vanderhoof rating scale for girls, test battery for golf skills (12), and an eight iron approach test (70).

Gymnastics

Actual performance in gymnastic events that are judged by competent judges is the best evaluation of gymnastic performance. The following may prove useful: screening test for gymnastic events (36) and objectivity of judging (25).

Handball

Cornish Handball Test

Clayton Cornish (19) developed this test to measure specific skills in handball. He selected five test items (30-second volley, front wall placement, back wall placement, service placement, and the power test) which correlated .69 with actual playing ability. Alone the power test correlated .58 with the criterion, and in combination with the 30-second volley test the power test correlated .67 with the criterion measure. Therefore, Cornish recommends that the power test be used with the 30-second test. About 15 students can be tested at each station in 40 minutes.

Procedure: The two recommended tests are performed as follows:

1. *Power Test.* The floor of a court is divided into five playing areas as illustrated in Figure 14-8. The student stands in the service zone and throws the ball against the front wall, letting it hit the floor on the rebound before striking it. He or she then hits the ball as hard as possible, making sure it strikes the front wall below the 6-foot line. The student repeats this procedure until he or she has made five strokes with each hand. The student has another trial if he or she steps into the front court or if the ball fails to hit the wall below the 6 foot line. The score for each trial is the value of the scoring zone on the floor where the ball lands. The final score is the total points for the 10 trials.

2. *Thirty-second Volley.* The student stands behind the service line, drops the ball to the floor, and volleys it against the front wall as many times as possible in 30 seconds. All strokes should be made from behind the service line, but if the ball fails to return to the service line, the student may step forward of the line to play that particular stroke and then return behind the service line for the succeeding stroke. If the student misses the ball, the instructor gives another ball and he or she continues volleying. The score is the total number of times the ball hits the wall in 30 seconds.

Scoring: Each test is scored separately. Achievement scales are not available.

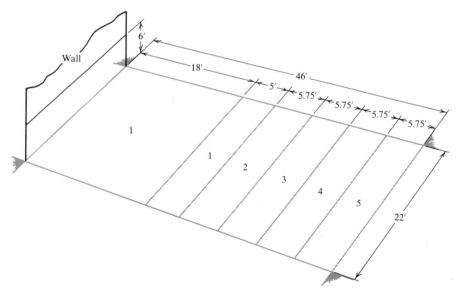

FIGURE 14-8.   Cornish handball test floor plan.

Other Handball Tests

In addition, the following sources may prove useful when evaluating handball skills: use of a tournament (51) and a measure of playing ability (51).

Ice Hockey and Ice Skating

The following tests may be useful when evaluating ice hockey and ice skating: a battery of ice hockey skill tests (48) and a test for beginners in figure skating (57).

Rhythm Tests

Heaton Dance Rating Scale

This rating scale (31) applies at all levels of ballroom dance—beginners through advanced. One couple at a time dances across the floor. A maximum of nine points is possible for each fundamental. The points can be converted to letter grades if one point is considered an F (failing), three points a D, five points a C, seven points a B, and nine points an A (excellent). This same system of rating can be used with other forms of dance by changing the items in the left hand column as desired.

·	1	2	3	4	5	6	7	8	9	Points	Grade
Posture											
Walking											
Rhythm											
Etiquette											
Position											
Leading											
Following											
Styling											
Relaxation											
Steps											

Total =

Soccer

McDonald Soccer Test

This test (46) measures general soccer playing ability of college men, but it is also useful for high school boys. When results of the test were correlated with coaches ratings of playing ability, validity coefficients ranging from .63 to .94 were obtained on different occasions. Reliability has not been established.

A wall or backboard 30 feet wide and at least 11½ feet high is needed. A restraining line is drawn 9 feet from the wall. With a stopwatch and three soccer balls about 15 students can be tested at each station in 40 minutes.

Procedure: At the signal, the student begins kicking the ball against the wall from behind the restraining line and continues to do so as many times as possible in 30 seconds. He may kick the ball on the fly or on the bounce, and may use his hands to retrieve it. However, to score a point he must make the kick from behind the restraining line. If the ball goes out of control, he has the option of playing one of the spare balls instead of retrieving the loose ball. The two spare balls are placed nine feet behind the restraining line. The student is given four trials.

Scoring: The score is the highest number of legal kicks in any one of the four trials.

Johnson Soccer Test

This test (37) measures general soccer playing ability of college men. It is also useful for high school boys. The test has produced validity coefficients ranging from .58 to .98 on various occasions. It has a reliability coefficient of .92.

A backboard 24 feet wide and at least eight feet high is required. (This dimension is the same as that for a regulation soccer goal.) The restraining line is placed 15 feet from the wall. A ball container for spare balls is placed 15 feet behind the restraining line. About 18 students can be tested at each station in 40 minutes.

Procedure: The student holds a soccer ball while standing behind the restraining line. On the starting signal, he or she kicks the ball against the backboard, either on the fly or after a bounce. When the ball rebounds, he or she kicks it again and continues kicking the ball against the backboard as many times as possible in 30 seconds. He must kick the ball from behind the restraining line with a legal soccer kick. If the ball goes out of control the student may use a spare ball rather than chase the loose ball. The student has three 30-second trials.

Scoring: The score is the total number of legal kicks during the three trials.

Other Soccer Tests

In addition to the aforementioned tests the following are useful measures of soccer ability: Shaufele soccer test for girls (62) and Warner test of soccer skills (69).

Softball

O'Donnell Softball Test

Doris O'Donnell (54) designed this test to measure basic softball playing skills of high school girls. The test is also useful for college women and there is no reason why it could not be used for college men and high school boys. The total test consists of six items. O'Donnell suggests that two simplified versions should be considered, consisting of test items three, four, and six or test items three and four. With all six items included, the test has produced a validity coefficient of .91. Its reliability has not been established. When all six stations are operated simultaneously, about 30 students can be tested in 40 minutes.

Procedure: The six specific tests are performed as follows:

1. *Speed Throw.* The student stands behind a restraining line 65 feet from the wall. On the starting signal she or he throws a ball as fast as possible at the wall. The score is the time that elapses from the starting signal until the ball hits the wall. The student is allowed three trials, and the best is recorded to the nearest tenth of a second.
2. *Fielding Fly Balls.* Holding a softball, the student stands behind a restraining line 6 feet from the wall. On the signal she or he throws the ball against the wall and catches the rebound on the fly. This procedure is repeated as many times as possible in 30 seconds. The ball must strike the wall above a line 12 feet from the floor. The student must throw the ball from behind the restraining line but may catch it in front of the line if she or he desires. One practice trial is allowed. The score is the number of legal catches made in one official trial.
3. *Throw and Catch.* A rope is stretched 8 feet directly above a starting line which is drawn on the floor. The student stands behind the starting line, throws a softball over the rope, and then runs and catches the ball. The objective is to cover the maximum distance and still catch the ball. The score is the distance from the rope to the position of the heel of the student's front foot at the time she or he catches the ball. The student is allowed one practice throw and three official throws. The score of the best official throw is recorded.
4. *Repeated Throws.* The student stands behind the restraining line which is 15 feet from the wall. On the signal she or he throws the ball against the wall, attempting to hit the wall above a line placed 7½ feet from the floor. She or he catches the ball on the rebound and repeats throwing the ball above the 7½-foot line as many times as possible in 30 seconds. Each throw must be made from behind the restraining line. The score is the number of legal throws in 30 seconds.

5. *Fungo Batting.* Standing in the batter's box, the student tosses a softball into the air and bats it. A ball that lands in the outfield counts 5 points: one that lands in the infield, 3 points; and a foul ball, 1 point. The score is the sum of the points on 10 trials. Only tosses that are swung at count as trials.

6. *Overhand Accuracy Throw.* A target is drawn on a wall consisting of four circles with the center of the target 2 feet from the floor. The inner circle has a radius of 3 inches. The radii of the other circles are 11 inches, 21 inches, and 33 inches. The value of each circle from the center is 4, 3, 2, and 1, respectively. From a restraining line 45 feet from the target, the student throws 10 softballs at the target. The score is the number of points in the 10 trials.

Scoring: Each of the six tests is scored separately. Achievement scales are not available.

Fox–Young Batting Test

This test (30) measures batting distance and accuracy. Validity and reliability coefficients of .64 and .87, respectively, have been recorded. Supplies needed at each testing station include a bat, a batting tee, and eight softballs. About 20 students can be tested at each station in a 40-minute period.

Procedure: The student stands in the batter's box, places a ball on the tee, and knocks the ball as far as possible. Three practice trials and five official trials are allowed.

Scoring: Each trial is measured from the batter's box to the point where the ball first strikes the ground. The total score is the sum of the distances of the five official trials. (Experience and practice with a batting tee should be prerequisite for this test.)

Dexter Batting Test

The following scale (21) rates softball batting skill.

Other Softball Tests

Additional references to evaluate the skills of softball are: Fringer Battery (28), defensive softball skills for college women (63), and the American Alliance for Health, Physical Education and Recreation softball tests for boys and for girls (5) (6).

Dexter Batting Test

Student's Name _____ Date _____

Rated by _____ Score _____

Directions: First check the student's performance as good, fair, or poor on each item and then check deviations noted. Determine the student's score by assigning one point for poor, two for fair, and three for good; then total the points.

Rating		*Deviations from Standard Performance*
1. Grip	____ Good	____ Hands too far apart
	____ Fair	____ Wrong hand on top
	____ Poor	____ Hands too far from end of bat
2. Preliminary	____ Good	____ Stands too near the plate
	____ Fair	____ Stands too far from plate
	____ Poor	____ Stands too far forward toward pitcher
		____ Stands too far backward toward catcher
		____ Feet not parallel to line from pitcher to catcher
		____ Rests bat on shoulder
		____ Shoulders not horizontal
3. Stride or footwork	____ Good	____ Fails to step forward
	____ Fair	____ Fails to transfer weight
	____ Poor	____ Lifts backfoot from ground before swing
4. Pivot or body twist	____ Good	____ Fails to "wind up"
	____ Fair	____ Fails to follow-through with body
	____ Poor	____ Has less than 90 degree pivot
5. Arm movement or swing	____ Good	____ Arms held too close to body
	____ Fair	____ Bat not held approximately parallel to ground
		____ Not enough wrist motion used
		____ Wrists not uncocked forcefully enough
6. General (Eyes on ball, judgment of pitches, and the like)	____ Good	____ Body movements jerky
	____ Fair	____ Tries too hard; "presses"
	____ Poor	____ Fails to look at center of ball
		____ Judges pitches poorly
		____ Appears to lack confidence
		____ Does not use suitable bat

Speedball

Buchanan Speedball Test

This test (14), designed for high school girls, measures fundamental skills required in speedball. Validity and reliability ratings for the test are not available. When four stations are operated simultaneously, about 20 students can be tested in 40 minutes.

Procedure: The test consists of the following four specific tests:

1. *Lift to Others.* A volleyball, badminton, or tennis net is stretched between two standards so that the top of the net is 2½ feet above the

ground. The student stands behind a restraining line 6 feet from the net and attempts to lift the speedball with either foot, passing it over the net so that it lands within a 3-foot square diagonally opposite from where he is standing (see Figure 14-9). He is allowed 10 trials and scores one point for each pass that lands within the proper square.

2. *Throwing and Catching.* A restraining line is marked 6 feet from the parallel to an unobstructed wall. On the starting signal the student throws the ball against the wall and catches it in the rebound as many times as possible in 30 seconds. The score is the average number of catches made in five trials.

3. *Dribbling and Passing.* The field is marked according to Figure 14-9 with a starting line 60 yards from the end line of the field. Five Indian clubs or similar objects are placed in a line 10 yards apart, beginning at the starting line. At the end line two goals are marked, one to the right and one to the left of the dribbling course. The goal areas are 6 yards long, and their inner borders are 4 feet to the left and 4 feet to the right of the dribbling line. The student stands behind the starting line and on the signal starts dribbling the ball down the field. She or he dribbles to the right of the first Indian club, to the left of the second, and so on. Immediately after dribbling to the right of the last club, she or he attempts to kick the ball to the left into the goal area. The student follows

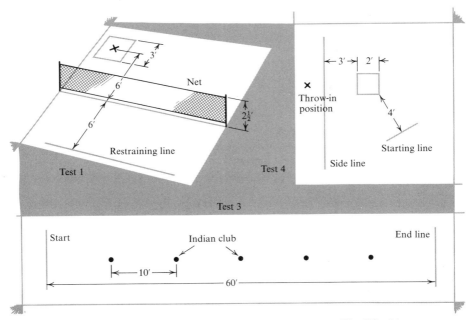

FIGURE 14-9. Field plan for Buchman speedball test. (Modified.)

this procedure for 10 trials, five to the right and five to the left. Three scores are obtained: The dribbling score is the sum of the 10 trials in seconds: the passing score is the number of accurate passes (goals) made in the 10 trials; and the combined score is the sum of the times for the 10 trials recorded in seconds, minus 10 times the number of accurate passes (goals) on the 10 trials.

4. *Kick-Ups.* For this test each testing station consists of a 2-foot square with the inner side 3 feet from the sideline of the field. A starting line is placed 4 feet from the outside corner of the square, following an imaginary extension of the diagonal of the square (see Figure 14-9). Two students work as partners with one student throwing the ball from behind the sideline directly opposite the square. The thrower tosses the ball from overhead so that it lands in the 2-foot square. The performer (partner) stands behind the starting line until the thrower releases the ball. At that instant, the performer runs forward and does a kick-up to self. The score is the number of successful kick-ups in 10 trials.

Scoring: Each of the four items is scored separately. There are no achievement scales for the test.

In addition to the Buchanan speedball test the Smith speedball test (64) is also a useful measure.

Swimming

Fox Swimming Power Test

This test (29) measures the power of swimmers in the sidestroke and front crawl stroke. It was constructed especially for college women but is useful for high school girls and boys and for college men. Validity coeficients of .83 and .69 were reported for the sidestroke and crawl stroke, respectively, when the scores were compared with experts' ratings on swimming form. Reliability coeficients of .97 for the sidestroke and .95 for the crawl stroke have been reported.

A rope measuring about 20 feet longer than the width of the pool should be stretched across the pool at a distance of 20 feet from the end. One end of the rope should be attached to the bank while the other end remains free so that when the free end is released the rope will drop to the bottom of the pool. Adhesive tape, masking tape, or other such material is used for markers along the bank of the pool.The markers are placed at 5-foot intervals beginning at the rope. About 30 students can be tested at each station in 40 minutes.

Procedure: With the starting point at the middle of the pool the rope is pulled tight so that it is about 1 foot under the water at the starting point. The student is in a floating position (on the side for the sidestroke, on his front for the crawl stroke) with the ankles resting on the rope. On the starting signal the rope is dropped, at which time the student begins swimming from a motionless float, taking six powerful strokes.

Scoring: The score for the sidestroke is the distance, measured to the nearest foot, from the starting line to the position of the ankles at the beginning of the recovery of the sixth stroke. The score for the front crawl stroke is the distance, measured to the nearest foot, from the starting line to the point where the ankles are when the fingers enter the water at the beginning of the sixth stroke.

Other Swimming Tests

Additional tests of swimming skill are: revision of the power test (58), method of rating synchronized swimming stunts (23), and the Wilson Achievement Test (71).

Tennis

Broer-Miller Forehand–Backhand Test

This test (11) measures the tennis playing ability of college women. However, it can be used for college men and high school boys and girls. Validity and reliability of the test have not been determined.

The court is marked with chalk lines and numbers indicating the point value of each zone, as shown in Figure 14-10. A rope is stretched across the court directly above the net at a height of 7 feet. About 20 students can be tested at each station in 40 minutes.

Procedure: The student stands behind the baseline on the unmarked side of the court. He or she bounces the ball and hits it between the net and the rope, aiming for the nine-foot zone nearest the baseline on the opposite side of the court. The student has 28 trials, 14 with the forehand and 14 with the backhand.

Scoring: Each trial counts the number of the zone in which the ball first lands. A ball that is obstructed does not constitute a trial and is taken over, but a ball that is missed on the first bounce constitutes a trial. Balls that go over the top of the rope are scored half the value of the zone in which they land.

Dyer Tennis Test

The Dyer tennis test (24) measures the tennis playing ability of college women. It has also proved useful for college men and high school boys and girls. When results of the test were compared with experts' ratings, the test

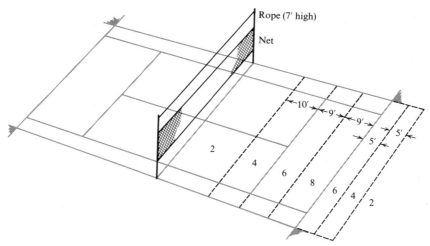

FIGURE 14-10.   Broer-Miller forehand—backhand test floor plan.

produced validity coefficients of .85 and .90; it has a reliability coefficient of .90.

A backboard or unobstructed wall space approximately 10 feet high and 15 feet wide is needed at each testing station as well as the following equipment: a stopwatch, a tennis racket, several tennis balls and a box for extra balls. About 15 students can be tested at each station in a 40-minute period.

Procedure: A line 3 inches wide is painted on the backboard to represent the height of a tennis net (36 inches from the floor to the top of the line). A restraining line 15 feet long, running parallel to the wall, is marked on the floor 5 feet from the wall. The box holding extra balls is placed at the left end of the restraining line (at the right end for left-handed players).

The students are divided into groups of four, and the students in each group are numbered one through four. They have the following responsibilities: student 1 takes the test; student 2 counts the points; student 3 watches for fouls at the restraining line; and student 4 collects the balls. The players rotate duties until all have performed the test three times.

Student 1 stands anywhere behind the restraining line holding a racket and two balls. At the starting signal he or she puts a ball into play by bouncing it on the floor and then hitting it against the wall so that it strikes above the net line. When it rebounds he hits the ball again. The objective is to volley the ball legally against the wall as many times as possible in 30 seconds. If the student loses control of the ball, he or she quickly takes another ball from the box and puts it into play. After the ball rebounds, the student may strike it again before it bounces, or may let it bounce one or more times before striking it.

Student 2 counts the number of times the ball strikes the wall on or above the net line and enters the score of student 1 on the score card. If student 3 reports any infringements, student 2 deducts them beore recording the score. A ball striking coincident with the word "stop" does not count.

Student 3 watches the player in relation to the restraining line and reports to the scorer (student 2) at the end of the trial the number of hits made while the player (student 1) was across the restraining line.

Student 4 collects the balls that have gone out of control and returns them to the box.

Scoring: The final score is the sum of the legal hits during the three trials.

Hewitt Revision of the Dyer Tennis Test

The Hewitt revision of the Dyer tennis test (32) measures the general tennis playing ability of students and classifies them for instruction. It is useful for both males and females at college and high school levels. When scores on the test were compared to the results of a round-robin tournament, validity coefficients ranging from .68 to .73 were produced for beginning players and .84 to .89 for advanced players. With the test–retest method, reliability coefficients of .82 and .93 were produced for beginning and advanced players, respectively.

A smooth wall 20 feet high and 20 feet wide is needed as well as the following equipment: a stopwatch, a tennis racket, and a basket with at least a dozen new tennis balls. A line 1 inch wide and 20 feet long is marked on the wall at a height of 3 feet from the floor to simulate the net. A restraining line about 20 feet long is placed 20 feet away from the wall. About 15 students can be tested at each station in 40 minutes.

Procedure: The student stands behind the restraining line with two balls in hand. On the signal he or she hits one of the balls against the wall above the net line, using a stroke. When the ball strikes the wall, the timer starts the stopwatch. The student rallies the ball against the wall as many times as possible in 30 seconds, using any kind of stroke desired. If the ball goes out of control, he or she serves the other ball. If the second ball goes out of control, additional balls may be taken from the basket which should be close by. Each time a new ball is taken the student must put it into play with a service stroke. The student has three trials.

Scoring: One point is counted for each time the ball hits above the 3-foot net line. No points are given for balls that strike the wall below the line or for balls that hit in front of the restraining line. A ball that hits on the net line counts. The average of the three trials is the final score.

Hewitt Tennis Achievement Test

The Hewitt tennis achievement test (32) measures a student's ability in the service, forehand, and backhand strokes. It can be used effectively for both males and females at college and high school levels. Based on the results with beginners, advanced, and varsity tennis players validity coefficients ranged from .52 to .93. The service placement test had the highest validity for varsity players, the revised Dyer wall test had the highest validity for advanced players, and the speed of service test had the highest validity for beginners. Reliability coefficients ranging from .75 to .94 have been obtained. About 20 students can be tested at each station in 40 minutes.

Procedure: Hewitt's achievement test consists of the following three test items:

1. *Service Placement Test.* The court is marked as illustrated in Figure 14-11. A small rope is stretched above the net at a height of 7 feet. Prior to administering the test the examiner should clearly describe it and demonstrate its procedure. A 10-minute warm-up should precede the performance of the test. From behind the baseline, the student serves 10 balls into the marked service court. The ball must pass between the net and the 7-foot rope. The score for each trial is the point value of the zone in which the ball hits. A ball that goes over the rope receives a score of zero. The student's final score is the sum of the points for the 10 trials.

2. *Speed of Service Test.* Four zones are designated on the court as illustrated in Figure 14-12. The objective is to cause the ball to bounce a

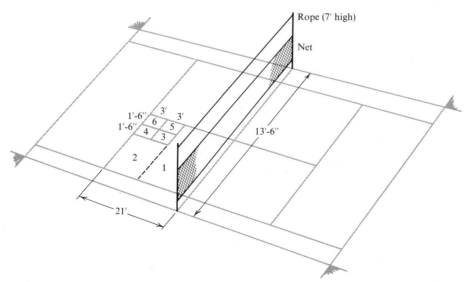

FIGURE 14-11.   Hewett tennis service placement test layout.

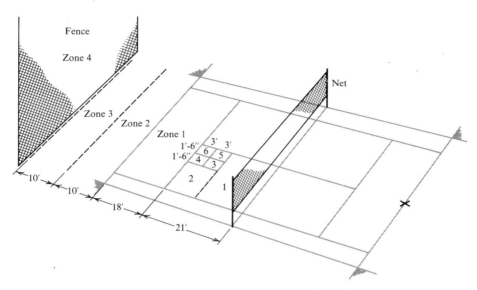

FIGURE 14-12.   Hewett tennis speed service test layout.

long distance after it strikes inside the service court. The student serves
10 balls. For each good serve the scorer notes the zone in which the
ball hits after the first bounce. The number of that zone represents the
score for that ball. The total score is the sum of the 10 serves.

3. *Forehand and Backhand Drive Tests.* The court is marked as illustrated
in Figure 14-13. A small rope is stretched above the net at a height of 7
feet. The student taking the test stands at the center mark of the baseline, while the instructor, with a basket full of balls, takes a position
across the net at the intersection of the center line and the service line
(see Figure 14-12). The instructor (or a ball-throwing machine) hits
five practice balls to the student just beyond the service court. Then
the student takes 20 official trials, 10 for the forehand and 10 for the
backhand. The student may choose which balls to hit forehand and
which to hit backhand. He or she tries to hit the ball between the net
and the rope so that the ball goes deep into the court. The same instructor should hit to all students in order to standardize the procedure
as much as possible. The score for each trial is the number of the zone
in which the ball lands.

Scoring: Each test item is scored separately. Achievement scales are not
available.

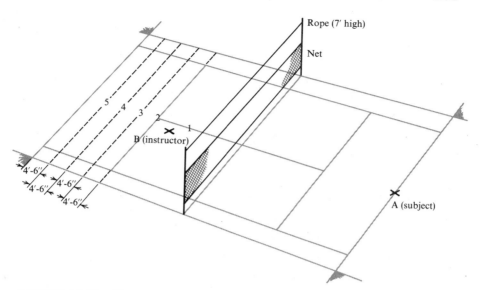

FIGURE 14-13.   Hewett tennis forehand and backhand drive test layout.

Other Tennis Tests

In addition to the forenamed tests the following tests may prove useful: Forehand and backhand drive and service tests (22), Hulac rating scale (35), and Kemp–Vincent rally test (38).

Volleyball

Chamberlain Forearm Bounce Pass Test

The Chamberlain forearm bounce pass test (15) measures the ability of college women to perform the volleyball bounce pass. A validity rating of 12.4 was determined with the use of Fisher's test of significance to determine the differences in performance by highly skilled and poorly skilled players. The test was found to be highly discriminative, with skilled players scoring high and poorly skilled players scoring low. The reliability coefficient was .78 with the use of the odd-even method. Both figures were significant at the .01 level of confidence.

Three ropes, standards to which the ropes can be attached, and three volleyballs are needed for each testing station. The floor markings are illustrated in Figure 14-14. About 15 students can be tested at each station in 40 minutes.

Procedure: A set-up person tosses the ball underhand between two ropes (5 feet and 7 feet high) to the student taking the test (see Figure 14-15). The per-

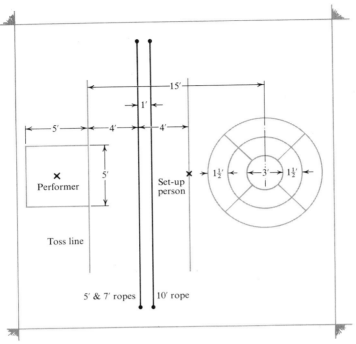

FIGURE 14-14. Floor plan for Chamberlain test (top view).

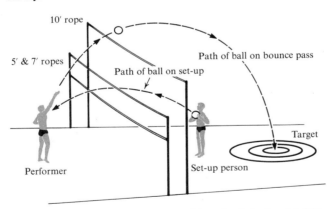

FIGURE 14-15. Floor plan for Chamberlain test (side view).

former makes a bounce pass which should go over the 10-foot rope and land on a target placed on the floor. She may move forward beyond the toss line to bounce pass the ball. The performer has 14 consecutive trials. She takes over a trial in which the ball hits any of the three ropes.

Scoring: The student scores 2 points if the ball travels over the 10-foot rope, and she receives additional points if the ball lands on one of the concentric circles of the target, which have point values of 4, 3, and 2. The inner circle has the highest point value. For balls that land on a line between concentric circles the student scores the higher value. The student does not score a target point if the ball fails to go over the 10-foot rope. A total of 6 points is possible for each trial when the height score is added to the target score.

Brady Volleyball Test

The Brady volleyball test (*10*) is a relatively simple and practical test of general volleyball playing ability. It is highly useful for classifying students for instruction or for measuring their progress in volleyball skill. Validity and reliability coefficients of .86 and .93, respectively, have been established for the test. Each testing station should have a stopwatch, a volleyball, and a smooth wall at least 15 feet high, marked according to Figure 14-16. About 2 minutes is required for each person taking the test. Several testing stations may be used.

Procedure: The student stands at the desired position in front of the wall. At the starting signal he or she throws the ball against the wall. As it rebounds he or she volleys the ball against the wall within the boundaries of the lines and continues the volley as many times as possible for one minute. If the student catches or loses control of the ball, she or he starts as at the beginning of the test by throwing the ball against the wall. Only legal volleys that hit the wall within the rectangle on or above the 11-foot 6-inch line are counted. A legal volley is determined by the definition in the official volleyball rule book.

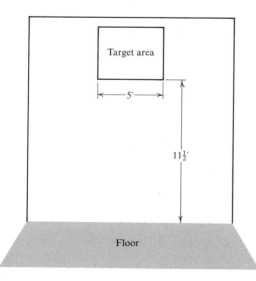

Target area

5′

$11\frac{1}{2}'$

Floor

FIGURE 14-16. Brady volleyball test floor plan.

Scoring: The number of legal volleys in 1 minute constitutes the score. When the test is used for classifying students, the scores may be arranged according to size and then divided into as many subgroups as desired. As a basis for determining skill improvement, the difference in scores made by students before and after a program of instruction may be compared. When it seems desirable to take into account differences in the starting levels of the students along with the skill development, progress may be measured by computing the difference between the scores on the first test and the last test, then adding the score on the last test. For example, if a student scored 16 at the beginning of a unit of instruction and 24 at the end of the unit, the score would be $24 - 16 = 8$, plus 24. The total score would be 32. Achievement scales are not available for this test.

Clifton Single Hit Volley Test

The single hit volley test (17) measures volleying ability of college women. It may also be used for college men and high school boys and girls. With experts' ratings of volleying as the criterion measure the test produced a validity coefficient of .70. With the test–retest method it produced a reliability coefficient of .83.

The test requires a stopwatch, an official volleyball, and a smooth wall. A Line 10 feet long is placed on the wall 7½ feet above the floor. A restraining line 10 feet long is placed on the floor 7 feet from the wall. The ceiling should be high enough to permit ample space for volleying above the 7½ foot line. If the students are alternated so that the testing station is in continuous use, about 20 students can be tested at each station in 40 minutes.

Procedure: The student stands behind the restraining line and on the signal tosses the ball underhand against the wall. Then she or he volleys the ball as many times as possible above the 7½ foot line on the wall. All volleys must be legal hits, according to the official volleyball rules, and should be made from behind the restraining line. If the student loses control of the ball, the student must recover it and put the ball back into play with an underhand toss from behind the restraining line. At the end of the first 30-second trial the student takes a two-minute rest after which she or he begins another 30-second trial.

Scoring: The score is the number of legal volleys touching on or above the 7½ foot line on the wall. No score is allowed for illegal hits or for hits made from on or in front of the restraining line. The total score is the sum of the scores for both trials.

Brumbach Volleyball Service Test

The Brumbach volleyball service test (13) measures the student's ability to serve the volleyball low and deep into the opponent's court. A rope is stretched 4 feet above the volleyball net. (In most cases extensions will need to be at-

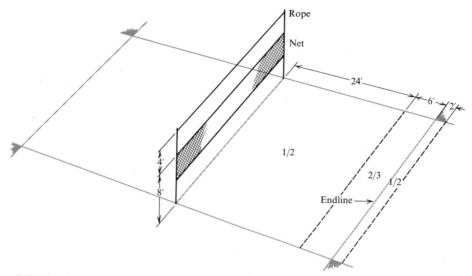

FIGURE 14-17. Brumbach service test floor plan.

tached to the standards.) The floor is marked as illustrated in Figure 14-17. About 20 students can be tested at each station in 40 minutes.

Procedure: The student stands behind the baseline. Without a practice trial he or she attempts to serve a volleyball so that the ball crosses the net without touching, goes underneath the rope, and lands in the opposite court. The student tries to have the ball land as near the baseline of the court as possible.

Scoring: A ball that passes between the rope and net is given the higher of the two values for the particular zone in which the ball lands. A ball that goes over the rope receives the smaller value. A foot fault, a ball that hits the net, and a ball that lands outside the scoring zones count zero. The student is given 12 trials in two sets of six. The final score is the sum of the point values for the 10 best trials. A perfect score would be 30.

Other Volleyball Tests

Additional tests for evaluating volleyball skills are: test for the pass (*43*), test for high school boys (*40*), a High Wall Volley Test (*20*), and AAHPER Volleyball Test (*7*).

Selected References

1. American Alliance for Health, Physical Education and Recreation: *Archery Skills Test Manual*. Washington D.C.: American Alliance for Health, Physical Education and Recreation, 1967.
2. American Association for Health, Physical Education and Recreation: *Basketball Skills Test Manual for Boys*. Washington, D.C.: AAHPER, 1966.
3. American Association for Health, Physical Education and Recreation: *Basketball Skills Test Manual for Girls*. Washington, D.C., AAHPER, 1966.
4. American Alliance for Health, Physical Education and Recreation: *Football Skills Test Manual*. Washington D.C.: AAHPER, 1966.
5. American Alliance for Health, Physical Education, and Recreation: *Softball Skills Test Manual for Boys*, Washington, D.C.: AAHPER, 1967.
6. American Alliance for Health, Physical Education and Recreation: *Softball Skills Test Manual for Girls*, Washington, D.C.: AAHPER 1967.
7. American Alliance for Health, Physical Education, and Recreation: *Volleyball Skills Test Manual*, Washington, D.C.: AAHPER, 1967.
8. Borleske, S. C.: A study of achievement of college men in touch football. *Research Quarterly*, 8:73, 1937.
9. Brace, D. K.: Validity of football achievement tests as measures of motor learning and as a partial basis for the selection of players. *Research Quarterly*, 14:372, 1943.
10. Brady, G. F.: *Preliminary investigations of volleyball playing ability*. *Research Quarterly*, 16:14–17, 1945.
11. Broer, M. R., and Miller, D. M.: Achievement tests for beginning and intermediate tennis. *Research Quarterly* 21:303, 1950.
12. Brown, H. S.: A test battery for evaluating golf skills. *Texas Association for Health, Physical Education, and Recreation Journal*, pp. 4–5, 28–29, May 1969.
13. Brumbach, W.: *Beginning Volleyball, A Syllabus for Teachers*, rev. ed. Eugene, Ore.: Wayne Baker Brumbach (distributed by University of Oregon), 1967.
14. Buchanan, R. E.: A Study of Achievement Tests in Speedball for High School Girls. Unpublished master's thesis, State University of Iowa, 1942.
15. Chamberlain, D.: Determination of Validity and Reliability of a Skill Test for the Bounce Pass in Volleyball. Unpublished master's thesis, Brigham Young University, 1968.
16. Clevett, M. A.: An experiment in teaching methods in golf. *Research Quarterly*, 2:104, 1931.
17. Clifton, M. A.: Single hit volley test for women's volleyball. *Research Quarterly*, 33:208–211, 1949.
18. Cochrane, J. F.: The Construction of an Indoor Golf Skills Test as a Measure of Golfing Ability. Unpublished master's thesis, University of Minnesota, 1960.
19. Cornish, C.: A study of measurement of ability in handball. *Research Quarterly*, 20:215–222, 1949.
20. Cunningham, P. and Garrison, J.: High wall volley test for women's volleyball. *Research Quarterly*, 29:480–490, 1968.
21. Dexter, G.: *Teachers' Guide to Physical Education for Girls in High School*. Sacramento, Calif.: State Department of Education, 1957, p. 316.

22. **DiGennaro, J.**: Construction of forehand drive, backhand drive, and service tennis tests. *Research Quarterly*, 40:496–501, 1969.

23. **Durrant, S. M.**: An analytical method of rating synchronized swimming stunts. *Research Quarterly*, 35:126–134, 1964.

24. **Dyer, J. T.**: The backboard test of tennis ability. *Supplement to the Research Quarterly*, 6:63, 1935.

25. **Faulkner, J.**, and **Loken, N.**: Objectivity of judging at the national collegiate athletic association gymnastic meet: A ten-year follow-up study. *Research Quarterly* 33:485–486, 1962.

26. **French, E.** and **Stalter, E.**: "Study of Skill Tests in Badminton for College Women." *Research Quarterly*, 20:257, 1949.

27. **Friedel J.**: The Development of a Field Hockey Skill Test for High School Girls. Microcarded master's thesis, Illinois State Normal University, 1956.

28. **Fringer, M. N.**: A Battery of Softball Skill Tests for Senior High School Girls. Unpublished master's thesis, University of Michigan, 1969.

29. **Fox, M. G.**: Swimming power test. *Research Quarterly* 23:233, 237, 1957.

30. **Fox, M. G.**, and **Young, Olive G.**: A test of softball batting ability. *Research Quarterly*, 25:26, 1954.

31. **Heaton, A.**: *Techniques of Teaching Ballroom Dance*. Provo, Utah: Brigham Young University press, 1965.

32. **Hewitt, J. E.**: Hewitt's tennis achievement test. *Research Quarterly*, 37:321–327, 1966.

33. **Hopkins, D. R.**: Factor analysis of selected basketball skill tests. *Research Quarterly*, 48:535–540, 1977.

34. **Hyde, E. I.**: National research study in archery. *Research Quarterly*, 7:64–73, 1936.

35. **Hulac, G. M.**: Hulac rating scale for the tennis serve in H. M. Barrow and R. McGee. in *A Practical Approach to Measurement in Physical Education*, Philadelphia, Pa., Lea & Febiger, 1972, pp. 325–326.

36. **Johnson, B. L.**: A Screening test for pole vaulting and selected gymnastic events. *Journal of Health, Physical Education and Recreation* 44:71–72, May 1973.

37. **Johnson, J. R.**: The Development of a Single-Item Test as a Measure of Soccer Skill. Microcarded master's thesis, University of British Columbia, 1963.

38. **Kemp, J.** and **Vincent, M. F.**: Kemp–Vincent rally test of tennis skill. *Research Quarterly*, 39:1000–1004, 1968.

39. **Knox, R. O.**: Basketball ability tests, *Scholastic Coach*, 17:45, 1947.

40. **Kronquist, R. A.** and **Brumbach, W. B.**: A modification of the Brady volleyball test for high school boys. *Research Quarterly*, 39:116–120, 1968.

41. **Lamp, N. A.**: Volleyball skills of junior high school students as a function of physical size and maturity. *Research Quarterly*, 25:189, 1954.

42. **Leilich, A.**: The Primary Components of Selected Basketball Tests for College Women. Unpublished doctoral dissertation, Indiana Unversity, 1952.

43. **Liba, M. R.**, and **Stauff, Marilyn R.**: A test for the volleyball pass. *Research Quarterly*, 34:56–63, 1963.

44. **Lockhart**, and **McPherson, Frances A.**: Development of a test of badminton playing ability. *Research Quarterly*, 20:402–405, 1945.

45. **Martin, J. L.**: Bowling norms for college men and women. *Research Quarterly*, 31:113, 1960.

46. **McDonald, L. G.**: The Contruction of a Kicking Skill Test as an Index of General Soccer Ability. Unpublished master's thesis, Springfield College, 1951.
47. **McKee, M. E.**: A test for the full swinging shot in golf. *Res. Q.* 21:40, 1950.
48. **Merrifield, H. H.** and **Walford, G. A.**: Battery of ice hockey skill tests. *Res. Q.* 40:146–152, 1969.
49. **Miller, F. A.**: A badminton wall volley test. *Res. Q.* 22:208, 1951.
50. **Miller, W. K.**: Achievement levels in basketball skills for women physical education majors. *Res. Q.* 25:450, 1954.
51. **Montoye, H. J.** and **Brotzmann, J.**: An investigation of the validity of using the results of a doubles tournament as a measure of handball ability. *Res. Q.* 22: 214–218, 1951.
52. **Nelson, J. K.**: An Achievement Test for Golf. Unpublished study, Louisiana State University, 1967.
53. **Nelson, J. K.**: The Measurement of Shooting and Passing Skills in Basketball. Unpublished study, Louisiana State University, 1967.
54. **O'Donnell, D. J.**: Validation of Softball Skill Tests for High School Girls. Unpublished master's thesis, Indiana University, 1950.
55. **Olson, J. K.** and **Liba, M. R.**: A device for evaluating spot bowling ability. *Res. Q.*
56. **Phillips, M.**, and **Summers, D.**: Bowling norms and learning curves for college women. *Res. Q.* 21:377, 1950.
57. **Recknagal, D.**: A test for beginners in figure skating. *Journal of Health and Physical Education* 16:91–92, 1945.
58. **Rosentswieg, J.**: A revision of the power swimming test. *Res. Q.* 39:818–819, 1968.
59. **Russell, N.** and **Lange, E.**: Achievement tests in volleyball for junior high school girls. *Res. Q.* 25:189, 1954.
60. **Schmithals, M.** and **French, E.**: Achievement tests in field hockey for college women. *Res. Q.* 11:84, 1940.
61. **Scott, M. G.** and **French, E.**: *Measurement and Evaluation in Physical Education.* Dubuque, Iowa: William C. Brown Co. Publishers, 1959, pp. 199–202.
62. **Shaufele, E. F.**: The Establishment of Objective Tests or Girls of the Ninth and Tenth Grades to Determine Soccer Ability. Unpublished master's thesis, State University of Iowa, 1940.
63. **Shick, J.**: Battery of defensive softball skills tests for college women, *Res. Q.* 41:82–87, 1970.
64. **Smith, G.**: Speedball Skill Tests for College Women. Unpublished study, Illinois State Normal University, 1947.
65. **Stroup, F.**: Game results as a criterion for validating basketball skill tests. *Res. Q.* 26:353, 1955.
66. **Thorpe, J.** and **West, C.**: A test of game sense in badminton. *Perceptual and Motor Skills*, 28:159–69, 1969.
67. **Vanderhoof, E. R.**: Beginning Golf Achievement Tests. Microcarded master's thesis, University of Oregon, 1956.
68. **Voltmer, E. F.**, and **Watts, T.**: A rating scale of player performance in basketball. *J. Health and Physical Education*, 11:94, 1940.
69. **Warner, F. H.**: Warner soccer test, *Newsletter of the National Soccer Coaches Association of America*, 6:13–22, 1950.
70. **West, C.** and **Thorpe, J.**: Construction and validation of an eight-iron approach test. *Res. Q.* 39:1115–1120, 1968.

71. **Wilson, M. R.**: A Relationship Between General Motor Ability and Objective Measures of Achievement in Swimming at the Intermediate Level for College Women. Unpublished master's thesis, The Women's College of the University of North Carolina, 1962.

72. **Young, G.**, and **Moser, H.**: A short battery of tests to measure playing ability in women's basketball. *Res. Q.* 5:3, 1934.

73. **Zabick, R. M.** and **Jackson, A. S.**: Reliability of archery achievement. *Res. Q.* 40:254–255, 1969.

V

Non Physical
Performance
Measures

15

Measures of Body Structure and Mechanics

Sculptors in ancient India, Egypt, Athens, and Rome measured individuals in various ways in attempts to find the ideal structure and proportions of man. Throughout history great athletic performers have been studied to determine the unique features of their structures. In the United States Edward Hitchcock at Amherst College in the 1860s, and Dudley A. Sargent, first at Yale and later at Harvard, made many structural measurements of college students and prepared profile charts. Since then numerous other studies have been completed. At present, with our knowledge about body structure and with the aid of measurements, we can recognize individual differences and appraise individual potential with more insight.

Body Fat Measurements

Skinfold Measurement

With the current emphasis on improving physical fitness and function, it is appropriate to include in this text tests for measuring body fat. The skinfold test which makes use of calipers is the most accurate method that is usable outside the research laboratory for measuring body fat. Age–height–weight charts can give only an estimate of a person's desirable weight, but the skinfold test provides an accurate measure of the amount of fat on the body as well as the distribution of the fat.

Equipment: A calibrated set of skin calipers that measures in millimeters. (See Figure 15-1.)

213

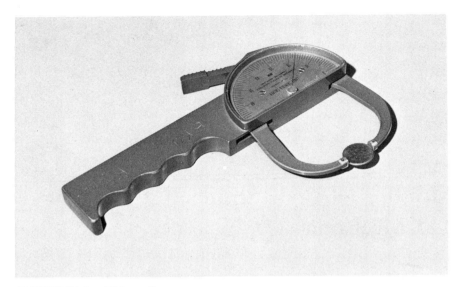

FIGURE 15-1. Skin calipers.

Procedures: Make all measurements on the right side of the body. Grasp
the skin between the thumb and index finger. Include skin and subcutaneous
fat without any muscle tissue. The skinfold should be in the vertical direction.
Apply the calipers about 1 centimeter from the fingers that are holding the
skinfold, and at a depth about equal to the thickness of the fold. Repeat the
procedure three times from the same location and average the measurements.

Precaution: All measurements should be made by trained technicians at
about the same time of day for each subject.
  Specific instructions for men:
  The following sites should be used for determining total body fat:

  1. *Thigh*—Locate a vertical skinfold in the anterior midline of the thigh,
     halfway between the inguinal ligament and the top of the patella. (See
     Figure 15-2.)
  2. *Subscapular*—Locate a skinfold running downward and laterally in the
     natural fold of the skin from the inferior angle of the scapula. (See Fig-
     ure 15-3.)

With a straightedge, align the thigh value in colum A with the subscapular
value in column B. Read the percent body fat where the straightedge crosses
the middle column.

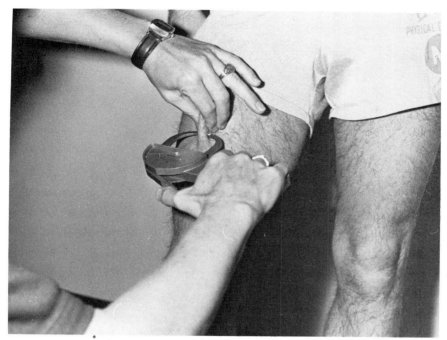

FIGURE 15-2. Skinfold in the midline of the thigh.

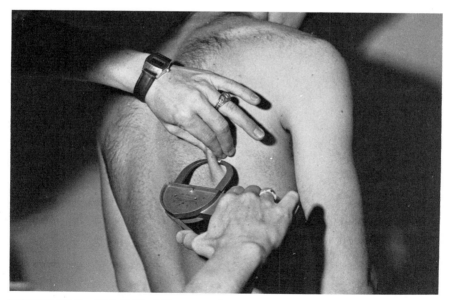

FIGURE 15-3. Skinfold of the scapula.

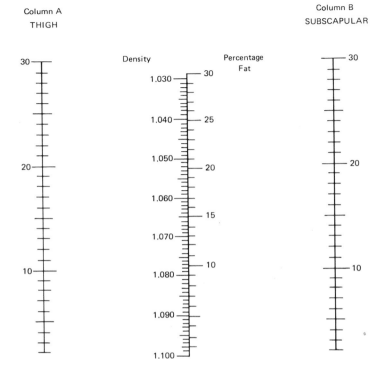

Sloan-Weir nomogram for prediction of body density and total body fat—MEN.

Specific instructions for women:
The following sites should be used for determining total body fat:

1. *Iliac crest*—Locate an almost horizontal skinfold on the hip crest at the
   point on the body where the front of the arm touches the hip when the
   arm is hanging vertically. (See Figure 15-4.)
2. *Triceps*—Locate the point halfway between the tip of the shoulder and
   the tip of the elbow with the elbow at a 90-degree angle. Measure the
   skinfold with the arm relaxed and hanging vertically. (See Figure
   15-5.)

With a straightedge, align the iliac crest measurement in column A with the
triceps value in column B. Read the percent body fat value where the straightedge crosses the middle column.
The following table is presented for college-age persons as an indication of
body fat categories for use in evaluating the skinfold measurements.

Percent Body Fat Norms

Category	Men (%)	Women (%)
I. Very Poor	20+	28+
II. Poor	18–19	23–27
III. Fair	15–17	18–22
IV. Good	11–14	13–17
V. Excellent	8–10	10–12

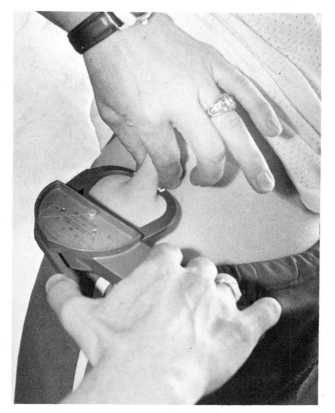

FIGURE 15-4. Skinfold on the hip crest.

Hydrostatic Weighing

Hydrostatic weighing is a method of assessing body volume that is based on Archimedes' principle of water displacement. This method of assessing body fat is used in the research laboratory and is not a practical method to be used in a classroom or gymnasium. The weighing of the subject under water is usually

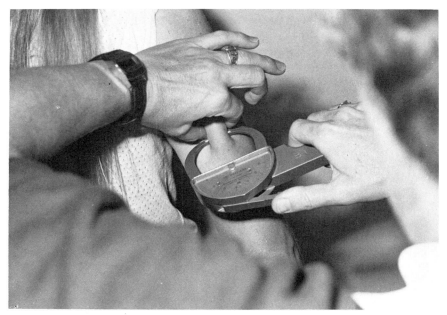

FIGURE 15-5. Skinfold on the triceps.

accomplished by having the subject sit in a chair that is supported by a weight scale and is lowered into a specially constructed tank that is filled with water.

Measures of Body Type

Amount of body fat, extent of muscular development, and dimensions of body structure are factors generally used in evaluating physique or body type. Within certain limits diet and exercise may affect the development of musculature and amount of fatty tissue, but not basic body type (morphology), which results from heredity.

Observation of individual athletes and research both indicate that body build relates considerably to one's ability to perform. A certain body build may be an advantage or a disadvantage in performance, depending on the nature of the activity. For example, height is clearly an advantage in basketball and volleyball. Generally it is less advantageous in skating, ice hockey, and football and still less advantageous in soccer, gymnastics, and wrestling. A tall and heavy stature is an advantage in the shot put, discus throw, and hammer throw but a distinct disadvantage in the two-mile run and in several gymnastic activities. People of medium structure with well-developed muscles are generally good

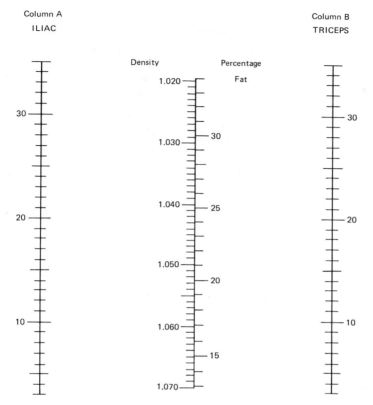

Column A
ILIAC

Column B
TRICEPS

Density   Percentage
           Fat

Sloan-Weir nomogram for prediction of body density and total body fat—WOMEN.
Young women. X_1 = suprailiac skinfold thickness (mm) and X_2 = back of arm skinfold thickness (mm).

performers in such sports as swimming, gymnastics, and wrestling; and people with slight builds tend to do reasonably well in track events, especially distance running, and in some individual and dual sports.

A study of the physiques and ages of the champions in the Olympic Games furnishes evidence of the relationship of body build to performance. The Olympic basketball players and the volleyball net players were lean and tall, did not have excessive weight, and did not have a great deal of muscularity. The hockey and soccer players were rather small but stout. The gymnasts were generally small but strong. The weight lifters had short arms and were heavy and strong. The shot, discus, and hammer throwers were large and strong; the high jumpers, tall and lean. The pole vaulters were shorter and heavier because of the strength needed in the arms and shoulder girdle muscles. The distance runners, requiring much endurance, tended to be lean and small, more so as the distances increased, and the short-distance runners were heavier because of the demand for strength and speed. In addition to the Olympic athletes described, football linemen tend to be large and heavy; ends, tall and lighter; and backs, lighter than the linemen. Of course there are exceptions to these generalizations.

Knowledge that body build and size influence performance in certain ways can be useful to physical education teachers and coaches. This knowledge is especially useful for predictive purposes among those who coach athletic teams. However, no student should be deprived of opportunities to excel in any activity simply because his or her body build deviates from those who *usually* excel in the activity.

Sheldon's Somatotype System

Of the various methods used to classify people by physique or body build the somatotype classification (13) designed by William H. Sheldon, is generally the most useful in physical education. Somatotyping may be applied to boys, girls, men, and women. With Sheldon's system individuals may be classified accord-

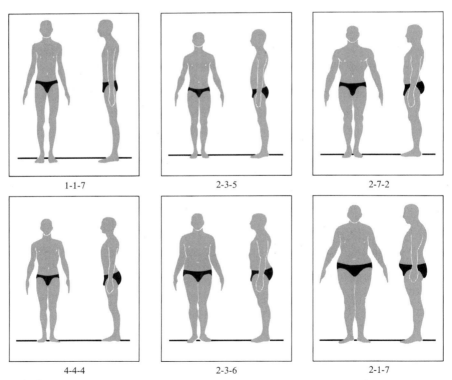

1-1-7	2-3-5	2-7-2
4-4-4	2-3-6	2-1-7

FIGURE 15-6.   Examples of somatotypes rated according to Sheldon's Somatotype System.

ing to endomorphic, mesomorphic, or ectomorphic characteristics (see Figure 15-6).

The endomorph tends to be thickset, and the body has a large amount of viscera and fatty tissue. He or she has a large round head; relatively short, thick neck; short, thick arms; thick chest with fatty breasts; thick, fatty abdomen, heavy buttocks, and thick legs. In general the endomorph has a pear-shaped structure and tends toward obesity.

The mesomorph, often referred to as the athletic type, has heavy, well-defined muscles throughout, large bones, broad shoulders, relatively narrow hips, large hands and arms. In general the mesomorph has a V-shaped structure.

The ectomorph has small bones; light, fairly undefined musculature; long, slender arms; small chest; flat, slender abdomen; narrow hips, and slender legs. The ectomorph may be described as the beanpole type.

Nearly all persons possess a mixture of the traits of the three primary body types. Therefore, three ratings are used to identify a person's body types, one rating for each component. Each rating is signified by a number between 1 and 7, with the higher numbers indicating dominance of that particular component. The first number refers to endomorphy, the second to mesomorphy, and the third to ectomorphy. Thus a person rated 7–1–1 would have dominant endomorphic characteristics and would lack mesomorphic and ectomorphic characteristics. A person with prominent mesomorphic characteristics might be rated 1–7–1, and one with prominent ectomorphic traits might receive a 1–1–7 rating. Most people would not receive a 1 or 7 rating. More typical would be ratings of 2–6–4 or 5–3–2.[4]

Except for research purposes somatotyping in the schools will probably continue to be done by judgment based on observation, rather than detailed objective measurements.

Parnell's M.4 Deviation Chart

Parnell (10) divided height by the cube root of weight to determine ectomorphy; used the skinfold measures for the triceps, subscapular, and suprailiac measures to determine endomorphy; the bone diameter of humerus and femur and girth measures of biceps and calf to determine mesomorphy. Photography was used to provide a permanent record of the physique.

Heath and Carter Somatotype Rating Method

Heath and Carter (4) added skinfold to Parnell's measures in the assessment of mesomorphy. Parnell's scoring methods were changed and the measurement scales were reused.

---

[4] For greater detail about somatotyping refer to Sheldon's *Atlas of Man* in which he describes the entire somatotyping process and uses a large number of photographs to identify different body types.

Posture and Body Mechanics

Posture refers to the relative positions of the different body segments. Posture is both static (body position while sitting and standing) and dynamic (body position during movement). Because dynamic posture is difficult to judge, there is a tendency to evaluate posture in only the standing and the sitting position. Silhouettes, photographs, posture charts, and posture rating scales have been used in evaluating the posture of students.

Correct posture is important because it enhances the functioning of the organic systems; reduces the strain on muscles, ligaments, and tendons and thereby retards the onset of muscle fatigue; increases the attractiveness of the person; and may influence the self-concept of the person and the view of others toward him or her.

Although there are postural guides that apply in general, no precise standard of posture can be applied to all persons. Individual differences in structure and function result in part from heredity, and posture must be evaluated from the physiological, anatomical, and aesthetic points of view.

Physiological Correctness

Posture is physiologically correct when it allows the body systems to function efficiently. Posture which restricts circulation, respiration, digestion, and elimination is less than correct. Research indicates that changes in posture can influence heart rate in static positions and also can affect cardiac output during exercise.

Anatomical Correctness

Posture is anatomically correct when the body is in good balance and alignment for the least amount of muscle strain. Posture with each weight-bearing segment balanced upon the segment beneath demands less muscular effort than posture with segments formed in a zigzag alignment. Anatomically the best posture has body structure in good alignment and muscles as relaxed as possible.

Aesthetic Correctness

Posture is aesthetically correct when it contributes most to the attractiveness of the person. Aesthetically correct posture also tends to be anatomically and physiologically correct (see Figure 15-7). The concept of aesthetic posture may change slightly from time to time and from one segment of society to another: What is aesthetically correct for fashion models and for military personnel is indeed different.

Posture has strong psychological implications. A shy person may display a withdrawn type of posture to be less obvious, while a highly aggressive person may display a straight and outgoing type of posture to be more obvious.

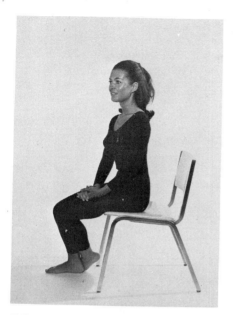 

FIGURE 15-7. Illustrations of good posture, sitting and standing.

Evaluation of Posture

Postural evaluation considers both the lateral and anteroposterior alignments of the different body segments. Spinal deviations include kyphosis (hunchbacked curvature), lordosis (exaggerated forward curvature in the lower part of the back), scoliosis (lateral curvature), and forward tilt of the head. Other deviations are rounded shoulders and sunken chest, lateral or medial rotation of the legs and feet, and abdominal ptosis (sagging). The following guides should be considered in the evaluation of posture:

1. The weight-bearing body segments should be correctly aligned.
2. The extension of the weight-bearing joints should be an easy extension, not rigid and tense.
3. The feet should point straight forward and be placed far enough apart to form a base of support so that the body can be easily balanced.
4. Excessive forward or lateral tilt of the pelvis should be avoided.
5. The spinal column, viewed from the rear, should be straight and the natural curves of the spine, viewed laterally, should not be excessive.
6. The abdominal wall should have good tone and should be kept flat.
7. The chest should not be sunken and the shoulders should not rotate forward.
8. The neck should be held straight so that the neck muscles are not under unnecessary strain.

Postural Screening Tests

Even though most postural deviations are apparent to one who knows correct posture, there are some postural screening tests that may be helpful to teachers who have little or no instruction on posture deviation and correction.

The manual for the New York State Fitness Test (9) includes a convenient

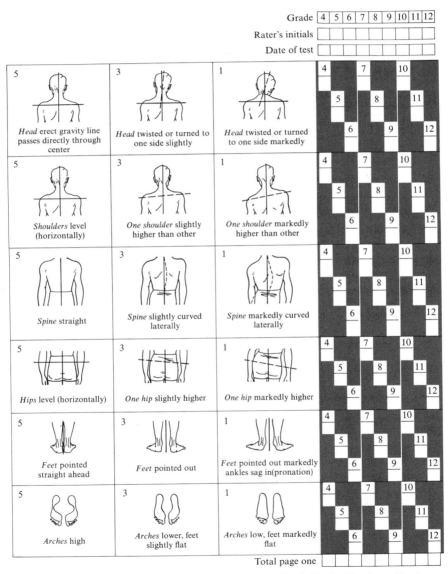

FIGURE 15-8.   Posture profiles from the New York State Posture Test.

posture rating system. This system includes a series of profiles (see Figure 15-8 against which any student's posture may be compared).

Procedure: The examiner hangs a plumb line from a stationary support about 4 feet in front of a screen or other suitable background against which to

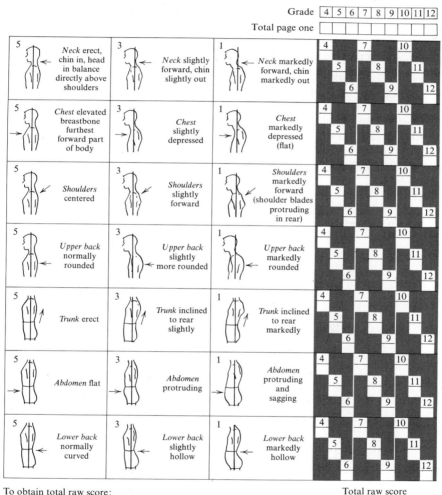

To obtain total raw score:
1. Determine the score for each of the above 13 items as follows:
    5 points if description in left hand column applies
    3 points if description in middle column applies
    1 point if description in right hand column applies
2. Enter score for each item under proper grade in the scoring column
3. Add all 13 scores and place total in appropriate space

FIGURE 15-8. (continued)

view the student. Then at a right angle from the screen he or she passes a line of masking tape directly under the plumb line and extends it 10 feet toward him or her (see Figure 15-9). In the first part of the examination the student stands between the screen and the plumb line facing the screen, directly over the line of masking tape so the plumb line passes directly up the middle of the back. The examiner then rates the student's posture from the rear view by comparing the student with the rear view profiles (see Figure 15-9). In a similar fashion the student assumes a side position and the examiner completes the examination.

Scoring: The examiner assigns a score of 5, 3, or 1 for each body area, according to the profile that best matches the student and records the score in the square corresponding to the student's grade level. Then the 13 scores are totaled to obtain a final score and the final score is compared to the norm based on a percentile scale (see Table 15-1).

Other useful posture tests are the Kraus–Weber Refined Posture Test (5) the Massey Posture Test (7), the Wellesley Posture Test (6) and the Wickens and Kiphuth Posture Test (15)

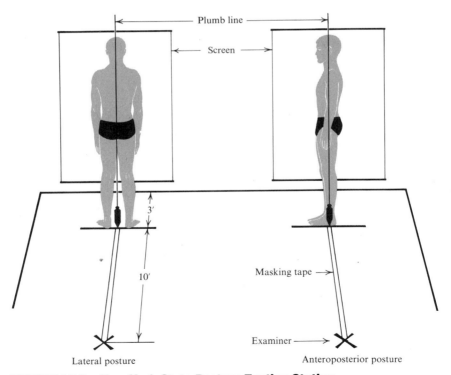

FIGURE 15-9. New York State Posture Testing Station.

TABLE 15·1 Norms for the New York State Posture Test

Final Score	Percentile
65	98
63	93
61	84
59	69
55–57	50
49–53	31
39–43	7
35–37	2
0–33	1

Growth and Nutrition

In combination growth (change in size) and development (change in function) are a process of maturation. In some cases development may affect growth, since growth changes are largely a result of maturation rate. The teacher has more influence over and more concern with development than with growth and therefore may only indirectly affect growth.

Growth tends to be continuous, but its rate is not constant; it follows a pattern of spurts and plateaus. Variations in growth rate occur among different individuals and also in the same individual from time to time. Many variations in growth rate are simply normal irregularities, but some variations may result from illness, body defects, nutrition changes, and environmental changes. Glandular malfunctions may produce excessive growth or may retard growth. Because of irregularities in growth rate, a child's present growth status and rate are best compared with his or her own record of the past rather than with the growth rate of other persons.

Wetzel Grid

Norman C. Wetzel (15) developed a chart known as the Wetzel Grid based on age, height, and weight and used to show the growth rate of children.

Wetzel classified physique into nine categories on the grid so that the plottings of a child's age, height, and weight determine his or her position on the chart. Plottings at reasonable age intervals (at least once a year) show the child's growth status in relation to the normal growth expectation. Children who proceed normally tend to remain in their channel on the chart. If they deviate from their channel, they should be given special attention to determine the cause of deviation and the means for correction. Its primary purpose is to identify children who need special attention because of abnormal growth patterns. The chart is especially useful for early identification of malnourishment.

In his original study Wetzel compared the grid ratings of 2093 children, in kindergarten through grade 12, with physicians' appraisals. There was an 87.5 percent agreement between the physicians' ratings and the grid ratings. When one of the categories (fair) was omitted from the comparison of results, the percentage of agreement between the physicians and the grid increased to 94.5 percent.

Since Wetzel's original study, several other studies involving the Wetzel Grid have been completed.[1] The evidence indicates that this technique is useful for identifying abnormal growth patterns, provided the child is located in the correct channel in the beginning.

Pryor Weight–Width Tables

Because of the inadequacy of age–height–weight standards for evaluating nutritional status, Helen Pryor (12) developed a set of weight–width tables for persons between the ages of 1 and 41 years. The tables are designed to serve as a basis for screening individuals with nutritional deficiencies. This useful system for measuring nutritional status takes into account the bony framework and body structure in addition to age, height, weight, and sex.

To use these tables the teacher records the child's age to the nearest year, height to the nearest one-quarter inch, and weight to the nearest pound. Hip width (biilliac diameter) is measured with calipers to the nearest one-tenth centimeter. Chest width is also measured with calipers to the nearest one-tenth centimeter. Then the teacher selects the appropriate table according to the child's age, sex, and chest width, and opposite the child's height and under his or her biilliac diameter the appropriate weight in pounds can be determined. Finally, the child's actual weight is compared with the appropriate weight. On the basis of such a comparison the teacher can identify students who show signs of malnutrition.[2] Students identified as malnourished should be placed under the direction of the school medical staff.

Meredith Height–Weight Chart

Howard Meredith (8) constructed a useful zone classification system for height and weight of boys and girls ages 4 through 18 years. His chart contains curved zones for height and weight on which the child's growth progress can be plotted. There are five zones for height: *tall, moderately tall, average, moderately short,* and *short.* Similarly there are five zones for weight: *heavy, moderately heavy, average, moderately light,* and *light.* The height zones are at the top of the chart and the weight zones at the bottom.

After the child's height and weight are plotted at the appropriate age columns, an immediate check is available to see whether the child's height and weight are in similar zones; a moderately short child is expected to be light; a tall child, heavy; and so on. If the zones are dissimilar, the child's physique

---

[1] Copies of the Wetzel Grid chart along with specific instructions for its use may be obtained from the NEA Service, Inc., 1200 West 3rd St., Cleveland, Ohio.

[2] Pryor's Weight–Width Tables may be obtained from the Stanford University Press, Stanford, California. The tables are accompanied by specific instructions for measuring and scoring.

may account for the dissimilarity, for example, a child may be naturally tall and slender, or short and stocky. If this is not the case, then further examination should be made for possible health problems such as malnutrition, obesity, and illness. Moreover, as successive plottings are made, growth patterns can be observed. A child's height and weight will essentially parallel each other in that they will proceed along the same zones. Any marked deviation from one zone to another is usually cause for referral.[3]

Selected References

1. **Allsen, P., J. Harrison,** and **Vance, B.** *Fitness for Life: An Individualized Approach.* Dubuque, Iowa: Wm. C. Brown Co., 1977
2. **Behnke, A. R.,** and **Wilmore H. H.**; *Evaluation and Regulation of Body Build and Composition.* Englewood Cliffs, N.J.: Prentice-Hall, 1974.
3. **Hafen, B. Q.** (Ed.): *Overweight and Obesity: Causes, Fallacies, Treatment,* Provo, Utah: Brigham Young University Press, 1975.
4. **Heath, B. H.,** and **J. E. L. Carter.** A Modified Somatotype Method, *American Journal of Physical Anthropology* 27–57, July 1967.
5. **Kraus, H.,** and **Weber, S.**: Evaluation of posture based on structural and functional measurements, *Physiotherapy Review, 26* (6), 1945.
6. **MacEwan, C. G.,** and **Howe, E. C.**: An objective method of grading posture *Research Quarterly* 3 (3), 1932.
7. **Massey, W. W.**: A critical study of objective methods for measuring anteriorposterior posture with a simplified technique, *Research Quarterly 14* (1), 1943.
8. **Meredith, H. V.**: A physical growth record for use in elementary and high schools, *American Journal of Public Health,* 39:878–885, 1949.
9. *The New York State Physical Fitness Test: A Manual for Teachers of Physical Education.* Albany, N.Y.: Division of Health, Physical Education and Recreation, New York State Education Department, 1958.
10. **Parmel, R. W.**: *Behavior and Physique* London: Edward Arnold Ltd.
11. *Physical Fitness Research Digest,* Series 5, No. 2, April 1978. Published by the President's Council on Physical Fitness and Sports, Washington, D.C.
12. **Pryor, H. B.**: *Weight–Width Tables.* Stanford, Calif.: Stanford University Press, 1940.
13. **Sheldon, W. H.**: *The Treatment of Growth Failure in Children.* Cleveland, Ohio: NEA Service, 1948.
14. **Sloan, A. W.,** and **J. B. deVe Weir**: Nomograms for prediction of body density and total body fat prediction: from skinfold measurements. *Journal of Applied Physiology,* 28:221, 1970.
15. **Wetzel, N.C.**: The treatment of growth failure in children. Cleveland, Ohio: NEA Service, 1948.
16. **Wickens, J.,** and **Kiphuth, O.**: Body mechanics analysis of Yale University freshmen. *Research Quarterly,* 3(4), 1937.

[3] Copies of Meredith's chart along with specific instruction may be obtained from the American Medical Association, 535 N. Dearborn St., Chicago, Illinois or from the National Education Association, 1201 Sixteenth St., N.W., Washington, D.C.

16

Measures of Personality Traits

There are only a few noteworthy instruments in physical education that measure personality traits (interests, attitudes, emotional behavior, and character). Much additional work needs to be done in this area of measurement.

Ratings of Interests

People involved in physical education are interested in participating in physical activities as well as in learning about their organization, techniques, and environment. In addition, rather than participate, other people may enjoy watching the active participants or reading in newspapers and magazines about such participation. This widespread interest on the part of participants and observers helps to maintain the interscholastic, intercollegiate, and professional sports.

When making studies of human interests physical educators frequently formulate a list of items and then have the students rate themselves as to their degree of interest in each item. The rating scale generally provides for several degrees of interest: high, above average, average, below average, and little interest. Teachers often find profitable the use of interest rating scales related to physical education activities or to the expected outcomes from participation in the activities.

Ratings of Attitudes

An attitude is a predisposition to feel favorably or unfavorably toward something. A person's attitudes strongly influence his thinking and behavior and have an important influence on the learning process. Attitudes may relate to activities, people, leadership, and the environment. Since attitudes impel one to act, they may be inferred from observed behavior.

To be effective, teachers of physical education must be concerned with the appraisal of student attitudes and with the development of favorable attitudes. However, since objective tests of attitudes are impossible, teachers must rely on careful observation of behavior, student reactions to attitude inventories, anecdotal records, and the information from rating scales.

Ratings of Behavior

Emotional behavior is involved in most motor performances. The emotional elements inherent in swimming (fear of water, for example) are different from the emotional elements in gymnastics, wrestling, basketball, football, or golf. Each activity has its own type and level of emotional involvement. Active participation offers unusual opportunities for evaluation of emotional behavior and for the development of favorable behavior patterns.

Ratings of Character

Character is a complex of one's behavior traits; hence ratings of behavior are essentially ratings of character traits. Behavior rating scales are the result of efforts to evaluate character as a whole or some aspect of character as exhibited in physical education activities. The following examples are desirable behavior traits: friendly attitude toward teammates and opponents; accuracy in keeping score; loyalty to self, the team, coach, and school; modesty in winning; courage in contact sports; refinement in manners; appropriate expression and emotion; sense of humor in appropriate situations; tact at necessary times.

Construction and Use of Rating Scales

Several factors must be considered in the construction of rating scales for the evaluation of personality traits: How should the traits be selected? How many traits should be selected? How should the traits be defined? Should general or specific traits be listed? Should both desirable and undesirable traits be listed? Should different degrees of a trait be measured? To what degree is the trait desirable or undesirable? Who is to do the rating? How frequently does the person exhibit the trait?

A teacher should attempt ratings of character traits only after intentional and accurate observation over a reasonable period of time. He or she should use these ratings as an aid in changing undesirable forms of student conduct, not for the purpose of grading.

The teacher might make the process of rating a class project and allow students with some training to assist in the evaluation process by rating themselves or their classmates. In this way students may learn the importance of good behavior and become interested in improving their own ways of behaving.

Useful Measures of Personality Traits

The following selected measuring instruments have proved to be useful in evaluating how students feel about their participation in physical education activities:

Neilson Character Rating Scale

This scale was prepared by N. P. Neilson to measure how well a student of junior high school, high school, or college age demonstrates desirable character traits. The evaluator, usually the teacher, rates the student on each of the 24 items and records the appropriate score (listed at the top of each column) opposite the item. Five is the highest possible score on each item. There are 120 points possible.

Cowell's Social Adjustment Index

This index (3) was developed to measure how well students of junior high school through college age are adjusted to their social environment. The index has a reported validity coefficient of .63 and a reliability coefficient of .82 for high school students.

Procedure: The teacher rates each student on both Form A and Form B.

Scoring: He then computes the score (listed at the top of the columns) in the appropriate column opposite each item and computes the raw score by subtracting the total score on Form B from the total score on Form A. The higher scores are indications of good social adjustment.

Mercer Attitude Inventory

The Mercer Inventory (8) was constructed to evaluate the attitudes of high school girls toward the psychological, sociological, moral, and spiritual values of their physical education experience. The inventory has a reported validity coefficient of .72 and a reliability coefficient of .92.

Procedure: The student responds to each of the statements by placing a check mark on the answer sheet to indicate the appropriate answer from the following choices:

Neilson Character Rating Scale

Name _____ Age _____ Grade _____

Date _____ Evaluator _____

CHARACTER TRAITS	poor 1	fair 2	average 3	good 4	excellent 5
1. *Accuracy:* precise, correct.					
2. *Alertness:* watchful; ready to act.					
3. *Cheerfulness:* joyous; in good spirits.					
4. *Confidence:* reliant; sure; free from doubt.					
5. *Cooperation:* ability to work harmoniously with other persons.					
6. *Courage:* meets difficulties with firmness or valor.					
7. *Dependability:* trustworthy; reliable.					
8. *Enthusiasm:* inspired; ardent; interested.					
9. *Honesty:* truthful; having integrity.					
10. *Industry:* diligent; not slothful or idle.					
11. *Initiative:* to begin action in new fields.					
12. *Judgment:* making intelligent decisions.					
13. *Language:* good choice of words; avoids profanity.					
14. *Leadership:* directing action; being followed by others.					
15. *Loyalty:* giving active support to a cause.					
16. *Modesty:* not boastful or egotistical; absence of arrogance.					
17. *Neatness of dress:* being clean and appropriately dressed.					
18. *Obedient:* compliance with requests of one in authority.					
19. *Refinement in manners:* actions are pleasing and in good taste.					
20. *Self-control:* control over emotions; self-direction.					
21. *Sense of humor:* ability to appreciate amusing situations.					
22. *Social adaptability:* friendly with people and at ease in their presence.					
23. *Sportsmanship:* fairness; respect for rights of others; a good loser and graceful winner.					
24. *Tact:* ability to deal with others without giving offense.					

Cowell's Social Adjustment Index (Form A)

Name _____ Age _____ Grade _____

Date _____ Describer's name _____

Behavior Trends	Descriptive of the Student			
	Markedly (+3)	Somewhat (+2)	Only Slightly (+1)	Not at All (+0)
1. Enters heartily and with enjoyment into the spirit of social intercourse.				
2. Frank; talkative and sociable, does not stand on ceremony.				
3. Self-confident and self-reliant, tends to take success for granted, strong initiative, prefers to lead.				
4. Quick and decisive in movement, pronounced or excessive energy output.				
5. Prefers group activities, work or play; not easily satisfied with individual projects.				
6. Adaptable to new situations, makes adjustments readily, welcomes change.				
7. Is self-composed, seldom shows signs of embarrassment.				
8. Tends to elation of spirits, seldom gloomy or moody.				
9. Seeks a broad range of friendships, not selective or exclusive in games and the like.				
10. Hearty and cordial, even to strangers, forms acquaintanceships very easily.				

strongly   neutral—   strongly
disagree   disagree   undecided   agree   agree
(   )   (   )   (   )   (   )   (   )

Scoring: The statements included on the inventory are both positive and negative as marked on the answer sheet. The best answer on positive statements would be five, indicating strong agreement. The best answer on negative statements would also be 5, indicating strong disagreement. The final score is the total of all the score values for the 40 items. There are 200 points possible. Achievement scales are not available.

Behavior Attitude Checklist

This checklist (5) was constructed to provide junior and senior high school students with a self-appraisal of behavior in physical education classes. The objective is to motivate the students to develop good behavior and to make them aware of poor behavioral traits.

Procedure: Each student rates himself or herself on each item by placing a check mark in the column opposite the appropriate item. The test may be

Cowell's Social Adjustment Index (Form B)

Name _____ Age _____ Grade _____

Date _____ Describer's name _____

Behaviors Trends	Descriptive of the Student			
	Markedly (−3)	Somewhat (−2)	Only Slightly (−1)	Not at All (−0)
1. Somewhat prudish, awkward, easily embarrassed in social contacts.				
2. Secretive, seclusive, not inclined to talk unless spoken to.				
3. Lacking in self-confidence and initiative, a follower.				
4. Slow in movement, deliberative, or perhaps indecisive. Energy output moderate or deficient.				
5. Prefers to work and play alone, tends to avoid group activities.				
6. Shrinks from making new adjustments, prefers the habitual to the stress of reorganization required by the new.				
7. Is self-conscious, easily embarrassed, timid or "bashful."				
8. Tends to depression, frequently gloomy or moody.				
9. Shows preference for a narrow range of intimate friends and tends to exclude others from association.				
10. Reserved and distant except to intimate friends, does not form acquaintanceships readily.				

given periodically during the year to determine whether the physical education course has motivated the student toward better behavior.

Scoring: There are no numerical score values involved. The examiner simply evaluates the responses to determine which behavioral traits need to be improved.

Blanchard Behavior Rating Scale

This rating scale (1) was constructed to measure behavior characteristics of students. The scale has a reported validity coefficient of .93 and a reliability coefficient of .71.

Procedure: The teacher rates each student on the scale of circling the appropriate number opposite each of the 24 items.

Scoring: The score for each item is the circled number. The higher scores are indications of better behavior. There are 120 points possible.

Mercer Attitude Inventory

Name _____ Age _____

Date _____ Grade _____

1. Physical education activities are likely to be emotionally upsetting to many girls and boys.
2. The saying, "Rules are made to be broken," is true in highly competitive sports.
3. It would be better to study than to spend time in physical education classes.
4. Physical education contributes nothing toward character development.
5. Girls who are skilled in active games and sports are not popular with boys.
6. Social dancing helps one to improve in grace and poise.
7. Competitive activities break down emotional self-controls.
8. Physical education classes are not looked forward to with enthusiasm.
9. Learning to accept situations as they are rather than as they should be is learned through participation in competitive sports.
10. An appreciation for art and beauty can be learned from physical education.
11. Archery is an activity in which one learns to score honestly.
12. Opportunities for making friends are provided more in other classes than in physical education.
13. Feelings of joy and happiness may be expressed through physical activities.
14. Girls and boys who excel in sports are not as intellectual as other girls and boys.
15. A good team is composed of individuals each working for his or her own particular good.
16. The spending of money for "exercise" and "play" is unnecessary and wasteful.
17. There is no apparent spiritual basis for physical education.
18. Working together as a team does not reduce the value of human relationships.
19. Being dishonest in calling balls good or bad in tennis is not related to personal integrity and honesty.
20. Physical education is not related to any other subject in the school program.
21. Learning to play by the rules of the game is not related to learning good moral and spiritual conduct.
22. Participation in competitive games and sports gives an opportunity for self-control.
23. Girls who enjoy physical activities are "unfeminine."
24. Individual student interests are not considered in physical education classes.
25. Accepting defeat graciously is not learned from participation in games and sports.
26. Physical education activities offer many opportunities for emotional expression.
27. Accepting your own capabilities is learned from participation in physical education.
28. Physical education activities do not provide opportunities for learning moral and spiritual values of living.
29. Physical education should be required in grades 1–12, and in college.
30. Just playing is not as important as having instruction in physical education.
31. A team should play according to the rules regardless of how unfairly the opposing team plays.
32. Associating with others in physical education activities is fun.
33. Physical education should be concerned with the learning of physical skills.
34. Physical activities are embarrassing for girls and boys who are not skilled.
35. Each player on a team should play in every game regardless of his or her skill.
36. Physical education makes important contributions to the mental health of an individual.
37. Physical education offers little of importance to the general education of high school students.
38. No opportunities are offered for students to become leaders in the physical education classes.
39. Physical education activities provide no opportunity for learning emotional control.
40. Physical education activities develop socially desirable standards of conduct.

Scoring Key

Code	Strongly Disagree	Disagree	Negative	Agree	Strongly Agree		Code	Strongly Disagree	Disagree	Negative	Agree	Strongly Agree		Code	Strongly Disagree	Disagree	Negative	Agree	Strongly Agree
− 1.	5	4	3	2	1		−14.	5	4	3	2	1		+27.	1	2	3	4	5
− 2.	5	4	3	2	1		−15.	5	4	3	2	1		−28.	5	4	3	4	5
− 3.	5	4	3	2	1		−16.	5	4	3	2	1		+29.	1	2	3	2	1
− 4.	5	4	3	2	1		−17.	5	4	3	2	1		+30.	1	2	3	4	5
− 5.	5	4	3	2	1		+18	1	2	3	4	5		+31.	1	2	3	4	5
+ 6.	1	2	3	4	5		−19.	5	4	3	2	1		+32.	1	2	3	4	5
− 7.	5	4	3	2	1		−20.	5	4	3	2	1		−33.	5	4	3	2	1
− 8.	5	4	3	2	1		−21.	5	4	3	2	1		−34.	5	4	3	2	1
+ 9	1	2	3	4	5		+22.	1	2	3	4	5		+35.	1	2	3	4	5
+10.	1	2	3	4	5		−23.	5	4	3	2	1		+36.	1	2	3	4	5
+11.	1	2	3	4	5		−24.	5	4	3	2	1		−37.	5	4	3	2	1
−12.	5	4	3	2	1		−25.	5	4	3	2	1		−38.	5	4	3	2	1
+13.	1	2	3	4	5		+26.	1	2	3	4	5		−39.	5	4	3	2	1
														+40.	1	2	3	4	5

Evaluation of Accomplishment of Objectives

This evaluation form was prepared by Neilson to help students of junior high school through college age evaluate how well they accomplished certain important objectives.

Procedure: The form should be completed at the end of a unit instruction or at the end of a semester. Usually the student completes the form but the teacher can fill in the information if he or she so desires.

Scoring: The student or teacher records the score in the appropriate column opposite each of the 20 items. The highest score for each item is 5. There are 100 points possible.

How Is Your Physical Education Coming Along?

This checklist (7) was established to assess a student's progress in achieving the objectives of physical education. Students may use it as a periodical ap-

Behavior Attitude Checklist

Name _____ Age _____

Date _____ Grade _____

Always	Often	Seldom	Never	
				Self-Direction
				1. I work dilligently even though I am not supervised.
				2. I practice to improve the skills I use with least success.
				3. I follow carefully directions that have been given me.
				4. I willingly accept constructive criticism and try to correct faults.
				5. I play games as cheerfully as I can.
				6. I appraise my progress in each of my endeavors to learn.
				Social Adjustment
				1. I am considerate of the rights of others.
				2. I am courteous.
				3. I am cooperative in group activities.
				4. I accept gladly responsibility assigned me by a squad leader.
				5. I accept disappointment without being unnecessarily disturbed.
				6. I expect from the members of my group only the consideration to which I am entitled.
				Participation
				1. I am prompt in reporting for each class.
				2. I dislike being absent from class.
				3. I ask to be excused from an activity only when it is necessary.
				4. I do the best I can regardless of the activity in which I am participating.
				5. I give full attention to all instructions that are given in class.
				6. I encourage others with whom I am participating in an activity.
				Care of Equipment and Facilities
				1. I use equipment as I am supposed to use it.
				2. I return each piece of equipment to its proper place after using it.
				3. I avoid making my dressing area untidy.
				4. I arrange my clothes neatly in my locker.
				Personal Attractiveness
				1. I am particular about my personal appearance.
				2. I take a shower after I have participated in any vigorous activity.
				3. I wear clean clothes in physical education.
				4. I dress appropriately for each activity.
				5. I bathe regularly even during my menstrual period.

Blanchard Behavior Rating Scale

Name_____ Age _____ Grade_____

Date_____ Name of rater _____

	No Opportunity to Observe	Frequency of Observation					Score
		Never	Seldom	Fairly often	Frequently	Extremely Often	
Leadership							
1. He or she is popular with classmates.		1	2	3	4	5	
2. He or she seeks responsibility in the classroom.		1	2	3	4	5	
3. He or she shows intellectual leadership in the classroom.		1	2	3	4	5	
Positive Active Qualities							
4. He or she quits on tasks requiring perseverance.		5	4	3	2	1	
5. He or she exhibits agressiveness in relationships with others.		1	2	3	4	5	
6. He or she shows initiative in assuming responsibility in unfamiliar situations.		1	2	3	4	5	
7. He or she is alert to new opportunities.		1	2	3	4	5	
Positive Mental Qualities							
8. He or she shows keenness of mind.		1	2	3	4	5	
9. He or she volunteers ideas.		1	2	3	4	5	
Self-Control							
10. He or she grumbles over decisions of classmates.		5	4	3	2	1	
11. He or she takes a justified criticism by teacher or classmate without showing anger or pouting.		1	2	3	4	5	
Cooperation							
12. He or she is loyal to the group.		1	2	3	4	5	
13. He or she discharges group responsibilities well.		1	2	3	4	5	
14. He or she is cooperative in attitude toward the teacher.		1	2	3	4	5	
Social Action Standards							
15. He or she makes loud-mouthed criticisms and comments.		5	4	3	2	1	
16. He or she respects the rights of others.		1	2	3	4	5	
Ethical Social Qualities							
17. He or she cheats.		5	4	3	2	1	
18. He or she is truthful.		1	2	3	4	5	
Qualities of Efficiency							
19. He or she seems satisfied to "get by" with tasks assigned.		5	4	3	2	1	
20. He or she is dependable and trustworthy.		1	2	3	4	5	
21. He or she has good study habits.		1	2	4	5	5	
Sociability							
22. He or she is liked by others.		1	2	3	4	5	
23. He or she makes a friendly approach to others in the group.		1	2	3	4	5	
24. He or she is friendly.		1	2	3	4	5	

Evaluation of Accomplishment of Objectives

Name _____ Age _____ Grade _____

Date _____ Evaluator _____

To what extent did you:	1	2	3	4	5
1. Make new friends?					
2. Develop a sense of humor?					
3. Learn to know your own limitations?					
4. Work hard in order to succeed?					
5. Do your best under difficult situations?					
6. Respect the ability of opponents?					
7. Respect the ability of teammates?					
8. Become tolerant of the success of others?					
9. Share with teammates in the struggle to accomplish a goal?					
10. Sacrifice your own desires, when necessary, for the good of the group?					
11. Exhibit loyalty to the leader and the school?					
12. Strive for an ideal?					
13. Learn to make decisions quickly when necessary?					
14. Understand the strategy in the activities?					
15. Learn to be a leader?					
16. Keep your body clean?					
17. Abide by training rules (eating, sleeping, and avoiding tobacco, alcoholic drinks, and drugs)?					
18. Develop strength?					
19. Develop skill?					
20. Develop endurance?					

praisal of themselves or as a goal toward achievement of various items. Boys and girls of junior and senior high school age may use the checklist.

Procedure: Students answer yes or no to each of the questions listed under A, B, C, and D according to their best judgment.

Scoring: Students should achieve the indicated score on each set of questions to pass the evaluation in good standing. They record their total score at the end of the checklist (see checklist on page 291).

Edgington Attitude Scale

The Edgington Attitude scale (6) was designed to measure attitudes of high school freshman boys toward physical education. The reliability of the final form was determined to be .92 (see directions on page 242).

Physical Education Checklist

Name_____ Age _____

    Date _____ Grade_____

A. Developing Good Living Habits (6 out of 6)
    1. I get enough sleep (8–10 hours each night) so that I am rested and refreshed
        in the morning.
    2. I drink milk every day and eat three good meals that include plenty of fruit
        and vegetables.
    3. I take a bath or shower frequently.
    4. I am concerned about my personal appearance and try to be neat and clean
        at all times.
    5. I always take reasonable precautions for the safety of myself and others.
    6. I have regular dental and medical examinations and seek correction of any
        defects that are found.

B. Acquiring Skills in Sports and Other Recreational Activities (6 out of 7)
    1. I swim well enough to feel safe in, on, or about the water.
    2. I can play well one or more individual sports like archery, bowling, golf, or
        tennis. I am a good player in one or more team sports (softball, soccer,
        volleyball, and the like) and take part in several others.
    3. I am a member of an intramural or a varsity team.
    4. I have a hobby that I hope to enjoy the rest of my life.
    5. I participate regularly throughout the year in some vigorous activity outside
        school hours.
    6. I enjoy a vigorous activity (modern dancing, gymnastics, tumbling, wres-
        tling, track and field, and the like) that helps to develop my strength, en-
        durance, agility, coordination, and balance.
    7. I dance well enough to enjoy school dances and similar social functions.

C. Learning Facts about Sports (4 out of 6)
    1. I enjoy watching and discussing sports because I understand the rules,
        vocabulary, and basic strategy of the popular sports.
    2. I know the rules of one or more sports well enough to officiate in class or
        intramural contests.
    3. In each sport I play, I know the proper safety precautions to take in order
        to avoid injuring myself and others.
    4. I have learned to recognize and appreciate good sports equipment and know
        how to care for it to obtain maximum service.
    5. I know the origin of many popular sports and how they have affected the
        life of my community.
    6. I know about several outstanding sports personalities and their achieve-
        ments.

D. Learning and Living the Good-Sportsman's Code (10 out of 10)
    1. I consider athletic opponents and officials to be guests of my school and
        treat them accordingly.
    2. I respect the rights and feelings of those who cheer the rival team.
    3. I respect the authority and judgment of the coach.
    4. I respect the property of the school and the authority of school officials.
    5. I cheer good plays and good sportsmanship whether displayed by my
        school's team or its opponents.
    6. I appreciate the responsibility of sports officials and accept their decisions.
    7. I maintain self-control at all times during and after the game.
    8. I try to be modest in victory and gracious in defeat.
    9. I do what I can to encourage both players and spectators to act in the spirit
        of fair play and sportsmanship.
    10. I try to observe the code of the good sportsman not only on the playing
        field but wherever I go.

            Yes: _____   No: _____

Directions (for Edgington Attitude Scale)

Below you will find a list of statements about physical education. We would like to know how you feel about each statement. Feelings about these statements vary among people. There are no right or wrong answers. Please answer each statement according to your own feelings about physical education. Put your answers on the provided answer sheet. Denote your feelings of the statement by making an **X** in the bracket which best indicates your agreement or disagreement.[1]

1. Physical education is mainly concerned with muscle building. (−)
2. Physical education should be eliminated from the curriculum. (−)
3. Physical education is too strenuous for the average student. (−)
4. Knowledge of various sports learned in physical education helps students to become more understanding spectators. (+)
5. Physical education should develop in students an understanding of the importance of exercise to health. (+)
6. Respect for human personality should be one of the qualities sought in a physical education class. (+)
7. Credit should not be given for physical education. (−)
8. Physical education has little value and should be eliminated. (−)
9. Skills learned in physical education are of value in social life. (+)
10. Cooperation is not necessary in physical education activities. (−)
11. Physical education is not as important as other academic classes. (−)
12. Emotional expressions can be brought under control through participation in games. (+)
13. Physical education helps students to develop poise. (+)
14. The main purpose of physical education is to cause fatigue in students. (−)
15. Physical education should not be considered a part of general education. (−)
16. The intellectual processes are related to the physical processes of the body. (+)
17. Physical education should be a required subject. (+)
18. Physical education should introduce only activities that are useful during the teen-age years. (−)
19. Grades should not be given in physical education. (−)
20. A student should learn to respect the opponent in physical education. (+)
21. Physical education helps students adapt to group situations. (+)

---

[1] + after the statement indicates a favorable attitude; − indicates an unfavorable attitude. These symbols, of course, do not appear on the student's list of statements, but are included for the information of the scorer.

22. Physical education does little in developing desirable standards of conduct. (−)
23. Tolerance, obedience, and respect for the rights of others are learned in physical education. (+)
24. Physical education should be an elective subject after the ninth grade. (−)
25. Exercise is of little importance in maintaining good health. (−)
26. There is a scientific basis for physical education. (−)
27. To participate in games is undignified. (−)
28. Physical education once or twice a week is inadequate. (+)
29. Written tests should be given in physical education. (+)
30. Physical education is mainly concerned with team games. (−)
31. Physical education should be required in every grade. (+)
32. Students have little opportunity in physical education to receive recognition and status. (−)
33. Physical education classes provide opportunities to make friends. (+)
34. Physical conditioning is an important part of the physical education class. (+)
35. No real learning takes place in a physical education class. (−)
36. Physical education is harmful if an individual is physically weak. (−)
37. Credit should be given for physical education. (+)
38. Physical education has little to offer for the unskilled individual. (−)
39. Varsity athletes should be excused from physical education classes. (−)
40. The program in physical education should be organized so there is progression in the learning of skills. (+)
41. Calisthenics should be eliminated from physical education. (−)
42. Participants in physical education learn to cooperate as a member of the group. (+)
43. Physical education is important in the growth and development of students. (+)
44. The physical education program should include activities leading to sports appreciation. (+)
45. Activities in physical education offer students opportunities to make quick decisions and responses. (+)
46. Physical education contributes to physical development. (+)
47. Physical education should be a relaxation period between academic classes. (−)
48. The activities in the physical education program do little to develop physical fitness. (−)
49. The program in physical education is the same year after year. (−)
50. Students get all the physical activity they need outside of school. (−)
51. Taking a long walk would be a good substitute for physical education. (−)

52. Learning the rules of activities is an important part of physical education. (+)
53. The rules of sportsmanship should be practiced in physical education. (+)
54. Physical education is not an important phase of education. (−)
55. There is little carry-over value from physical education. (−)
56. Physical education classes should not be free play periods. (+)
57. Flexibility is important in physical education. (+)
58. Some calisthenics should be included in physical education. (+)
59. Physical education is needed for a complete education. (+)
60. Little intelligence is required for physical education. (−)
61. Physical education classes should provide challenging activities. (+)
62. Physical education is a waste of time in school. (−)
63. Individual sports learned in physical education can be useful in later life. (+)
64. Physical education is mainly for the physically gifted. (−)
65. Coordination can be developed in physical education. (+)
66. Strength cannot be developed in physical education. (−)

Other Measurements of Impulsive Traits

In addition to the aforementioned measurements of impulsive traits the following are also useful: Action-Choice Tests for Competitive Sports Situations, Cowell Personal Distance Scale (3), Outcomes of Sports: An Evaluation Checksheet, Social Evaluation Score Card, A Subjective Rating Scale for Social, Personal, and Emotional Development, Carr Attitude Inventory, Kneer Attitude Inventory and Diagnostic Statements, Scale to Measure Attitudes Toward Intensive Competition for High School Girls, Wear Attitude Inventory (7).

Selected References

1. **Blanchard, B. E., Jr.:** A behavior frequency rating scale for the measurement of character and personality in physical education classroom situation. *Research Quarterly*, 1936, 7, 56–66. The Blanchard Behavior Rating Scale is reprinted by permission of the American Association for Health, Physical Education, and Recreation.
2. **Campbell, D. E.:** Wear attitude inventory applied to junior high school boys. *Research Quarterly* 39 (4), 1968.
3. **Cowell, C. C.:** Our function is still education! *The Physical Educator* 14: 6–7, 1957.
4. **Cowell, C. C.:** Validating an index of social adjustment for high school use. *Research Quarterly*, 29:7–18, 1958. Form A and B of the Index are reprinted by permission of the American Association for Health, Physical Education, and Recreation.
5. **Dexter, G. (Ed.):** *Teachers' Guide to Physical Education for Girls in High School.* Sacramento: California State Department of Education, 1957, p. 318.

6. **Edgington, C. W.**: Development of an attitude scale to measure attitudes of high school freshman boys toward physical education. *Research Quarterly* 39 (3), 1964.
7. **National Education Association:** How is your physical education coming along? *NEA Journal.* 1955, 44, 353.
8. **Mercer, E. L.**: An Adaptation and Revision of the Galloway Attitude Inventory for Evaluating the Attitudes of High School Girls Toward Psychological, Moral–Spiritual, and Sociological Values in Physical Education Experiences. Unpublished master's thesis, The Women's College of the University of North Carolina, 1961.
9. **Wear, C. L.**: The evaluation of attitudes toward physical education as an activity course. *Research Quarterly*, 22:114–26, 1951.

17

Student Classification Plans

Students are often classified for competition and instruction according to age or grade, but sometimes other methods are preferred. Experience and research have led to the conclusion that age, height, and weight measures form a sound basis for the classification of elementary and junior high school boys and girls and for high school boys. Height and weight may be used for the classification of college men. Age, height, and weight measures are no more satisfactory than age or grade for classifying high school girls or college women. For students other than high school girls and college women, age, height, and weight classification plans have been used successfully to establish achievement scales for evaluating a student's performance, measuring his or her improvement in skills, stimulating his or her interest in total development, and helping the teacher select activities to meet individual needs.

The examiner can determine height with a stadiometer and weight with a balance scale. Age can be conveniently and accurately computed by the method shown in the table on the following page.

First the examiner finds the difference between the year during which the age is being computed and the year the student was born. This number will be the base years. Since the teacher will usually be working with similar age groups, the base years for a given group will not vary widely. Then the classification chart shown here is used to determine the month difference to be added to, or subtracted from, the base years to produce an accurate age in years and months. For example, if the difference between the present year and the year the student was born is 14, this number will be the base years. If the computation is made in February and the student was born in September, then using the classification chart, the examiner looks down the February column and across the September row to find that the month difference is 7. Then this

246

Month Age Is Being Computed

		Jan.	Feb.	Mar.	Apr.	May	June	July	Aug.	Sept.	Oct.	Nov.	Dec.	
	Jan.	0	1	2	3	4	5	6	7	8	9	10	11	
	Feb.	1	2	1	2	3	4	5	6	7	8	9	10	
	March	2	1	0	1	2	3	4	5	6	7	8	9	
	April	3	2	1	0	1	2	3	4	5	6	7	8	
Birth Month	May	4	3	2	1	0	1	2	3	4	5	6	7	Add
	June	5	4	3	2	1	0	1	2	3	4	5	6	
	July	6	5	4	3	2	1	0	1	2	3	4	5	
	Aug.	7	6	5	4	3	2	1	0	1	2	3	4	
	Sept.	8	9	6	5	4	3	2	1	0	1	2	3	
	Oct.	9	8	7	6	5	4	3	2	1	0	1	2	
	Nov.	10	9	8	7	6	5	4	3	2	1	0	1	
	Dec.	11	10	9	8	7	6	5	4	3	2	1	0	

Subtract

number is subtracted from the base years, 14. The result is 13 years 5 months. The chart, of course, can be used with any base years.

Classification Plan for Elementary and Junior High School Students

The Neilson and Cozens age–height–weight classification plan has been used extensively for elementary and junior high school students. It was first developed in the Oakland, California, public schools as an adaptation of the classification scheme used in connection with the California Decathlon Charts, which were outgrowths of Frederick Reilly's plan of rational athletics. Through research Frederick W. Cozens clearly established the validity of the Neilson and Cozens plan. Use of the plan for the classification of students is illustrated by the following example:

Age–Height–Weight	Exponent*
Height = 59 inches	8
Age = 13 years and 7 months	8
Weight = 119 pounds	12
Sum of exponents	28
Class of student	E

The following achievement scales (7) are based on the Neilson and Cozens classification plan.

For Girls

Agility Run (Shuttle Run)	Run—60 yards
Basketball Throw for Goal	Soccer Dribble
Jump and Reach (Vertical Jump)	Softball Throw for Accuracy
Run and Catch	Standing Long Hop
Run—50 yards	Standing Three Hops

For Boys

Agility Run (Shuttle Run)	Run—75 yards
Basketball Throw for Goal	Running High Jump
Jump and Reach (Vertical Jump)	Soccer Dribble
Pull-up	Softball Throw for Accuracy
Push-up	Standing Hop, Step, Jump
Run—50 yards	Standing Long Jump

TABLE 17-1 Classification Chart for Elementary and Junior High School Boys and Girls

Exponent	Height in Inches	Age in Years	Weight in Pounds
1	50 to 51	10 to 10-5	60 to 65
2	52 to 53	10-6 to 10-11	66 to 70
3		11 to 11-5	71 to 75
4	54 to 55	11-6 to 11-11	76 to 80
5		12 to 12-5	81 to 85
6	56 to 57	12-6 to 12-11	86 to 90
7		13 to 13-5	91 to 95
8	58 to 59	13-6 to 13-11	96 to 100
9		14 to 14-5	101 to 105
10	60 to 61	14-6 to 14-11	106 to 110
11		15 to 15-5	111 to 115
12	62 to 63	15-6 to 15-11	116 to 120
13		16 to 16-5	121 to 125
14	64 to 65	16-6 to 16-11	126 to 130
15	66 to 67	17 to 17-5	131 to 133
16	68	17-6 to 17-11	134 to 136
17	69 and over	18 and over	137 and over

Sum of Exponents	Class	Sum of Exponents	Class
9 and below	A	25 to 29	E
10 to 14	B	30 to 34	F
15 to 19	C	35 to 38	G
20 to 24	D	39 and above	H

Using 20,000 performance records of boys in a wide variety of individual athletic events, Cozens arrived at the Best-Fit Index of $2A + .475H + .16W$, where A refers to age in years, H to height in inches, and W to weight in pounds. Table 17-2 was produced from the Best-Fit Index. In this classification plan junior high school boys predominate in classes, F, E, D, and C, while senior high school boys fall mainly in classes C, B, and A.

The following example uses Table 17-2 for the classification of a boy who is 12 years old, 54 inches tall, and weighs 160 pounds.

Age–Height–Weight	Exponent
Height = 54 inches	26
Age = 12.0 years	24
Weight = 160 pounds	26
Sum of exponents	76
Class of student	D

TABLE 17-2   Classification Plan for Secondary School Boys Grades 7 to 12 Inclusive

Expo-nent	Age	Height	Weight	Expo-nent	Age	Height	Weight
9			53– 59	24	11:9–12:2	49.5–51.5	147–153
10			60– 65	25	12:3–12:8	52 –53.5	154–159
11			66– 71	26	12:9–13:2	54 –55.5	160–165
12			72– 78	27	13:3–13:8	56 –57.5	166–171
13			79– 84	28	13:9–14:2	58 –59.5	172–178
14			85– 90	29	14:3–14:8	60 –62	179–184
15			91– 96	30	14:9–15:2	62.5–64	185–190
16			97–103	31	15:3–15:8	64.5–66	191–up
17			104–109	32	15:9–16:2	66.5–68	
18			110–115	33	16:3–16:8	68.5–70.5	
19			116–121	34	16:9–17:2	71 –72.5	
20			122–128	35	17:3–17:8	73 –74.5	
21			129–134	36	17:9–18:2	75 –up	
22	10:9–11:2	47–down	135–140	37	18:3–18:8		
23	11:3–11:8	47.5–49	141–146	38	18:9–19:2		

Sum of Exponents	Class	Sum of Exponents	Class
88 and over	A	75–78	D
83–87	B	70–74	E
79–82	C	69 and below	F

Classification Indexes

On the basis of extensive study Charles H. McCloy established three age–height–weight indexes:

For high school:	Classification Index I	20 (age in years) + 6 (height in inches) + weight in pounds
For college:	Classification Index II	6 (height in inches) + weight in pounds
For elementary school:	Classification Index III	10 (age in years) + weight in pounds

McCloy (6), in recommending the indexes for different age levels, found that age ceased to make a contribution at 17 years and that height was not an important factor at the elementary school level.

Selected References

1. **Barrow, H. M.**: Classification in physical education. *Physical Education* 17:101, 1960.
2. **Clarke, H. H.**, and **Degutis, E. W.**: Comparison of skeletal age and various physical and motor factors with the pubescent development of 10, 13, and 16 year old boys. *Research Quarterly*, 33:356–368, 1962.
3. **Clarke, H. H.**, and **Harrison, J. C. E.**: Differences in physical and motor traits between boys of advanced, normal, and retarded maturity. *Research Quarterly*, 33:13–25, 1952.
4. **Espenschade, A. S.**: Restudy of relationships between physical performances of school children and age, height, and weight. *Research Quarterly*, 34:144–53, 1963.
5. **Gross, E. A.**, and **Casciani, J. A.**: Value of age, height, and weight as a classification device for secondary school students in the seven AAHPER youth fitness tests. *Research Quarterly*, 33:51–58, 1962.
6. **McCloy, C. H.**, and **Young, Norma D.** *Tests and Measurements in Health and Physical Education*, 3rd ed. New York: Appleton-Century-Crofts, 1954, p. 59.

7. **Neilson, N. P.**, and **Comer, J. L.**: *Physical Education for Elementary Schools*, 3rd ed. New York: Ronald Press, 1966.
8. **Pierson, W. R.**, and **O'Connell, E. R.**: Age, height, weight, and grip strength. *Research Quarterly*, 33:439–443, 1962.

VI

Construction
and Application
of Measurements

18

Construction of Tests and Measurements

Before he or she can measure skill or knowledge, the teacher must either select a test from the available standardized tests or construct one to serve his or her particular purpose. Either a written test or a motor performance test may be needed, both of which are important yet serve different purposes. The construction of such tests is a difficult task requiring ample concentration and effort.

Written Tests

Written tests fall into two general categories, standard tests and teacher-made tests. Standard tests are usually designed to measure general traits, such as intelligence, personality, general academic achievement, and general knowledge. A standard test, such as an IQ (intelligence quotient) test supposedly produces comparable results when it is administered to different people at different times and in different localities. Conversely, a teacher-made test is highly local in nature, that is, designed for a specific group of people who have had particular experiences which prepare them for the test. For example, a teacher-made test may be constructed to evaluate the learning that occurred as a result of a unit of instruction on tennis.

Construction of Standardized Written Tests

Construction of a standard written test is an involved project because the test must be designed to produce valid and reliable results when administered at different times and places. Thus the test items may not be localized or confined to a particular situation or group of people. Usually these tests have evolved from research projects which are done or supervised by testing experts.

To develop a standard written test, the test author must:

1. Determine the purpose of the test and define its scope and delimitations.
2. Determine the kinds of test questions to be considered: multiple choice, true–false, matching, or completion.
3. Accumulate all test items that should be considered for inclusion in the test.
4. Administer the test items to groups of people who represent the population for which the test is intended. Then from the results, determine the relative validity and reliability of the test items by correlating the results of each item with a selected criterion measure.
5. Eliminate poor items and items that cause duplication.
6. Select the items to be included in the semifinal draft.
7. Administer the semifinal draft at least two times to a randomly selected sample of the population for which the test is designed. Then make a final check for validity and reliability of each item. Check validity by correlating the results with the best criterion available; check reliability by correlating the results of the first administration of the test with the second administration to the same people.
8. Arrange the items in order from the least to the most difficult.
9. Prepare the test in final form and include standard written instructions and score sheets.
10. Develop norms for other test.
11. Make a sufficient number of copies of the test and make known their availability to the potential users.

Construction of Teacher-Made Written Tests

No standard written tests have been designed to measure the progress students make during a five-week unit in tennis, soccer, or any other activity. Such tests must be carefully prepared on the basis of information that has been included in the instruction. Only the teacher, perhaps with the help of the students, is in a position to design such tests because only he knows what has been covered and what should have been learned. Even though such tests are constructed to measure the students' knowledge of important facts and concepts, they may also stimulate additional interest in the subject, help the students evaluate themselves, and reemphasize the most important information.

To construct a teacher-made test, the test author must:

1. Review thoroughly the curricular content which the test will cover and select the specific points that should receive emphasis in the test. The

test should reflect approximately the content emphasis as included in the instructional unit.

2. Determine the kinds of questions, true-false, multiple choice, matching, completion, or essay, that best suit the nature of the test.
3. Formulate more questions than are needed for the desired length of test; then carefully evaluate each question and select the better ones.
4. Arrange the questions into logical sequence on the basis of type and difficulty.
5. Make a final appraisal of the test before administering it; then reappraise the test after each administration to determine if it can be improved. In appraising the test retain each test item only on the basis that it contributes to the intent and purpose of the test.

Kinds of Written Test Items

Written test items fall into two general categories: *subjective* and *objective*. Essay questions are subjective; the answers are not clearly correct or incorrect, but require careful evaluation and judgment by the person scoring the test. Conversely, objective-type questions include the use of facts and are clearly correct or incorrect. True–false, multiple choice, matching, and completion questions are objective items. Objective questions should be used when the material to be evaluated is predominated by specific facts and little, if any, subjective judgment is involved.

Essay Questions   Essay questions can best evaluate learning about the application of concepts, strategies, and ideas. They do not test specific facts like dates, names, etc., as well as objective questions do. Essay items allow the student to organize and use his own words in answering the question. All answers may contain a certain degree of correctness, and therefore must be evaluated for content, organization, and thoroughness.

Essay questions should be considered when (1) the material is best suited to essay answers, (2) when the time to prepare the test is short, (3) when the group size is small, (4) when there is no equipment to reproduce the test and the questions will be written on the chalkboard.

Essay questions have the following characteristics:

1. They are advantageous to students who express themselves well in writing.
2. They afford the student more freedom to explain what he or she knows and believes about the subject.
3. They tend to guide students toward learning the fundamental facts and broad concepts as opposed to specific facts and figures.
4. Their correction is time-consuming, and must be done by a person who thoroughly understands the subject.

When scoring essay questions:

1. Decide what factors are to be measured and score the answers accordingly. A good approach is to prepare a model answer for each question at the time the question is prepared. Show what points are desired in the answer and the amount of credit to be given.
2. Read all of the answers to one question for the entire class before going on to the next question. This will result in more uniformity in evaluation for the whole class.
3. Grade all questions without knowing who the student is who wrote the answer.
4. Have another person who is qualified also read the answers to the questions whenever possible—resulting in two evaluations of each answer.

Some sample essay questions about kinesiology follow. Directions: Respond to each of the following by writing thorough, but concise statements.

1. Describe the all-or-none law of muscle contraction.
2. Describe the differences between the first, second, and third class levers in the human body.
3. Explain how increased strength of certain muscle groups may improve a person's speed in swimming.

True or False Items. True–false statements must be clearly true or false in order not to confuse the student. They are useful for measuring specific and isolated material. True–false items are said to have two weaknesses: (1) they encourage emphasis on trivial material, and (2) they encourage guessing. Well-stated true–false statements are difficult to write and require a high level of writing skill on the part of the test maker.

True–false statements have the following characteristics:

1. They are more difficult to construct than some other kinds of questions because of the importance of clear, concise statements.
2. They are not good measures of major concepts because each statement can deal with only a small amount of information.
3. They are easy to correct and can be corrected by anyone with the answer sheet, or by machine.

When writing true–false statements:

1. Avoid using such words as *always, all, no, never,* because they almost always cause the statement to be false.
2. Avoid such words as *frequently, greatly, often, seldom,* because these words are too general and they add ambiguity.
3. Avoid statements that contain more than one idea, especially if one portion of the statement is true and the other false.
4. Avoid extremely long statements because they are hard to comprehend.

Following are some sample true–false questions on skiing. Directions: Indicate whether each statement is true or false by circling T or F in the space opposite the statement. Any statement that is not completely true should be marked false.

T   F   1. Skiing is an activity that was invented and developed during the last century.
T   F   2. The herringbone is a climbing technique on skis.
T   F   3. As he or she increases speed, the skier should decrease the amount of forward lean and leg flexion.
T   F   4. It is considered discourteous to cover sitzmarks.

Multiple-Choice   This kind of question is the most flexible and possibly the most effective of the objective types. Multiple-choice questions are divided into two parts—the *stem* that presents the problem and is in the form of a statement, and the *list*, which includes three or more possible answers. A high level of skill is required to design this kind of question well.

Multiple-choice questions have the following characteristics:

1. They are among the most difficult questions to construct.
2. Multiple-choice questions are more thought provoking than true–false questions.
3. They allow guessing by the student.
4. They are easy to correct and can be corrected by almost anyone who has the answer sheet.
5. They are not good measures of large and fundamental concepts. They test exact knowledge and they tend to encourage trivial information.

When writing multiple-choice questions, remember:

1. The stem should clearly formulate a problem, and all answer options should be possible, with one option being better than the others.
2. Include all the essential information in the stem, but don't load the stem with irrelevant material.
3. There is to be one and only one correct or clearly best answer.
4. Avoid taking statements directly from the textbook or other class material.
5. Avoid grammatical cues like *an* or *a* or *the* in the stem.

Following are sample multiple choice questions about golf. Directions: After each statement, there are several choices, each preceded by a letter. In the space provided, write the letter that represents the best answer.

_____ 1. Two strokes under par for a hole is called
    a. a bogie.
    b. an honor.
    c. a birdie.
    d. an eagle.
    e. par.
_____ 2. Turf chopped loose during a stroke is called a
    a. chop.
    b. dormie.
    c. slice.
    d. divot.
    e. hook.
_____ 3. A ball that curves to the right after it has been hit is called a
    a. hooked ball.
    b. good ball.
    c. sliced ball.
    d. whiffle ball.

Matching Questions　These are really a form of the multiple-choice because all of the options are available to the student and he has only to connect the two together. Matching questions can measure factual information, meanings of words, dates, names, and events. Knowledge about maps, drawings, charts, and symbols are also often measured with matching questions.

Matching questions have the following characteristics:

1. They are fairly easy to construct.
2. Matching questions tend to measure recall rather than understanding.
3. Such questions allow guessing by the student.
4. They can be corrected by almost anyone with an answer sheet.
5. They tend to measure trivial information.
6. A large number of questions can be answered in a short period of time.

When writing matching-type questions, remember to

1. Make diagrams and drawings as clear as possible, if they are involved.
2. Include more choices than are needed to match, but all options might be possible.
3. Get depth into the matching and limit trivial facts in the statements as much as possible.

Here are some sample matching questions about swimming. Directions: Find the answer in the right column that corresponds to each item in the left column and record the corresponding number in the blank.

_____flutter kick
_____whip kick
_____dolphin kick
_____scissors kick
_____scissors and flutter kick
_____tuck position

1. Sidestroke
2. Front crawl stroke
3. Elementary backstroke
4. Butterfly stroke
5. Jellyfish float
6. Back crawl stroke
7. Single trudgeon
8. Trudgeon crawl
9. Skulling
10. Vertical float

Completion Questions Completion questions can be used to measure a variety of specific knowledge. They have the following characteristics:

1. They are relatively easy to construct.
2. They encourage memorization rather than understanding.
3. Such questions need to be scored by someone who knows the various answers that might be acceptable.
4. Completion questions tend to encourage trivial information.

When preparing completion questions, remember:

1. Organize each statement so that the answer can be placed appropriately in the statement.
2. Avoid lifting statements directly from the textbook or other class material.
3. Do not include more than three blanks in a single completion statement.

Following are examples of completion type questions about tennis. Directions: One or more blanks appear in each of the following statements. Write the word to the left of the statement that makes the statement correct.

_____1. When playing singles, one person has won one point and the other no points. The score is _____.
_____2. In singles, when both competitors have won three points, the score is _____.
_____3. The height of the net should be _____ feet at the center and _____ feet at the posts.

Motor Performance Tests

Athletic performance tests may be classified into two categories, *standard* tests and *teacher-made* tests. There are many standard performance tests, some of which are highly useful in instructional programs while others are useful only in research. Standard tests have been constructed to measure such traits as strength, power, agility, endurance, general athletic ability, and specific sports skills. For examples of standardized motor performance tests, see the tests in Chapter 14.

Frequently at the beginning, during, or at the completion of a unit of instruction, the teacher wants to measure specific performance characteristics, and sometimes standard tests are not suited to the particular need. In such cases, the teacher has to design a performance test that will suit the situation.

Construction of Standard Tests

Construction and standardization of a performance test is an involved process. To develop such a test the teacher should:

1. Keep in mind the reason for giving the test, and identify the particular traits the test will measure, such as strength, power, general athletic ability, or a specific sport skill.
2. Select all test items that measure the specific qualities to be tested.
3. Eliminate items that are not feasible in terms of time, equipment, facilities, or cost.
4. Determine the validity and reliability of each of the remaining items. Validity can be determined by administering the item to a representative group and then correlating the results with a selected criterion measure. Reliability can be determined by the test–retest method.
5. Make the final selection of items to be included, eliminating invalid, unreliable, and duplicate items.
6. Determine the order in which test items should be administered and the exact procedure to be followed in administering the items.
7. Establish final ratings of validity and reliability for the test as a whole. The final validity can be established by administering the test to a sample of the population for which it is designed, and then correlating the results with the best criterion measure available. The final reliability rating can be established by correlating the two sets of scores obtained by the test–retest method.
8. Prepare written instructions explaining exactly how the test should be administered.
9. Prepare norms for the test by administering the test to as many students as possible (this is optional).

Construction of Teacher-Made Tests

Such tests should include skills that are frequently used in the sport and can be accurately measured. For example, a unit in basketball might have items on shooting, straight dribbling speed, dribbling speed over a zigzag course, or passing the ball repeatedly against a wall. After a unit of instruction on wrestling, the teacher might test the students on their ability to perform certain holds, take downs, and escapes. At the end of a unit on tennis the teacher might conduct a tournament to determine the relative performance ability of the students.

Other Methods of Measuring Performance

Rating Scales. When subjective judgment is the basis for a performance score, a rating scale is often used. A 5-point scale is used most frequently and consists of the following:

Poor   Fair   Average   Good   Excellent

This scale may then be converted to corresponding letter grades, or it may be converted to numbers on a 100-point scale (for example, 20, 40, 60, 80, 100) and the numbers may be added to other such scores to form the basis for the letter grade. A rating scale may be used in gymnastic events, diving, swimming, or dance.

Tournament Play. Tournament play can be a type of skill test for individual sport activities. A ladder tournament in badminton singles will result in an indication of relative skill level. Win/loss results and tournament standing can be considered in determining the letter grade.

Races. In activities in which speed is a factor, such as track, swimming, or skiing, students can be tested with a racing event. The performance can be against time or against other students.

Skill Tests. A well-designed skill test is a very useful evaluating tool. A skill test should have the following characteristics:

1. The skill being tested should be a part of the activity of the unit of instruction. The students should have been taught the skill being used in the test.
2. Direction for the various tests must be clearly written for understanding. The students should have practiced the skill before the day of the skill test.
3. It must be possible for the students to complete the test in one class period. It would be better to divide the test for two days testing than to have a percentage of the students not finish the test.

Establishment of Norms

Norms provide a convenient way to find the relative status of any raw score and thereby greatly enhance the ability to interpret the score. To establish norms the test should be administered to a large, representative sample of the population for which the norms are to be developed, and a standard scale should be made to fit the scores from the sample. Norms may be based on the percentile scale, or the Z or T scales.

19

Application of Measurement Results

In Chapter 3 several guides for the administration of a testing program were presented and should be reviewed again at this point. These guides are the test management controls that will provide meaningful scores. Results of the tests are useful in several ways: they can motivate students toward achievement; they can assist in evaluating the effectiveness of the educational program; they can be used to classify students; and they can provide information for evaluating progress and establishing grades.

Motivation of Students

To perform well in school, students must be motivated to achieve. Both written tests and motor performance tests can assess goals that students want to attain. The results of such tests provide students with evidence of progress or lack of progress in attaining these goals. The lack of such evidence detracts from motivation.

Students generally want to be more knowledgeable, more fit, and more skillful. They are stimulated by goals and want to demonstrate their achievements, and be recognized for their achievements. Furthermore, they want to see evidence that they are progressing, and are stimulated by such evidence.

Program Evaluation

A student's progress is the best indication of a successful program. To determine progress, the goals toward which the students ought to strive should be clearly defined and sound methods for evaluating progress should be employed.

One means that a teacher has for determining progress is periodic measurement of student achievement. Measures of achievement in tennis help to evaluate the effectiveness of the that phase of the program. Measures of achievement in gymnastics, swimming, basketball, and other sports help to measure the success of these phases. When achievement is low and progress is slow, the teacher should look seriously at the program content, and the methods of instruction.

Part of program evaluation should be concerned with how well individual weaknesses of students are dealt with, and the effectiveness of meeting the needs of the exceptional students.

Establishment of Marks

Every teacher should develop and use effective evaluation procedures and an accurate method of marking students (the term *marking* is preferred over the term *grading*). A student's marks in school are important because they determine to some extent whether he or she will secure a good position of employment, be admitted into college, win a scholarship, be eligible for lower automobile insurance, or gain prestige among classmates. Most important of all, marks represent to the student and to his or her parents an evaluation of success in school. Because of the importance placed on marks, an accurate system for determining and reporting marks must be adopted.

Purpose of Marking

Grades serve different purposes for students, teachers and guidance counselors, parents, and school administrators. A mark should inform the student how nearly he or she has met the standards on which the mark is based. It should clearly indicate how well he or she performed as contrasted to how well he or she might be expected to perform. If it is not accurate or justifiable and if it has a weak basis, then the mark loses its value to the student. It may even destroy the student's interest and incentive and result in a negative attitude toward the subject and the teacher.

Teachers and guidance personnel may use marks for guidance and counseling. If accurately determined, marks can help the teacher predict how successful a student might be in certain pursuits and may also help the teacher evaluate the effectiveness of his teaching.

Parents are usually eager to learn of their children's success in school and also desire to know the reason for the absence of success. Marks that are properly obtained, reported, and interpreted will furnish desired facts. As a result, guidance from home may help overcome deficiencies.

In the present school systems marks are essential to administrators, who interpret them as symbols of progress and indicators of achievement levels. Since marks become permanent records of achievement, they are also used as a basis for promotion and scholastic honor awards. It is essential, then, that marks be established on a solid, equally fair basis and that they be accurately reported and interpreted.

Criteria for Useful Marks.

Marks should be valid. They must truly represent the quality and quantity of pupil achievement for which they purportedly stand.

Marks should be reliable. They must accurately and consistently represent the same results for each student.

Marks should be highly objective. Different teachers, given the same data on a student, should arrive at the same mark. This quality is dependent upon a clearly defined marking system.

Marks should be assigned on the basis of definite standards. The standards should not differ for each pupil nor should they fluctuate widely from one year to the next.

Marks should be capable of clear interpretation with regard to what they signify. If the significance of an A is not evident in terms of quality and quantity of achievement, then the grade lacks meaning.

Marks should be based on a system that allows for the most economical use of the teacher's time and effort. Since marking is only one of the teacher's many tasks, only a reasonable amount of time can be justified for it.

Marks should be timely. Final marks are recorded only at the end of semesters, but for purposes of incentive students should frequently be informed of their progress and present standing.

Methods of Reporting Marks.

There are many methods for evaluating students. The method used must be the one that best evaluates the student on his or her knowledge of the material being tested. The method used must be consistent with the evaluation method used in the school system. The following methods of reporting grades are used:

Five Letter Method. This method results in subjective evaluation by the teacher unless concrete measures are used to determine what is meant by the words, excellent, good, poor, average.

Pass or Fail Method. In this system a standard of acceptability is established. If the student performs up to the standard, he or she passes, if performance is below the standard he or she fails. Sometimes *satisfactory* or *unsatisfactory* are terms used in place of *pass* or *fail*.

Percent Method.   In this method the student is given a percentage score as a mark, with 100 percent representing excellent performance. Percentages can then be converted to letter marks in order to make them more meaningful in the school system. Usually it is assumed the 90–100 percent = A; 80–89 percent = B; 70–79 percent = C; 60–69 percent = D; below 60 percent = F.

Accumulative Points Method.   In this method the student is awarded points for performing the various activities throughout the unit of instruction. The highest number of points accumulated receive the highest grades. The teacher must make subjective judgments as to the cutoff points for distinguishing between the different marks.

Contract Method.   Many options for evaluation are presented with the point values of each during the early part of the marking period. The student decides which projects or experiences he or she will complete and presents these decisions in the form of a contract. The grade contracted for will be received if the student completes what was established that he or she would complete.

Descriptive Statement.   This method consists of a short paragraph explaining the student's status and stating the student's strengths and weaknesses in the subject. This statement is reviewed by the teacher, student, and parent in reaching understanding on the student's progress.

Glossary

The physical educator is faced with the problem of choosing terms with clear meanings and relationships. The clarity of a term depends on the choice of words used in defining it. The importance of terminology in the areas of statistics and measurement necessitates the use of simple words with clear meanings.

The terms in this glossary have been selected and defined in the context of their use in this book.

Ability. Development that has occurred within the limitations of capacity; represented by the highest performance record or achievement score attained within a recent period of time.

Abscissa. Horizontal axis in the coordinate system.

Accomplishment. An individual's best level of achievement.

Accuracy. Freedom from errors.

Achievement. Evaluation of a person's performance record based on the performance records of a group of like persons.

A.D. Average deviation.

Agility. Ability to move quickly and change position and direction rapidly.

Anteroposterior posture. Posture as seen from a side view.

Anthropometry. Science of measurement of people relating to structure; measurement of body dimensions—lengths, widths, depths, and circumferences.

Aptitude. Talent or potential indicating probability of success in a line of endeavor.

AR. Abbreviation for arbitrary reference.

Athletic ability. Ability to perform in physical education activities (athletics).

Attitude. Readiness to act in a particular way; an expression of different degrees of acceptance or rejection.

Average deviation. Average of the amount that scores deviate from the mean of the distribution.

Badge test. Test in which a badge is given for a standard performance; not an appropriate name for a test.

Balance. Ability to keep the center of gravity over the base of support; ability to maintain equilibrium.

Bar graph. Type of histogram shown horizontally.

Battery of tests. Number of tests given to a person or group of persons usually within a short period of time.

Bimodal. A distribution of scores with two modes. A curve with the two high points of equal height.

Calipers. Instrument used to measure body dimensions.

Capacity. Limits (potential) determined by heredity and other factors within which ability may be developed.

Cf. Abbreviation for cumulative frequencies.

Chest expansion. Difference in girth of chest with one measurement taken after full expiration and one taken following a full inspiration.

Chronological age. Age in years, months, and days from time of birth.

Circulorespiratory endurance. Ability to sustain activity over a period of time; the efficiency with which the cardiovascular and respiratory systems work.

Coefficient of correlation. Numerical expression of relationship of two or more variables, varying between minus 1 and plus 1.

Coefficient of reliability. Numerical expression of relationship between scores obtained from two applications of the *same* test to the *same* students by the *same* examiner, separated by a short interval of time; in most cases, .90 is considered relatively high.

Coefficient of validity. Numerical expression of relationship between test scores and criterion scores by which the validity of the test is being judged.

Comparable measures. Measures expressed in terms of the same unit and with reference to the same zero point.

Conduct. Overt behavior that is measured as performance.

Continuous series. Series of data capable of any degree of subdivision (tenths or hundredths of a second).

Control group. Group not subjected to experimental procedures.

Correlation. Relationship between two series of measures of the same individuals.

CR. Abbreviation for critical ratio.

Criterion. Law, fact, or standard by which the validity of some factor is to be determined.

Critical ratio. Obtained difference between two measures divided by the standard error of the difference.

Crude score. Raw score; original score obtained.

Curvilinear correlation. Relationship between two sets of scores expressed by a curved line.

Data. Facts or scores that are used as sources of information.

Decathlon test. Test consisting of ten events.

Decils. Points that divide the total number of cases in a frequency distribution into 10 equal parts; 10th, 20th, 30th, etc., percentiles.

Development. Improvement in function or behavior.

Discrete series. Series of data that cannot be subdivided without destroying the unit (such as basketballs or people).

Divergency. Extreme deviation from a range of normality; an anomaly that may be structural (six fingers on one hand) or functional (pneumonia).

Dynamic strength. Strength exhibited in motion.

Dynamometer. Instrument used to measure muscular strength.

Endurance. Ability to postpone fatigue.

Evaluation. Process of determining the value of something using numbers or words.

Examination. Appraisal of present status in any respect; means used to make the appraisal.

Experimental group. Groups subjected to the experimental procedures.

f. Abbreviation for frequencies.

Flexibility. Range of movement with reference to joints in a body.

Frequency distribution. Scores listed in order of their size with the number of occurrence indicated opposite each other.

Frequency polygon. Line graph of a frequency distribution.

GA. Abbreviation for guessed average.

General ability test. A test that includes ability in art, music, physical education, and other fields.

General athletic ability. Ability exhibited in a considerable number of athletic activities.

General endurance. Ability to continue performance in a variety of activities.

General motor ability. Ability to perform effectively in a variety of motor activities.

Graph. Pictorial illustration of a frequency distribution.

Growth. Increase in size.

Health. Freedom from disease; condition that enables the body organs to function efficiently; quality of functioning of the human organism.

Histogram. Frequency distribution represented in a series of adjacent columns.

Impulsive traits. Traits involving feelings; interest, attitudes, emotions, and ideals.

Initial test. Test given at the beginning of an experimental period or period of time.

Interpretive traits. Ideas, concepts, comprehension, knowledge, and judgments.

Interquartile range. Distance between the 25th and 75th percentiles in a distribution of scores.

Knowledge. Facts; information.

Mark. Rating given a pupil.

Maturation. Degree of completion as a result of growth and development.

Mean (M). Arthimetic average; sum of the measures divided by the number of measures.

Measurement. Process of objective, precise evaluation; process by which a person tries to find the degree to which a trait is possessed by another person.

Measures of central tendency. Central points on a scale of scores.

Measures of variablity. Distances along the scale of scores.

Median (Mdn). Point on the scale above and below which half the scores occur.

Mode. Point on the scale at which the most frequencies occur.

Motor ability. Developed ability to perform a variety of motor activities.

Motor capacity. The limits (potential) determined by heredity and other factors within which motor ability may be developed.

Multimodal. A distribution with more than two modes.

Muscular power. Ability to use muscular force in one concentrated or explosive effort.

Muscular strength. Ability to exert muscular force against resistance.

Native ability. Native implies potential or capacity and should not be used in connection with ability which is developed as a result of activity.

Native capacity. Capacity determined by heredity which places limits on the structure and function of the human organism.

Neuromuscular development. Development of strength and skill (nerve–muscle coordinations).

Norm. Average or typical value (score) of a particular performance in a homogeneous population.

Normal curve. Bell-shaped curve with the mean, median, and mode equal, and with the curve fitting all other specifications of a normal curve as described in Chapter 6.

Objective. Goal, aim, or purpose; accurate test scores. (In an objective test different examiners use the same instrument to measure the same trait and obtain the same scores.)

Objectivity. Quality of dependence on factual evidence or established truth rather than on personal opinion or judgment.

Ogive curve. Cumulative frequency curve with a percentile scale added.

Ordinate. Vertical axis in the coordinate system.

Parameter. True statistic of the total population; True mean or true variance.

Pentathlon test. Test consisting of five events.

Performance. What a person does as distinguished from what his or her potential is.

Physique. Structural organization and body proportions; external appearance of the body.

Posture. Relative alignment and position of body segments.

Power. Rate at which work is performed; amount of work performed divided by the time taken to perform the work; the product of force and velocity.

PR. Abbreviation for percentile rank.

Proficiency. Less desirable term used to mean *efficiency* in performance.

Progress. Improvement indicated by the difference in scores obtained on two identical tests with an interval of time between the tests.

Pulse test. Test indicating the reaction of the human pulse to activity or other conditions.

Quality scale. Scale composed of a set of samples arranged in order of merit.

Questionnaire. Series of questions used in the collection of data only when there is not a more reliable technique to obtain the needed data.

Rándom sample. Representative sample that has been selected without bias from the total group.

Range. Difference between extreme scores.

Rank correlation. Method of finding relationship by computing the correlation between ranks rather than between exact scores.

Raw score. Original obtained score; crude score.

Rectilinear correlation. Relationship between two sets of scores expressed by a straight line.

Reliability of a test. The amount of agreement between the results secured from two applications of the *same* test to the *same* students by the *same* examiner (with a short interval of time between the tests).

SD (σ or sigma). Abbreviation for standard deviation.

Semi-interquartile range. Half the distance between the 25th and 75th percentiles.

SI. Abbreviation for the step interval used in a frequency distribution. In connection with Rogers strength test, *SI* means strength index.

Sigma difference. Standard deviation of a distribution of obtained differences.

Six sigma scale. A statistical scale (standard scale) covering 100 points (0–100) in six standard deviations. The mean of the scale is always 50, and the standard deviation is 16.67.

Skewed distribution. Condition whereby the mean, median, and mode are at different points and the balance of the curve is thrown to the left or to the right.

Skill. Ability to coordinate effectively the actions of the different muscles used in a body movement; neuromuscular functions.

Standard. Statement of the performance that students should reach at a certain time; standards may or may not be the same as norms.

Standard deviation. Square root of the average of the squared deviations in a distribution of scores; most reliable measure of variability.

Standard error. Standard deviation of the sample distribution of any measure (a mean, a sigma, or other such measure).

Standard score. Score expressed in terms of standard deviation units from the mean of the scores. Examples are z scores, T scores, and 6σ scores.

Standardized test. A test with satisfactory content for which norms and standard instructions have been established and which may be scored with a high degree of objectivity.

Static strength. Strength exhibited without overt motion.

Statistical method. Method of research based on the collection and interpretation of numerical data.

Strength. Ability of the muscles to exert force against resistance. (Strength is lessened by inadequate nutrition or inadequate exercise.)

Subjective. Dependence on personal judgment of truth rather than factual evidence or established truth.

Technique. Method or way of performing; technical form or skill.

Test. Device or procedure used to measure performance or ability.

T-scale. Statistical scale (standard scale) proposed by McCall and named in honor of Terman and Thorndike, consisting of 100 units and extending from five standard deviations below the mean to five standard deviations above the mean with the mean score always 50 on the scale, and the standard deviation of the scale is 10.

T score. Standard score based on a 10 standard deviation scale with the mean at 50.

Undistributed scores. Scores that fail to distinguish between degrees of student performances.

Unimodal. A distribution which has only one mode.

Validity of a test. Accurate measurement of that which the test is claimed to measure.

Variance. Average of the squared deviations taken from the mean of the distribution of scores.

Weighting scores. Assigning of values to be carried by each of a number of scores when determining a total or average score.

Work capacity. Potential for doing work.

z-scale. A statistical scale (standard scale) with the mean of the scale equalling zero and the standard deviation equalling one.

z scores. Standard scores based on a six standard deviation scale with the mean at zero.

Mathematical Review

The following is a review of basic mathematical procedures. (Refer to a mathematics textbook for a more extensive review.)

Addition. For numbers of like signs, add the numbers and use the sign common to both of them: $(15)+(10)=25$; $(-15)+(-10)=-25$. For numbers of different signs, find the difference between the numbers and apply the sign of the larger number: $(15)+(-10)=5$; $(-15)+(10)=-5$.

Subtraction. Change the sign of the number to be subtracted and then add the numbers algebraically: $(15)-(10)=5$; $(-15)-(10)=-25$; $(-15)-(-10)=-5$; $(15)-(-10)=25$.

Multiplication. When numbers of like signs are multiplied, the answer is positive: $(15)\times(10)=150$; $(-15)\times(-10)=150$. When the two numbers are of different signs, the answer is negative: $(15)\times(-10)=-150$; $(-15)\times(10)=-150$.

Division. As in multiplication, when two numbers are of like signs, the answer is positive: $(15)\div(10)=1.5$; $(-15)\div(-10)=1.5$. When the two numbers are of different signs, the answer is negative: $(15)\div(-10)=-1.5$; $(-15)\div(10)=-1.5$.

Percentage. Divide the total into the portion, or divide the larger number into the smaller number: 15 is what percent of 30? $(15\div30=.50=50$ percent); 29 is what percent of 80? $(29\div80=.36=36$ percent); 687 is what percent of 1560? $(687\div1560=.44=44$ percent).

Squares. To square a number, simply multiply it by itself: $25^2 = (25) \times (25) = 625$; $2.5^2 = (2.5) \times (2.5) = 6.25$. To check the answer, divide it by the original number: $625 \div 25 = 25$; $6.25 \div 2.5 = 2.5$.

Square Root. Square roots of many numbers are found in the Table of Square Roots in Appendix E. But the square roots of some numbers not in the table may be needed; therefore, it is important to recall the procedure for computing square roots. Following is a description of how to extract the square root of the number 4854.60:

```
               6 9. 6 7
            ┌─────────────
            │  4854.6000
     6   √    36
         ───────────────
   129       1254
             1161
         ───────────────
  1386        9360
              8316
         ───────────────
 13927      104400
             97489
         ───────────────
              6911
```

a. Begin at the decimal point and mark off two places at a time to the left and to the right.
b. Estimate the root of the first number, or pair of numbers (48), and place the root (6) as the divisor and also in the answer.
c. Multiply the divisor (6) by the answer (6) and subtract the result $(48 - 36 = 12)$.
d. Bring down the next pair of figures (54).
e. Multiply the present answer by 2 and add a zero to represent another digit $(2 \times 6 = 12$, add a zero $= 120)$. This figure is the new divisor.
f. Place the next root in the answer and replace the zero in the divisor by that same number (9). The divisor is now 129.
g. Multiply 9×129 and subtract the result (1161) from 1254.
h. Repeat the procedure until the answer appears in as many decimal places as desired.

PRACTICE PROBLEMS

1. Addition
   $(26) + (-92) =$
   $(-93) + (-13) =$
   $(56) + (112) =$
   $(-16) + (63) =$

2. Subtraction
   $(-62) - (-26) =$
   $(-47) - (32) =$
   $(113) - (-47) =$
   $(23) - (17) =$

3. Multiplication
$(-13) \times (43) =$
$(-28) \times (-69) =$
$(93) \times (-12) =$
$(67) \times (10) =$

4. Division
$(-73) \div (12) =$
$(-69) \div (-30) =$
$(24) \div (-6) =$
$(36) \div (14) =$

5. The following chart contains the season won–lost records for four professional baseball teams. Express the season record for each team in a percentage:

Team	Won	Lost	Percentage
A	101	51	
B	70	90	
C	78	83	
D	109	53	

6. Express the batting percentage of the following players:

Player	At Bat	Hits	Percentage
A	491	149	
B	432	135	
C	544	170	
D	540	132	

7. Squares
$16^2 =$
$132^2 =$
$44^2 =$
$220^2 =$

8. Square Roots
$\sqrt{1} =$
$\sqrt{144} =$
$\sqrt{10.46} =$
$\sqrt{1224} =$

APPENDIX **B**

Data for Problems

DATA I The Number of Sit-ups in 30 Seconds Performed by 50 High School Girls

13	20	9	15	16
7	17	17	18	11
10	16	19	17	17
11	14	17	13	15
19	21	14	12	13
15	16	11	14	18
17	17	17	18	21
15	19	17	18	16
13	17	16	20	14
18	19	9	17	18

DATA II Scores Made by 75 High School Boys on the Right Grip Test, Measured to the Nearest Pound

100	94	106	64	97
95	86	139	121	133
94	124	96	100	107
99	103	103	96	99
85	76	91	104	110
101	125	111	113	117
75	102	92	93	120
60	88	80	123	105
102	127	104	97	138
110	113	90	89	118
98	128	100	114	65
115	101	63	102	109
109	78	114	79	80
95	112	99	108	125
110	90	89	129	79

DATA III Data on Six Different Factors for 25 Junior High School Boys

Case	Height (Inches)	Weight (Pounds)	Leg Strength (Pounds)	High Jump (Inches)	100-yard Run (Seconds)	Long Jump (Inches)
1	65	126	560	55	12.4	199
2	66	156	720	58	10.7	196
3	68	143	616	59	10.3	193
4	67	125	592	55	12.3	197
5	69	132	472	57	13.0	168
6	66	121	513	52	13.0	166
7	62	97	460	49	12.4	176
8	69	147	614	42	10.1	199
9	68	145	520	58	12.8	187
10	60	124	480	51	13.7	149
11	63	111	470	54	12.6	177
12	63	100	450	41	12.9	174
13	69	145	736	58	12.4	214
14	58	61	372	45	15.6	112
15	64	112	510	53	12.6	185
16	70	136	615	61	12.5	177
17	68	138	662	58	12.9	196
18	67	137	640	56	12.5	170
19	70	143	687	59	13.6	166
20	67	129	532	53	13.5	167
21	65	118	510	55	14.0	177
22	60	90	470	45	14.8	141
23	68	157	767	56	12.0	204
24	68	150	620	59	13.0	187
25	68	127	540	60	15.8	185

DATA IV   Squares for Data III

Case	Height	Weight	Leg Strength	High Jump	100-Yard Run	Long Jump
1	4225	15876	313600	3025	153.76	37601
2	4356	24336	518400	3364	114.49	38416
3	4624	20446	379456	3481	106.09	37249
4	4489	15625	350464	3025	151.29	38809
5	4761	17424	222784	3249	169.00	28224
6	4356	14641	263169	2704	169.00	27556
7	3844	9409	211600	2401	153.76	30976
8	4761	21609	376996	1764	102.01	39601
9	4624	21025	270400	3364	163.84	34969
10	3600	15376	230400	2601	187.69	22201
11	3969	12321	220900	2916	158.76	31329
12	3969	10000	202500	1681	166.41	30276
13	4761	21025	541696	3364	153.76	45796
14	3364	3721	138384	2025	243.36	12544
15	4096	12544	260100	2809	158.76	34225
16	4900	18496	378225	3721	156.25	31329
17	4624	19044	438244	3364	166.41	38416
18	4489	18769	409600	3136	156.25	28900
19	4900	20449	471969	3481	184.76	27556
20	4489	16641	283024	2809	182.25	27889
21	4225	13924	260100	3025	196.00	31329
22	3600	8100	220900	2025	219.04	19881
23	4624	24649	588289	3136	144.00	41616
24	4624	22500	384400	3481	169.00	34969
25	4624	16129	291600	3600	249.64	34225
ΣX^2	108898	414082	8601282	73551	4175.78	807882

APPENDIX C

Table of Squares and Square Roots

Table of Squares and Square Roots of Numbers from 1 to 1000

Number	Square	Square Root	Number	Square	Square Root
1	1	1.000	41	16 81	6.403
2	4	1.414	42	17 64	6.481
3	9	1.732	43	18 49	6.557
4	16	2.000	44	19 36	6.633
5	25	2.236	45	20 25	6.708
6	36	2.449	46	21 16	6.782
7	49	2.646	47	22 09	6.856
8	64	2.828	48	23 04	6.928
9	81	3.000	49	24 01	7.000
10	1 00	3.162	50	25 00	7.071
11	1 21	3.317	51	26 01	7.141
12	1 44	3.464	52	27 04	7.211
13	1 69	3.606	53	28 09	7.280
14	1 96	3.742	54	29.16	7.348
·15	2 25	3.873	55	30 25	7.416
16	2 56	4.000	56	31 36	7.483
17	2 89	4.123	57	32 49	7.550
18	3 24	4.243	58	33 64	7.616
19	3 61	4.359	59	34 81	7.681
20	4 00	4.472	60	36 00	7.746
21	4 41	4.583	61	37 21	7.810
22	4 84	4.690	62	38 44	7.874
23	5 29	4.796	63	39 69	7.937
24	5 76	4.899	64	40 96	8.000
25	6 25	5.000	65	42 25	8.062
26	6 76	5.099	66	43 56	8.124
27	7 29	5.196	67	44 89	8.184
28	7 84	5.292	68	46 24	8.246
29	8 41	5.385	69	47 61	8.307
30	9 00	5.477	70	49 00	8.367
31	9 61	5.568	71	50 41	8.426
32	10 24	5.657	72	51 84	8.485
33	10 89	5.745	73	53 29	8.544
34	11 56	5.831	74	54 76	8.602
35	12 25	5.916	75	56 25	8.660
36	12 96	6.000	76	57 76	8.718
37	13 69	6.083	77	59 29	8.775
38	14 44	6.164	78	60 84	8.832
39	15 21	6.245	79	62 41	8.888
40	16 00	6.325	80	64 00	8.944

Number	Square	Square Root	Number	Square	Square Root
81	65 61	9.000	136	1 84 96	11.662
82	67 24	9.055	137	1 87 69	11.705
83	68 89	9.110	138	1 90 44	11.747
84	70 56	9.165	139	1 93 21	11.790
85	72 25	9.220	140	1 96 00	11.832
86	73 96	9.274	141	1 98 81	11.874
87	75 69	9.327	142	2 01 64	11.916
88	77 44	9.381	143	2 04 49	11.958
89	79 21	9.434	144	2 07 36	12.000
90	81 00	9.487	145	2 10 25	12.042
91	82 81	9.539	146	2 13 16	12.083
92	84 64	9.592	147	2 16 09	12.124
93	86 49	9.644	148	2 19 04	12.166
94	88 36	9.695	149	2 22 01	12.207
95	90 25	9.747	150	2 25 00	12.247
96	92 16	9.798	151	2 28 01	12.288
97	94 09	9.849	152	2 31 04	12.329
98	96 04	9.899	153	2 34 09	12.369
99	98 01	9.950	154	2 37 16	12.410
100	1 00 00	10.000	155	2 40 25	12.450
101	1 02 01	10.050	156	2 43 36	12.490
102	1 04 04	10.100	157	2 46 49	12.530
103	1 06 09	10.149	158	2 49 64	12.570
104	1 08 16	10.198	159	2 52 81	12.610
105	1 10 25	10.247	160	2 56 00	12.649
106	1 12 36	10.296	161	2 59 21	12.689
107	1 14 49	10.344	162	2 62 44	12.728
108	1 16 64	10.392	163	2 65 69	12.767
109	1 18 81	10.440	164	2 68 96	12.806
110	1 21 00	10.488	165	2 72 25	12.845
111	1 23 21	10.536	166	2 75 56	12.884
112	1 25 44	10.583	167	2 78 89	12.923
113	1 27 69	10.630	168	2 82 24	12.9€1
114	1 29 96	10.677	169	2 85 61	13.000
115	1 32 25	10.724	170	2 89 00	13.038
116	1 34 56	10.770	171	2 92 41	13.077
117	1 36 89	10.817	172	2 95 84	13.115
118	1 39 24	10.863	173	2 99 29	13.153
119	1 41 61	10.909	174	3 02 76	13.191
120	1 44 00	10.954	175	3 06 25	13.229
121	1 46 41	11.000	176	3 09 76	13.266
122	1 48 84	11.045	177	3 13 29	13.304
123	1 51 29	11.091	178	3 16 84	13.342
124	1 53 76	11.136	179	3 20 41	13.379
125	1 56 25	11.180	180	3 24 00	13.416
126	1 58 76	11.225	181	3 27 61	13.454
127	1 61 29	11.269	182	3 31 24	13.491
128	1 63 84	11.314	183	3 34 89	13.528
129	1 66 41	11.358	184	3 38 56	13.565
130	1 69 00	11.402	185	3 42 25	13.601
131	1 71 61	11.446	186	3 45 96	13.638
132	1 74 24	11.489	187	3 49 69	13.675
133	1 76 89	11.533	188	3 53 44	13.711
134	1 79 56	11.576	189	3 57 21	13.748
135	1 82 25	11.619	190	3 61 00	13.784

Number	Square	Square Root	Number	Square	Square Root
191	3 64 81	13.820	246	6 05 16	15.684
192	3 68 64	13.856	247	6 10 09	15.716
193	3 72 49	13.892	248	6 15 04	15.748
194	3 76 36	13.928	249	6 20 01	15.780
195	3 80 25	13.964	250	6 25 00	15.811
196	3 84 16	14.000	251	6 30 01	15.843
197	3 88 09	14.036	252	6 35 04	15.875
198	3 92 04	14.071	253	6 40 09	15.906
199	3 96 01	14.107	254	6 45 16	15.937
200	4 00 00	14.142	255	6 50 25	15.969
201	4 04 01	14.177	256	6 55 36	16.000
202	4 08 04	14.213	257	6 60 49	16.031
203	4 12 09	14.248	258	6 65 64	16.062
204	4 16 16	14.283	259	6 70 81	16.093
205	4 20 25	14.318	260	6 76 00	16.125
206	4 24 36	14.353	261	6 81 21	16.155
207	4 28 49	14.387	262	6 86 44	16.186
208	4 32 64	14.422	263	6 91 69	16.217
209	4 36 81	14.457	264	6 96 96	16.248
210	4 41 00	14.491	265	7 02 25	16.279
211	4 45 21	14.526	266	7 07 56	16.310
212	4 49 44	14.560	267	7 12 89	16.340
213	4 53 69	14.595	268	7 18 24	16.371
214	4 57 96	14.629	269	7 23 61	16.401
215	4 62 25	14.663	270	7 29 00	16.432
216	4 66 56	14.697	271	7 34 41	16.462
217	4 70 89	14.731	272	7 39 84	16.492
218	4 75 24	14.765	273	7 45 29	16.523
219	4 79 61	14.799	274	7 50 76	16.553
220	4 84 00	14.832	275	7 56 25	16.583
221	4 88 41	14.866	276	7 61 76	16.613
222	4 92 84	14.900	277	7 67 29	16.643
223	4 97 29	14.933	278	7 72 84	16.673
224	5 01 76	14.967	279	7 78 41	16.703
225	5 06 25	15.000	280	7 84 00	16.733
226	5 10 76	15.033	281	7 89 61	16.763
227	5 15 29	15.067	282	7 95 24	16.793
228	5 19 84	15.100	283	8 00 89	16.823
229	5 24 41	15.133	284	8 06 56	16.852
230	5 29 00	15.166	285	8 12 25	16.882
231	5 33 61	15.199	286	8 17 96	16.912
232	5 38 24	15.232	287	8 23 69	16.941
233	5 42 89	15.264	288	8 29 44	16.971
234	5 47 56	15.297	289	8 35 21	17.000
235	5 52 25	15.330	290	8 41 00	17.029
236	5 56 96	15.362	291	8 46 81	17.059
237	5 61 69	15.395	292	8 52 64	17.088
238	5 66 44	15.427	293	8 58 40	17.117
239	5 71 21	15.460	294	8 64 36	17.146
240	5 76 00	15.492	295	8 70 25	17.176
241	5 80 81	15.524	296	8 76 16	17.205
242	5 85 64	15.556	297	8 82 09	17.234
243	5 90 49	15.588	298	8 88 04	17.263
244	5 95 36	15.620	299	8 94 01	17.292
245	6 00 25	15.652	300	9 00 00	17.321

Number	Square	Square Root	Number	Square	Square Root
301	9 06 01	17.349	356	12 67 36	18.868
302	9 12 04	17.378	357	12 74 49	18.894
303	9 18 09	17.407	358	12 81 64	18.921
304	9 24 16	17.436	359	12 88 81	18.947
305	9 30 25	17.464	360	12 96 00	18.974
306	9 36 36	17.493	361	13 03 21	19.000
307	9 42 49	17.521	362	13 10 44	19.026
308	9 48 64	17.550	363	13 17 69	19.053
309	9 54 81	17.578	364	13 24 96	19.079
310	9 61 00	17.607	365	13 32 25	19.105
311	9 67 21	17.635	366	13 39 56	19.131
312	9 73 44	17.664	367	13 46 89	19.157
313	9 79 69	17.692	368	13 54 24	19.183
314	9 85 96	17.720	369	13 61 61	19.209
315	9 92 25	17.748	370	13 69 00	19.235
316	9 98 56	17.776	371	13 76 41	19.261
317	10 04 89	17.804	372	13 83 84	19.287
318	10 11 24	17.833	373	13 91 29	19.313
319	10 17 61	17.861	374	13 98 76	19.339
320	10 24 00	17.889	375	14 06 25	19.363
321	10 30 41	17.916	376	14 13 76	19.391
322	10 36 84	17.944	377	14 21 29	19.416
323	10 43 29	17.972	378	14 28 84	19.442
324	10 49 76	18.000	379	14 36 41	19.468
325	10 56 25	18.028	380	14 44 00	19.494
326	10 62 76	18.055	381	14 51 61	19.519
327	10 69 29	18.083	382	14 59 24	19.545
328	10 75 84	18.111	383	14 66 89	19.570
329	10 82 41	18.138	384	14 74 56	19.596
330	10 89 00	18.166	385	14 82 25	19.621
331	10 95 61	18.193	386	14 89 96	19.647
332	11 02 24	18.221	387	14 97 69	19.672
333	11 08 89	18.248	388	15 05 44	19.698
334	11 15 56	18.276	389	15 13 21	19.723
335	11 22 25	18.303	390	15 21 00	19.748
336	11 28 96	18.330	391	15 28 81	19.774
337	11 35 69	18.358	392	15 36 64	19.799
338	11 42 44	18.385	393	15 44 49	19.824
339	11 49 21	18.412	394	15 52 36	19.849
340	11 56 00	18.439	395	15 60 25	19.875
341	11 62 81	18.466	396	15 68 16	19.900
342	11 69 64	18.493	397	15 76 09	19.925
343	11 76 49	18.520	398	15 84 04	19.950
344	11 83 36	18.547	399	15 92 01	19.975
345	11 90 25	18.574	400	16 00 00	20.000
346	11 97 16	18.601	401	16 08 01	20.025
347	12 04 09	18.628	402	16 16 04	20.050
348	12 11 04	18.655	403	16 24 09	20.075
349	12 18 01	18.682	404	16 32 16	20.100
350	12 25 00	18.708	405	16 40 25	20.125
351	12 32 01	18.735	406	16 48 36	20.149
352	12 39 04	18.762	407	16 56 49	20.174
353	12 46 09	18.788	408	16 64 64	20.199
354	12 53 16	18.815	409	16 72 81	20.224
355	12 60 25	18.841	410	16 81 00	20.248

Number	Square	Square Root	Number	Square	Square Root
411	16 89 21	20.273	466	21 71 56	21.587
412	16 97 44	20.298	467	21 80 89	21.610
413	17 05 69	20.322	468	21 90 24	21.633
414	17 13 96	20.347	469	21 99 61	21.656
415	17 22 25	20.372	470	22 09 00	21.679
416	17 30 56	20.396	471	22 18 41	21.703
417	17 38 89	20.421	472	22 27 84	21.726
418	17 47 24	20.445	473	22 37 29	21.749
419	17 55 61	20.469	474	22 46 76	21.772
420	17 64 00	20.494	475	22 56 25	21.794
421	17 72 41	20.518	476	22 65 76	21.817
422	17 80 84	20.543	477	22 75 29	21.840
423	17 89 29	20.567	478	22 84 84	21.863
424	17 97 76	20.591	479	22 94 41	21.886
425	18 06 25	20.616	480	23 04 00	21.909
426	18 14 76	20.640	481	23 13 61	21.932
427	18 23 29	20.664	482	23 23 24	21.954
428	18 31 84	20.688	483	23 32 89	21.977
429	18 40 41	20.712	484	23 42 56	22.000
430	18 49 00	20.736	485	23 52 25	22.023
431	18 57 61	20.761	486	23 61 96	22.045
432	18 66 24	20.785	487	23 71 69	22.068
433	18 74 89	20.809	488	23 81 44	22.091
434	18 83 56	20.833	489	23 91 21	22.113
435	18 92 25	20.857	490	24 01 00	22.136
436	19 00 96	20.881	491	24 10 81	22.159
437	19 09 69	20.905	492	24 20 64	22.181
438	19 18 44	20.928	493	24 30 49	22.204
439	19 27 21	20.952	494	24 40 36	22.226
440	19 36 00	20.976	495	24 50 25	22.249
441	19 44 81	21.000	496	24 60 16	22.271
442	19 53 64	21.024	497	24 70 09	22.293
443	19 62 49	21.048	498	24 80 04	22.316
444	19 71 36	21.071	499	24 90 01	22.338
445	19 80 25	21.095	500	25 00 00	22.361
446	19 89 16	21.119	501	25 10 01	22.383
447	19 98 09	21.142	502	25 20 04	22.405
448	20 07 04	21.166	503	25 30 09	22.428
449	20 16 01	21.190	504	25 40 16	22.450
450	20 25 00	21.213	505	25 50 25	22.472
451	20 34 01	21.237	506	25 60 36	22.494
452	20 43 04	21.260	507	25 70 49	22.517
453	20 52 09	21.284	508	25 80 64	22.539
454	20 61 16	21.307	509	25 90 81	22.561
455	20 70 25	21.331	510	26 01 00	22.583
456	20 79 36	21.354	511	26 11 21	22.605
457	20 88 49	21.378	512	26 21 44	22.627
458	20 97 64	21.401	513	26 31 69	22.650
459	21 06 81	21.424	514	26 41 96	22.672
460	21 16 00	21.448	515	26 52 25	22.694
461	21 25 21	21.471	516	26 62 56	22.716
462	21 34 44	21.494	517	26 72 89	22.738
463	21 43 69	21.517	518	26 83 24	22.760
464	21 52 96	21.541	519	26 93 61	22.782
465	21 62 25	21.564	520	27 04 00	22.804

Number	Square	Square Root	Number	Square	Square Root
521	27 14 41	22.825	576	33 17 76	24.000
522	27 24 84	22.847	577	33 29 29	24.021
523	27 35 29	22.869	578	33 40 84	24.042
524	27 45 76	22.891	579	33 52 41	24.062
525	27 56 25	22.913	580	33 64 00	24.083
526	27 66 76	22.935	581	33 75 61	24.104
527	27 77 29	22.956	582	33 87 24	24.125
528	27 87 84	22.978	583	33 98 89	24.145
529	27 98 41	23.000	584	34 10 56	24.166
530	28 09 00	23.022	585	34 22 25	24.187
531	28 19 61	23.043	586	34 33 96	24.207
532	28 30 24	23.065	587	34 45 69	24.228
533	28 40 89	23.087	588	34 57 44	24.249
534	28 51 56	23.108	589	34 69 21	24.269
535	28 62 25	23.130	590	34 81 00	24.290
536	28 72 96	23.152	591	34 92 81	24.310
537	28 83 69	23.173	592	35 04 64	24.331
538	28 94 44	23.195	593	35 16 49	24.352
539	29 05 21	23.216	594	35 28 36	24.372
540	29 16 00	23.238	595	35 40 25	24.393
541	29 26 81	23.259	596	35 52 16	24.413
542	29 37 64	32.281	597	35 64 09	24.434
543	29 48 49	23.302	598	35 76 04	24.454
544	29 59 36	23.324	599	35 88 01	24.474
545	29 70 25	23.345	600	36 00 00	24.495
546	29 81 16	23.367	601	36 12 01	24.515
547	29 92 09	23.388	602	36 24 04	24.536
548	30 03 04	23.409	603	36 36 09	24.556
549	30 14 01	23.431	604	36 48 16	24.576
550	30 25 00	23.452	605	36 60 25	24.597
551	30 36 01	23.473	606	36 72 36	24.617
552	30 47 04	23.495	607	36 84 49	24.637
553	30 58 09	23.516	608	36 96 64	24.658
554	30 69 16	23.537	609	37 08 81	24.678
555	30 80 25	23.558	610	37 21 00	24.698
556	30 91 36	23.580	611	37 33 21	24.718
557	31 02 49	23.601	612	37 45 44	24.739
558	31 13 64	23.622	613	37 57 69	24.759
559	31 24 81	23.643	614	37 69 96	24.779
560	31 36 00	23.664	615	37 82 25	24.799
561	31 47 21	23.685	616	37 94 56	24.819
562	31 58 44	23.707	617	38 06 89	24.839
563	31 69 69	23.728	618	38 19 24	24.860
564	31 80 96	23.749	619	38 31 61	24.880
565	31 92 25	23.770	620	38 44 00	24.900
566	32 03 56	23.791	621	38 56 41	24.920
567	32 14 89	23.812	622	38 68 84	24.940
568	32 26 24	23.833	623	38 81 29	24.960
569	32 37 61	23.854	624	38 93 76	24.980
570	32 49 00	23.875	625	39 06 25	25.000
571	32 60 41	23.896	626	39 18 76	25.020
572	32 71 84	23.917	627	39 31 29	25.040
573	32 83 29	23.937	628	39 43 84	25.060
574	32 94 76	23.958	629	39 56 41	25.080
575	33 06 25	23.979	630	39 69 00	25.100

Number	Square	Square Root	Number	Square	Square Root
631	39 81 61	25.120	686	47 05 96	26.192
632	39 94 24	25.140	687	47 19 69	26.211
633	40 06 89	25.159	688	47 33 44	26.230
634	40 19 56	25.179	689	47 47 21	26.249
635	40 32 25	25.199	690	47 61 00	26.268
636	40 44 96	25.219	691	47 74 81	26.287
637	40 57 69	25.239	692	47 88 64	26.306
638	40 70 44	25.259	693	48 02 49	26.325
639	40 83 21	25.278	694	48 16 36	26.344
640	40 96 00	25.298	695	48 30 25	26.363
641	41 08 81	25.318	696	48 44 16	26.382
642	41 21 64	25.338	697	48 58 09	26.401
643	41 34 49	25.357	698	48 72 04	26.420
644	41 47 36	25.377	699	48 86 01	26.439
645	41 60 25	25.397	700	49 00 00	26.458
646	41 73 16	25.417	701	49 14 01	26.476
647	41 86 09	25.436	702	49 28 04	26.495
648	41 99 04	25.456	703	49 42 09	26.514
649	42 12 01	25.475	704	49 56 16	26.533
650	42 25 00	25.495	705	49 70 25	26.552
651	42 38 10	25.515	706	49 84 36	26.571
652	42 51 04	25.534	707	49 98 49	26.589
653	42 64 09	25.554	708	50 12 64	26.608
654	42 77 16	25.573	709	50 26 81	26.627
655	42 90 25	25.593	710	50 41 00	26.646
656	43 03 36	25.612	711	50 55 21	26.665
657	43 16 49	25.632	712	50 69 44	26.683
658	43 29 64	25.652	713	50 83 69	26.702
659	43 42 81	25.671	714	50 97 96	26.721
660	43 56 00	25.690	715	51 12 25	26.739
661	43 69 21	25.710	716	51 26 56	26.758
662	43 82 44	25.729	717	51 40 89	26.777
663	43 95 69	25.749	718	51 55 24	26.796
664	44 08 96	25.768	719	51 69 61	26.814
665	44 22 25	25.788	720	51 84 00	26.833
666	44 35 56	25.807	721	51 98 41	26.851
667	44 48 89	25.826	722	52 12 84	26.870
668	44 62 24	25.846	723	52 27 29	26.889
669	44 75 61	25.865	724	52 41 76	26.907
670	44 89 00	24.884	725	52 56 25	26.926
671	45 02 41	25.904	726	52 70 76	26.944
672	45 15 84	25.923	727	52 85 29	26.963
673	45 29 29	25.942	728	52 99 84	26.981
674	45 42 76	25.962	729	53 14 41	27.000
675	45 56 25	25.981	730	53 29 00	27.019
676	45 69 76	26.000	731	53 43 61	27.037
677	45 83 29	26.019	732	53 58 24	27.055
678	45 96 84	26.038	733	53 72 89	27.074
679	46 10 41	26.058	734	53 87 56	27.092
680	46 24 00	26.077	735	54 02 25	27.111
681	46 37 61	26.096	736	54 16 96	27.129
682	46 51 24	26.115	737	54 31 69	27.148
683	46 64 89	26.134	738	54 46 44	27.166
684	46 78 56	26.153	739	54 61 21	27.185
685	46 92 25	26.173	740	54 76 00	27.203

Number	Square	Square Root	Number	Square	Square Root
741	54 90 81	27.221	796	63 36 16	28.213
742	55 05 64	27.240	797	63 52 09	28.231
743	55 20 49	27.258	798	63 68 04	28.249
744	55 35 36	27.276	799	63 84 01	28.267
745	55 50 25	27.295	800	64 00 00	28.284
746	55 65 16	27.313	801	64 16 01	28.302
747	55 80 09	27.331	802	64 32 04	28.320
748	55 95 04	27.350	803	64 48 09	28.337
749	56 10 01	27.368	804	64 64 16	28.355
750	56 25 00	27.386	805	64 80 25	28.373
751	56 40 01	27.404	806	64 96 36	28.390
752	56 55 04	27.423	807	65 12 49	28.408
753	56 70 09	27.441	808	65 28 64	28.425
754	56 85 16	27.459	809	65 44 81	28.443
755	57 00 25	27.477	810	65 61 00	28.460
756	57 15 36	27.495	811	65 77 21	28.478
757	57 30 49	27.514	812	65 93 44	28.496
758	57 45 64	27.532	813	66 09 69	28.513
759	57 60 81	27.550	814	66 25 96	28.531
760	57 76 00	27.568	815	66 42 25	28.548
761	57 91 21	27.586	816	66 58 56	28.566
762	58 06 44	27.604	817	66 74 89	28.583
763	58 21 69	27.622	818	66 91 24	28.601
764	58 36 96	27.641	819	67 07 61	28.618
765	58 52 25	27.659	820	67 24 00	28.636
766	58 67 56	27.677	821	67 40 41	28.653
767	58 82 89	27.695	822	67 56 84	28.671
768	58 98 24	27.713	823	67 73 29	28.688
769	59 13 61	27.731	824	67 89 76	28.705
770	59 29 00	27.749	825	68 06 25	28.723
771	59 44 41	27.767	826	68 22 76	28.740
772	59 59 84	27.785	827	68 39 29	28.758
773	59 75 29	27.803	828	68 55 84	28.775
774	59 90 76	27.821	829	68 72 41	28.792
775	60 06 25	27.839	830	68 89 00	28.810
776	60 21 76	27.857	831	69 05 61	28.827
777	60 37 29	27.875	832	69 22 24	28.844
778	60 52 84	27.893	833	69 38 89	28.862
779	60 68 41	27.911	834	69 55 56	28.879
780	60 84 00	27.928	835	69 72 25	28.896
781	60 99 61	27.946	836	69 88 96	28.914
782	61 15 24	27.964	837	70 05 69	28.931
783	61 30 89	27.982	838	70 22 44	28.948
784	61 46 56	28.000	839	70 39 21	28.965
785	61 62 25	28.018	840	70 56 00	28.983
786	61 77 96	28.036	841	70 72 81	29.000
787	61 93 69	28.054	842	70 89 64	29.017
788	62 09 44	28.071	843	71 06 49	29.034
789	62 25 21	28.089	844	71 23 36	29.052
790	62 41 00	28.107	845	71 40 25	29.069
791	62 56 81	28.125	846	71 57 16	29.086
792	62 72 64	28.142	847	71 74 09	29.103
793	62 88 49	28.160	848	71 91 04	29.120
794	63 04 36	28.178	849	72 08 01	29.138
795	63 20 25	28.196	850	72 25 00	29.155

Number	Square	Square Root	Number	Square	Square Root
851	72 42 01	29.172	906	82 08 36	30.100
852	72 59 04	29.189	907	82 26 49	30.116
853	72 76 09	29.206	908	82 44 64	30.133
854	72 93 16	29.223	909	82 62 81	30.150
855	73 10 25	29.240	910	82 81 00	30.166
856	73 27 36	29.257	911	82 99 21	30.183
857	73 44 49	29.275	912	83 17 44	30.199
858	73 61 64	29.292	913	83 35 69	30.216
859	73 78 81	29.309	914	83 53 96	30.232
860	73 96 00	29.326	915	83 72 25	30.249
861	74 13 21	29.343	916	83 90 56	30.265
862	74 30 44	29.360	917	84 08 89	30.282
863	74 47 69	29.377	918	84 27 24	30.299
864	74 64 96	29.394	919	84 45 61	30.315
865	74 82 25	29.411	920	84 64 00	30.332
866	74 99 56	29.428	921	84 82 41	30.348
867	75 16 89	29.445	922	85 00 84	30.364
868	75 34 24	29.462	923	85 19 29	30.381
869	75 51 61	29.479	924	85 37 76	30.397
870	75 69 00	29.496	925	85 56 25	30.414
871	75 86 41	29.513	926	85 74 76	30.430
872	76 03 84	29.530	927	85 93 29	30.447
873	76 21 29	29.547	928	86 11 84	30.463
874	76 38 76	29.563	929	86 30 41	30.480
875	76 56 25	29.580	930	86 49 00	30.496
876	76 73 76	29.597	931	86 67 61	30.512
877	76 91 29	29.614	932	86 86 24	30.529
878	77 08 84	29.631	933	87 04 89	30.545
879	77 26 41	29.648	934	87 23 56	30.561
880	77 44 00	29.665	935	87 42 25	30.578
881	77 61 61	29.682	936	87 69 96	30.504
882	77 79 24	29.698	937	87 79 69	30.610
883	77 96 89	29.715	938	87 98 44	30.627
884	78 14 56	29.732	939	88 17 21	30.643
885	78 32 25	29.749	940	88 36 00	30.659
886	78 49 96	29.766	941	88 54 81	30.676
887	78 67 69	29.783	942	88 73 64	30.692
888	78 85 44	29.799	943	88 92 49	30.708
889	79 03 21	29.816	944	89 11 36	30.725
890	79 21 00	29.833	945	89 30 25	30.741
891	79 38 81	29.850	946	89 49 16	30.757
892	79 56 64	29.866	947	89 68 09	30.773
893	79 74 49	29.883	948	89 87 04	30.790
894	79 92 36	29.900	949	90 06 01	30.806
895	80 10 25	29.916	950	90 25 00	30.822
896	80 28 16	29.933	951	90 44 01	30.838
897	80 46 09	29.950	952	90 63 04	30.854
898	80 64 04	29.967	953	90 82 09	30.871
899	80 82 01	29.983	954	91 01 16	30.887
900	81 00 00	30.000	955	91 20 25	30.903
901	81 18 01	30.017	956	91 39 36	30.919
902	81 36 04	30.033	957	91 58 49	30.935
903	81 54 09	30.050	958	91 77 64	30.952
904	81 72 16	30.067	959	91 96 81	30.968
905	81 90 25	30.083	960	92 16 00	30.984

Number	Square	Square Root	Number	Square	Square Root
961	92 35 21	31.000	981	96 23 61	31.321
962	92 54 44	31.016	982	96 43 24	31.337
963	92 73 69	31.032	983	96 62 89	31.353
964	92 92 96	31.048	984	96 82 56	31.369
965	93 12 25	31.064	985	97 02 25	31.385
966	93 31 56	31.081	986	97 21 96	31.401
967	93 50 89	31.097	987	97 41 69	31.417
968	93 70 24	31.113	988	97 61 44	31.432
969	93 89 61	31.129	989	97 81 21	31.448
970	94 09 00	31.145	990	98 01 00	31.464
971	94 28 41	31.161	991	98 20 81	31.480
972	94 47 84	31.177	992	98 40 64	31.496
973	94 67 20	31.193	993	98 60 49	31.512
974	94 86 76	31.209	994	98 80 36	31.528
975	95 06 25	31.225	995	99 00 25	31.544
976	95 25 76	31.241	996	99 20 16	31.559
977	95 45 29	31.257	997	99 40 09	31.575
978	95 64 84	31.273	998	99 60 04	31.591
979	95 84 41	31.289	999	99 80 01	31.607
980	96 04 00	31.305	1000	100 00 00	31.623

Percentage of Cases within Standard Deviation Units of the Mean in a Normal Distribution Curve

σ	.00	.01	.02	.03	.04	.05	.06	.07	.08	.09
0.0	00.00	00.40	00.80	01.20	01.60	01.99	02.39	02.79	03.19	03.59
0.1	03.98	04.38	04.78	05.17	05.57	05.96	06.36	06.75	07.14	07.53
0.2	07.93	08.32	08.71	09.10	09.48	09.87	10.26	11.64	11.03	11.41
0.3	01.79	12.17	12.55	12.93	13.31	13.68	14.06	14.43	14.80	15.17
0.4	15.54	15.54	16.28	16.64	17.00	17.36	17.72	18.08	18.44	18.79
0.5	19.15	19.50	19.85	20.19	20.54	20.88	21.23	21.57	21.90	22.24
0.6	22.57	22.91	23.24	23.57	23.89	24.22	24.54	24.86	25.17	25.49
0.7	25.80	26.11	26.42	26.73	27.04	27.34	27.64	27.94	28.23	28.52
0.8	28.81	29.10	29.39	29.67	29.95	30.23	30.51	30.78	31.06	31.33
0.9	31.59	31.86	32.12	32.38	32.64	32.90	33.15	33.40	33.65	33.89
1.0	34.13	34.38	34.61	34.85	35.08	35.31	35.54	35.77	35.99	36.21
1.1	36.43	36.65	36.86	37.08	37.29	37.49	37.70	37.90	38.10	38.30
1.2	38.49	38.69	38.88	39.07	39.25	39.44	39.62	39.80	39.97	40.15
1.3	40.32	40.49	40.66	40.82	40.99	41.15	41.31	41.47	41.62	41.77
1.4	41.92	42.07	42.22	42.36	42.51	42.65	42.79	42.92	43.06	43.19
1.5	43.32	43.45	43.57	43.70	43.83	43.94	44.06	44.18	44.29	44.41
1.6	44.52	44.63	44.74	44.84	44.95	45.05	45.15	45.25	45.35	45.45
1.7	45.54	45.64	45.73	45.82	45.91	45.99	46.08	46.16	46.25	46.33
1.8	46.41	46.49	46.56	46.64	46.71	46.78	46.86	46.93	46.99	47.06
1.9	47.13	47.19	47.26	47.32	47.38	47.44	47.50	46.56	47.61	47.67
2.0	47.72	47.78	47.83	47.88	47.93	47.98	48.03	48.08	48.12	48.17
2.1	48.21	48.26	48.30	48.34	48.38	48.42	48.46	48.50	48.54	48.57
2.2	48.61	48.64	48.68	48.71	48.75	48.78	48.81	48.84	48.87	48.90
2.3	48.93	48.96	48.98	49.01	49.04	49.06	49.09	49.11	49.13	49.16
2.4	49.18	49.20	49.22	49.25	49.27	49.29	49.31	49.32	49.34	49.36
2.5	49.38	49.40	49.41	49.43	49.45	49.46	49.48	49.49	49.51	49.52
2.6	49.53	49.55	49.56	49.57	49.59	49.60	49.61	49.62	49.63	49.64
2.7	49.65	49.66	49.67	49.68	49.69	49.70	49.71	49.72	49.73	49.74
2.8	49.74	49.75	49.76	49.77	49.77	49.78	49.79	49.79	49.80	49.81
2.9	49.81	49.82	49.82	49.83	49.84	49.84	49.85	49.85	49.86	49.86
3.0	49.87									
3.5	49.98									
4.0	49.997									
5.0	49.99997									

* The data in this table were taken from *Tables for Statisticians and Biometricians*. Edited by Karl Pearson. Cambridge University Press.

APPENDIX **E**

t-Test Significance Levels

Df	.05	.01
1	12.71	63.66
2	4.30	9.92
3	3.18	5.84
4	2.78	4.60
5	2.57	4.03
6	2.45	3.71
7	2.36	3.50
8	2.31	3.36
9	2.26	3.25
10	2.23	3.17
11	2.20	3.11
12	2.18	3.06
13	2.16	3.01
14	2.14	2.98
15	2.13	2.95
16	2.12	2.92
17	2.11	2.90
18	2.10	2.88
19	2.09	2.86
20	2.09	2.84
21	2.08	2.83
22	2.07	2.82
23	2.07	2.81
24	2.06	2.80
25	2.06	2.79
26	2.06	2.78
27	2.05	2.77
28	2.05	2.76
29	2.04	2.76
30	2.04	2.75
40	2.02	2.70
60	2.00	2.66
125	1.98	2.62
200	1.99	2.60

Index